REMASTERED

BLACK DIVINITY

A Ghetto Theology for the Black Community
SHAHIDI COLLECTION VOL 1

SHAHIDI ISLAM

Copyright © 2012, 2014, 2017, 2019, 2024, 2026 by Shahidi Islam.
All rights reserved. No part of this book may be reproduced in any form or by any electronic or mechanical means, including information storage and retrieval systems, without permission in writing from the publisher, except by reviewers, who may quote brief passages in a review.

This publication has been made to provide accurate and authoritative information with regard to the subject matter discussed. It is sold with the understanding that neither the publisher nor the author are engaging in the offering of medical, psychological, or sociological service. If any of the above are required a competent professional person should be consulted.

All quotations provided throughout this book are strictly for the purpose of education and research, and fall well into the guidelines of fair dealing. Fair dealing is recognised in Canada, the United Kingdom, and Australia and allows for individuals, researchers, musicians, educators, and authors to use copyrighted material without permission from the copyright owner.

Book Ordering Information
Cover design provided by: https://www.fiverr.com/patrick_2013
Email: shahidiislam@godbodyinternational.com
https://godbodyinternational.com

Attention African American Theologians!!!
What if Everything you Thought you Knew About God Was Wrong?

Demystifying God: Redefining Black Theology in the Age of iGod [Remastered] is the second instalment in Shahidi Islam's Shahidi Collection series. With the world manipulating Black history we need to find a way to get to our truth.

Demystifying God

This book is dedicated to the Gods and
Goddesses of the foundation,
who dwell in a Nation of love, peace, and
happiness

Table of Contents

Preface to Shahidi Edition	viii
Preface to Third Edition	x
Preface to Second Edition	xii
Prologue	xvi
Introduction	xix

Part 1 Ecclesiology   1

1.	The Ghetto Saviour and the Game of Life	6
2.	When Her Poker Face Destroys His Flush	17
3.	Playing With the Cards We Were Dealt	36
4.	Pulling the Race Card and Other Absurdities	48
5.	The Great White Bluff … Why Everyone Loses!	64
6.	Deuces are Wild (With No Jokers)	75
7.	Know When to Fold'em	97

Part 2 Eschatology   111

8.	More Than Conquerors	119
9.	The Unstoppable Rise of an Insatiable Beast	132
10.	The Empire that Debt Built	144
11.	The Power of Absolute Power	155
12.	"Fear Not They Which Can Destroy the Body"	173
13.	The Voice that Shakes the Earth	194
14.	Judgment Day as Declared by the Prophets	211
15.	The Epistle of Revelation in Godbody Eschatology	220

Part 3 Soteriology   235

16.	Victorian Gardens	243
17.	The Real Bodily Resurrection	253
18.	Ancient Egyptian Theogonies	265
19.	"Don't Do That…"	274
20.	When Kings Die	283
21.	Blood Vengeance By Default	290

22. Where to Find the Real Ark of Noah	299
Conclusion	310
Epilogue	312

Appendage Christology 315

Bibliography	329

Preface to Shahidi Edition

For those who remember this book when it was still underground I must explain the need for this rewrite. See, I no longer go under the name Tony Saunders, which name is my slave name. My righteous name is now my government name properly and formally, and that is Shahidi Islam. For this reason I am re-releasing some of my former works under my new name so as to certify them. I have lots of other writings in circulation that go under the name Tony Saunders, some of which I am quite ashamed of. If you have found or read one of them please feel free to discard it. If it is not a book or writing under the name Shahidi Islam it is not something I am endorsing. Besides, Tony Saunders is a popular name and there are so many other people under that name I just got lost in the sea of them. To separate myself from all of them and to permanently remove the embarrassment of my former works I have chosen to release this Shahidi Collection featuring a correct explication of my doctrine as it stands. Again, if a work is not found either with the author name Shahidi Islam or endorsed by Shahidi Islam then I do not endorse what is written within, even if it is one of my own former writings, as some of them have ideas I no longer endorse or agree with. To wipe the slate clean and to endorse ideas that I do agree with look out for upcoming books and articles from Shahidi Islam, this Shahidi Collection is itself a precursor. As this book is in the Shahidi Collection not only am I endorsing it, but it is a part of my very philosophy and outlook on life. Therefore, I believe in what is written in these pages and believe the Black community would benefit substantially by paying close attention to what is being said.

Black Divinity: A Ghetto Theology for the Black Community Shahidi Collection Vol 1 [Remastered] was originally written to create a new kind of Black theology, a Black Godbody Theology, the starting point for which was to be that all Black people are divine. It is believed within the godbody, the ghetto organisation that propagates this philosophy, that once a city, a nation, the world, accepts the truth of Black Divinity then the true thearchy will exist on earth. This is a thearchy in which all Black people, as genuine Gods and Goddesses, rule. Not as oppressors, but as caretakers of the world and of the ecology. This will be a truly religionless, pollutionless, stateless, classless, exploitationless, povertyless, moneyless, marriageless, and pantyless society even as was ancient Ta Neteru (the land of the gods and goddesses). Indeed, as Ta Neteru was the only place in history in which there was no oppression on the basis of religion, race, class, gender, sexuality, or ecology, Ta Neteru is thereby the original blueprint for a Black thearchy that all we as a people should strive for. To such a world this book will be a companion.

Preface to Third Edition

Within months of publishing the second edition of *Black Divinity* it became apparent that there would need to be a third; however, having already begun the process of marketing the second edition I had to let that run its course. The current third edition is by far easier to reconcile to the 5 Percent philosophy than the first two editions were. However, as the basis for all three editions was notes taken in 2006 when I was still a Christian it is not completely fair to call any of these versions of *Black Divinity* a 5 Percent book. True the first two editions were written while I was a "new born" 5 Percenter and contain some 5 Percent embellishments; but no genuine 5 Percenter would respect either of them or the current as substantial 5 Percent theory. In that sense *Black Divinity* remains somewhat of a fossil, or at least an embryo.

I have chosen to remake *Black Divinity* this third time for the purpose of opening up an avenue for those who will read my next few books to see a more unified variation of my intellectual development: that, though certain substantial changes and transformations have occurred in my personal views and conclusions, my overall interpretation of life and of the solutions to the Black situation were already in existence over a decade ago. A final reason behind the current remake was to deal with certain issues that have arisen since the publication of the first edition, in particular the rising of ISIS. As the first two editions speak excessively of the Egyptian goddess Isis and her husband Isar, I felt it would be potentially confusing for future generations, and the young of the current generation, to read the word Isis so much and not associate it with a terrorist organisation; therefore I changed all mentions of the names Isar and Isis to their proper Egyptian names Ausar and Auset.

That said, this book is relatively faithful to the second edition with, however, certain big changes that bring the ideas closer to my current development. I do not want the reader to be confused, though, the book as a whole is and must be read as a Christian book. The Islamic and 5 Percent leanings do not in any way compensate for the heavily Christian philosophy expounded throughout. Nevertheless, the heart and soul of this book is to lead to a new interpretation of life and the Hebrew prophecies thereby bringing us to a place of fulfilment and salvation. Not that some outside saviour comes from the sky and saves us. Our salvation is self-performed. We become our own saviours through knowledge of self, love of self and love of neighbour as of self. In this is found the kingdom God promised to the Hebrew people and is found the pathway to that divine nature that is opened to us by accepting the message of truth.

Finally, this book is dedicated to my Sun and Enlightener who is currently a political prisoner doing time in Oklahoma State Prison, thank you for the jewels you dropped on me: it is much appreciated. And to all the Gods and Earths out there, peace – coming straight from Tony Saunders, whose righteous attribute is Shahidi Islam.

Preface to Second Edition

The first edition of this book was released in 2012 for the purpose of inspiring Black people to consider their potential for divinity. With the passing of time errors and inconsistencies became more evident. Also written for the purpose of representing the New York City street culture and showing some of its remarkable ideas and articulating them to the Black intelligentsia of America I found it ever more difficult to get a footing in this crowd and among this audience. Finding instead a home among African professionals I found it necessary to remove some of the more immature and gang related ideas of the first edition. I also found that the general message, that of demodernization, was not respectfully disclosed or given the conspicuousness it deserves in the last edition.

I feel at this time that perhaps the French were too soon to close the coffin on modernity. Modernity cannot be wished away it must, like any existing ruling force, be overthrown. Nothing has overthrown it. Nothing has taken its place. It still exists as the central basis of life in the Western world, as no new class of people has replaced it. No new movement has stood toe-to-toe with it and won. There has been no fight, not so to speak but literally.

Socialism may fight capitalism, but socialism on its own still cannot trump modernism. It is not the overthrow of modernism or a leap into a postmodern world. Even the anti-capitalist movement and the Make Poverty History movement come nowhere near to an overthrow of the system or its proper fight back.

I myself am simply laying the foundation for such an overthrow to occur. I may not see its completion and I do not expect to be that huge, just to be a foundation is more than enough for me; a stepping stone on which many giants tread. I do not think it too wise to go ahead of yourself, and expecting an imminent demise of modernism is stepping ahead of myself. True indeed, I must walk this straight and narrow path of anti-modernism but I must go at a pace that is credible and followable.

But how does one fight against something so stable and time honoured? What does one say to send tremors down the spine of modernity? It exists virtually everywhere. It is the all-seeing, all-controlling force of all forces. Modernism is so used to being in charge it seems almost impossible to dethrone her from her pre-eminence; built, as it is, on several shaky epistemological foundations. Modernism promised the uncovering of truth but brought in the propagation of opinion. It promised the reign of reason but brought in the reign of chaos. It promised us equal rights but brought us unequal privileges. It promised uninhibited freedom but brought in disguised subjugation. It promised universal prosperity but brought in abject poverty. These have been the real benefits of our surrendering to the machinism of modernism; but it is time for a change.

In this situation the first thing that needs to be adjusted is our views of systemic indoctrination. Everything in modernity is a system and everything is a machine. Machines called systems connecting to other machines called bureaucracies, to create further machines called institutions. Different structures form into systems which then become pandemic throughout modernism as a whole.

Systems are the central disease of modernity. They suck the life out of any and every thing they touch. This soulless enterprise is all-consuming as it infects the livelihoods of all living things in the human mind. It is abstract, absolutizing and objectifying. In fact, the objectivity of modernism is the basis for all its 'sciences.' But objectivity must give way to demodernizing intersubjectivity or we may all lose our souls.

By letting go of the grand theories of science, and by accepting that everything has a soul through which it vibrates transmissions and feedback at different velocities, amplitudes, frequencies and wavelengths, and through which it interprets all events and phenomena; we can begin to overthrow the first monster of modernism: the scientific method. True indeed, we should still hold to some of its classifications but overall grand sciences create only chaos and complexity. We need to appreciate that all these things are related. Without science taking a humbler seat in the banquet of life, modern theoretical ideologies will continue getting more and more dehumanizing.

So what does this mean, the abolition of objective theories? It means we appreciate that there are two or more sides to every truth. Even if one was to have all the facts of a specific event it still would not count for half the information necessary to make a reasonable judgment on the entire case. There is the observer's past experiences, feelings, hurts, pains, wins, gains and biases to consider also along with all manner of other subjective realities that have not been mentioned. But a truth is not only subjective, it is intersubjective as it is based on the subjective realities of every living being that exists. At the same time, if the truth is intersubjective then we are left with the irony of truth and the caricature of science.

In all this French Postmodernism was right; to destroy or surpass modernity we must begin at its philosophical precursors. Philosophically and ideologically that which is called postmodern would be better called anti-modern. It challenges the edifice of modern objectivity. Thus we have the understanding on its behalf of the intersubjective realities of each individual and the understanding that grand all-encompassing truths are an impossibility. So the French school is the best place to begin a full frontal assault against modernity. Having thus overthrown modernism in the mind and moved on to the postmodern it would be fair to prepare for the next level. This book is that.

Prologue

The starting point for the current theology is that all Black people are divine, yet this concept of Black divinity actually has a long history. It was first articulated by the ancient Ethiopians over twenty-eight millennia ago, in a land that was called in times past Ta Neteru (the land of the gods and goddesses). The message was then continued on in ancient Egypt by the various mystical traditions, around another nine millennia ago; and by the ancient Hebrew mystical traditions over three millennia ago. The message was eventually lost to the Hebrews during their many exiles, but it was still maintained in ancient Egypt and ancient Ethiopia over the vast centuries.

Then came the Baptist to revive among the Judeans the understanding of Black divinity. He would also start a liberation movement among the Judeans, predicting the coming of someone after him, in his own lifetime, who would bring the people back to their Black divinity through a baptism into holiness and into a fully independent monarchy. The very Messiah he prophesied, would continue on that message, which after his disappearance splintered off into several separate branches.

The mystics among his followers were called the gnostics and they combined the Messiah's message with the ancient Egyptian philosophy. The gnostic message thereby continued the idea of Black divinity secretly and underground during a time when even the mainstream messianic movement was also underground (due mainly to heavy persecution). Unfortunately, when the messianic movement, finally, did gain legality it was only the mainstream version. Gnosticism, however, would remain an outlaw movement, thus driving them even further underground.

At that time, within the mainstream movement the only Black person considered truly divine was the Messiah (back then the only images of the Messiah were as a Black man). Black divinity then re-emerged with Islamic mysticism, a tradition that combined the gnostic oral tradition with Islamic interpretations of the Quran. The Prophet himself was an ardent follower of gnostic ideas and beliefs. It is even likely that he was trained and mentored by a practicing gnostic. Whether this is true or not, we know for sure that he referenced several gnostic teachings and traditions in the Quran that he could not have possibly known without having some familiarity with their history.

Finally, Black divinity would ultimately reach its greatest height in America, starting with the Honorable Elijah Muhammad bringing to the Black communities of America that Islamic mystical tradition through his Lost-Found Nation of Islam. From the Nation of Islam would then eventually emerge the godbody movement: a movement in the ghetto that went on to define G.O.D. as guns over drugs – thereby interpreting that the militant Black man that gains Knowledge 120 becomes a God in his own right, having the power to give life (through spreading 120) and to take life (we all know how); and to build; and to destroy. Now for the most part we try to use this power, not to take life, but to build through it a Nation of Gods and Earths (hereafter to be called Goddesses).

That said, the 120 lessons we godbodies endorse are, again, only just the Supreme Wisdom lessons of the Honorable Elijah Muhammad. In that sense they have been read and mastered by several heroes and heroines within the Black community including: Minister Louis Farrakhan, Minister Malcolm X, Imam Warith Deen Muhammad, Dr. Khalid Muhammad, Dr. Sebi Alfredo Bowman, Dr. Malachi Z. York, the Champ Muhammad Ali, Erikah Badu, Bilal the 1st Born, D'Angelo, Jay Electronica, Busta Rhymes, Rakim Allah, Nas, Foxy Brown, Queen Latifah, all of the Fugees, the Wu-Tang Clan, Mobb Deep, and Brand Nubian. Even so, while the United States government has attacked and attempted to discredit many of these Black leaders, all of them are still well beloved by most Black people. The truth is, we Black people have always had the potential for divinity, but it is only now that we are starting to realise how to actually achieve it.

True, it may be currently accepted among the godbody – again, the ghetto organisation that is currently the central body propagating the message of Black divinity – that once a city, a nation, and the world comes to accept the truth of our destiny then a Black thearchy will begin to exist upon the earth. Indeed, as any true solarpunk/ecofuturist would much rather aim and strive for a low-tech and high-empath future; even so, within the godbody a more ghetto combination of solarpunk and Neo-Soul is believed to be more desirable; but that mainly through Black people taking their place as a God-Collective of the divine Black people we have always been.

Introduction

The current book is based on notes originally written in 2006 and edited in 2012 and again in 2019 for the purpose of liberating my people. Contained within are also a very large cross-section of quotations that break up a lot of the content making it seem at times frustrating and a little hard to read. This annoyance was unavoidable due to the current situation, and the unfortunate mistrust of those outside of the street life of the intelligence of anyone arising out of the street life. Again, hopefully no one within the street life, particularly within the Five Percent Nation, will be too offended by some of the language that I have chosen to use throughout, as it was mainly for the purpose of speaking to the uninitiated, not to ruin our image or desecrate our culture.

From an historical context all past developments in human progress have been correlated to philosophical precursors. From Aristotle's influence on ancient Greece and Plato's influence over the Roman *res publica*; to the influence of Rousseau on the French Revolution and Marx on the Russian; it is virtually impossible to separate historical epochs from their philosophical precursors. The initial philosophical bursts of light and hope, however, usually begin to dim as the pains of reaction begin to set in. This reactionary response to the new ideas and the hostility of its opposition usually bring great sorrow and disillusionment to the representatives of the new vision and ideal.

As these realities are the historical norm for all prior to revolutionary changes it is clear that anything of this calibre will meet also its own huge bursts of reactionary opposition and rage. From church pulpit to political gathering, from social clubs to cultural events all groups and sections of society claim allegiance to morality and against the dark cloud of the street life. True indeed, as the streets are considered a curse on society, and themselves cursed of God, we, in the eyes of those outside of the streets, should have nothing to do with anything even resembling the theocentric, let alone the thearchic. In fact, our anti-establishment makes us seem to any who are not affiliated to be more nihilistic than ritualistic. This anti-establishment being a product of our rejection by the establishment and being outcasts to it, has caused us to question our place in a society that would create and tolerate such vicious injustices as occur in the neighbourhoods of this so-called Western society.

But the godbody itself is really just a system based on the identification of a new Black theodicy, that is, a study of God's goodness and righteousness from a Black person's perspective. Having arisen from the backstreets of New York as the godbody, we have taken their general outlook and message, and added to them theological, psychological, ideological, sociological, ecological, and cosmological depth. Conversely, though, the godbody is primarily based on the use of ghetto codes and culture to achieve Black identity amid the difficult and adverse situations of racism, poverty, humiliation, demonisation, dyseducation, discrimination, marginalisation, criminalisation, and state-orchestrated incarceration.

As a people most of we Blacks have been separated from our history and a knowledge of our history; but as Nature expresses herself through a cyclical rhythm of spontaneous repetitions, I feel that a knowledge of recent Black history is worth acknowledging. Marcus Garvey inspired an entire generation with the thought of a Black God. A God, not White like their slave-masters (or like their job-managers in this current system of wage-slavery) but a God Black like them, who understood the trials and sufferings of the people and offered them the strength and power to redeem themselves from these sufferings.

This philosophy spread in Africa, America, and the Caribbean in many forms. Two most obvious forms were the Rastafarians, who claimed Negusa Negast Tafari was the Black God incarnate, and the Black theologians, who claimed the Messiah Jesus was the Black God incarnate. But you also had the Black Muslims, who claimed Master Fard Muhammad was the Black God incarnate. Then you had the Afrocentrics who claimed the ancestral gods of Africa (particularly those of ancient Egypt), which manifest themselves in Nature, were the Black gods incarnate. Even the Kemetic scholars (who are commonly and derisively called "Hoteps" by most Black people) would claim the Egyptian god Ra to be the Black God incarnated in all Black males; similar to the Five Percent, who claim Allah to be *the God* incarnated in all Black males who have mastered the 120 lessons and opened the third eye of astral vision.

All that said, the Five Percent movement contains six categorical systems which allow for our further continuance: Black divinity, Black revolutionism, Black eroticism, Black astralism, Black demodernisation, and Black syndicalism. These all effectively spell up to the words: Black DREADS; and all also make up the godbody ideology that I endorse – being generally accepted within the godbody movement as a whole – though never spelled-out or outlined in this sort of way before. What I thereby hope to accomplish with this undertaking is a complete renewal of our movement and the lessons of the movement as handed down to me by my mentor and enlightener so as to show where our movement can lead and why the actual teleology of godbodyism will be a positive and not a self-destructive one.

INTRODUCTION

In itself the godbody theory articulated throughout has been designed to be a form of Black ideology that incorporates ideas, language, and expressions from chaos theory, deconstruction theory, decolonising theory, post-colonial theory, critical race theory, pro-Black anarchist theory, and pro-sex womanist theory into the outlook and world vision of the Five Percent Nation. And as stated earlier the Five Percent Nation as a movement teaches that the Black man is God. Beginning in the 1960s under the leadership of a direct disciple of Malcolm X, who at that time was named Clarence 13X, but who we call Allah out of respect for the vision he received of the potential divinity of all Black men, obviously including himself, we seek also to enlighten our people as to their potential.

Even so, it must obviously also be noted that a lot of the ideas and practices encouraged throughout are not those of the entire godbody of the United States, but are add-ons I developed based on lessons I learned in the Socialist Workers Party as an anti-capitalist and in the Black Church as a Pentecostal. As I left America as a "newborn" godbody I never had the chance to fully master the 120 lessons; I did, however, take a lot of the lessons I learned in cipher with the godbody and expound on them to co-create with my enlightener: God Born Supreme Allah, a Black thearchy based on his own GBSA-ideology. This book therefore is mainly a union of all the previous movements I learned from so as to contribute to the further empowering of our people.

Recognising also that a lot of the Gods themselves have no tolerance for innovation; I concluded that we stand no hope of ever overthrowing White supremacy without making certain changes to our lessons. We will never elevate until we are willing to innovate. And if we were to find that something was emphatically wrong we would be obliged to destroy it and so elevate beyond it, even as we destroy the mathematics of anyone who does not backup their lessons with proof. It is my hope that

INTRODUCTION

these lessons, which are mainly based on quotations, can be used by all other newborns to understand how the Gods build, and by godbodies to bring us to a place of true divinity in our ways and actions based on knowledge, wisdom, and understanding. True indeed, as the highest form of understanding is love, even so, the love triad of empathic, agapic, and erotic love is the essence of true divinity, it is by this kind of divinity that we will be able to elevate beyond local hood heroes to become global superheroes.

Finally, this book has been through many revisions, however, it will go through no more. I am satisfied with what it is now and no longer feel it should be changed any further. It is my intention for the current version to be used to inform the course of the godbody movement in its rise to popularity, and to create an avenue for the acceptance of this theological perspective within the current discussions of African American theology. Within this context I pay homage to those who came before me in the classical schools: Anthony B. Pinn, William R. Jones, James H. Cone, Albert B. Cleage, Delores S. Williams, Kelly B. Douglas, Robert S. Beckford, Anthony G. Reddie, Creflo A. Dollar, and Thomas D. Jakes. Still, it must be said at this point, although this book may cause you to fall asleep, it is not because it is boring but more so because it will cause your mind to expand and work overtime to consolidate all the new information. Nevertheless, will I still take full responsibility for any negative opinions that you may have concerning it. Peace.

The Supreme Mathematics

Potentials

k = knowledge (1)

w = wisdom (2)

u = understanding (3)

f = freedom – I choose not to add culture as freedom is the most obvious elevation from understanding and culture is implied in the whole mathematics (4)

p = power – (I use the term power neither in the Marxian sense, as in to dominate nor in the Foucauldian sense, as in to discipline or surveille; but instead use it in the Adlerian sense as in empowerment) I choose not to add refinement as power is the next elevation from freedom and progresses till it reaches equality (5)

e = equality (6)

G = God – where God is equivalent to the omnipresent, and not to a state of pure perfection (7)

B = build – when adding on (8)

D = destroy – when subtracting (8)

$\forall$ = born (9)

$°$ = cipher (0)

INTRODUCTION

Symbols

D = dialectical moment where *pa* > *na* becomes *na* > *pa*, or vice versa.

Lm = the limitation

$\exists$ = when there is

$+$ = together with

$\in$ = the sum includes

$>$ = greater than

$\geq$ = greater than or equal to

$<$ = lesser then

$\leq$ = lesser than or equal to

$\rightarrow$ = leads on to

$\leftrightarrow$ = if and only if

$\nearrow$ = on the increase

$\searrow$ = on the decrease

$\propto$ = proportional to

Values

∞ = infinity

INTRODUCTION

o = zero

λ = wavelength

A = amplitude

d = displacement

t = time expended

v = rate of velocity

δ = astral forces $->x^1$

α = social forces $->x^{10}$

β = global forces $->x^{20}$

θ = environmental forces $->x^{30}$

ϕ = terrestrial forces (also called geomagnetic forces) $->x^{40}$

ϑ = solar forces (also called heliospheric magnetic forces) $->x^{50}$

∂ = globular forces (also called stellar magnetic forces) $->x^{60}$

φ = galactic forces (also called galactic magnetic forces) $->x^{70}$

ψ = super-clusteral forces (also called intercluster magnetic forces) $->x^{80}$

INTRODUCTION

$\mathcal{E}$ = cosmic forces $-> x^{90}$

Pa = positive action of an individual

pa = positive action of a social body

Na = negative action of an individual

na = negative action of a social body

x = social potential of a social body

n = level of social potentiality

g = a social movement

$opp.g$ = an oppressing social movement

$emp.g$ = an empowering social movement

(pa) = all the positive actions of a social body

(na) = all the negative actions of a social body

(v) = all the social velocity

(g) = the whole social movement

S = decelerative force caused by reaction of social body x_1

R = accelerative force caused by resistance of social body x_2

S = syndicalism

INTRODUCTION

The Godbody System

The Universal Laws of Existence

1. The law of interaction (whose corollary is the pleasure principle),

2. The law of intersubjectivity (whose corollary is the vibratory law),

3. The law of self-organisation (whose corollary is the identity law),

4. The law of opposition (whose corollary is the polarity law),

5. The law of repetition (whose corollary is the inertia law),

6. The law of self-similarity (whose corollary is the correspondence law),

7. The law of conservation (whose corollary is the reciprocity law),

8. The law of evolution (whose corollary is the power law),

9. The law of devolution (whose corollary is the entropy law),

10. The law of self-destruction (whose corollary is the phase-transition law),

11. The law of interconnectivity (whose corollary is the synchronicity law), and

INTRODUCTION

12. The law of interrelation (whose corollary is the eternalist law).

The 10 Principles

1. No God but Allah
2. No power imbalances
3. No non-authors
4. No non-fighters
5. No Divine fights alone
6. No problems handled in the Square should ever leave the Square
7. No marriage or marriages
8. No missing parliament meetings
9. No wearing underwear
10. No harassment or rape of any kind ever

What We Teach

1. That Black people are the Original people of the planet earth.
2. That Black people are the fathers and mothers of civilization.

INTRODUCTION

3. That the science of Supreme Mathematics is the key to understanding man's relationship to the universe.

4. That Islam is a natural way of life, not a religion.

5. That education should be fashioned to enable us to be self sufficient as a people.

6. That each one should teach one according to their knowledge.

7. That the Black man is God and his proper name is ALLAH. Arm, Leg, Leg, Arm, Head.

8. That our children are our link to the future and they must be nurtured, respected, loved, protected and educated.

9. That the unified Black family is the vital building block of the nation.

The Hedgehog Concept (The Build Allah Square)

1. Eat, Train, Read, Write, and Share

The Core Concepts

1. Black divinity, Black revolutionism, Black eroticism, Black astralism, Black demodernisation, and Black syndicalism

The Physical Concepts

1. biophysics, quantum physics, molecular physics, geophysics, astrophysics, and digital physics

INTRODUCTION

The Discursive Concepts

1. body, embody, and disembody
2. structure, infrastructure, and superstructure
3. subtle, subaltern, and subterranean
4. text, pretext, subtext, and context
5. discourse, discursive, pre-discursive, narrative, and performative
6. reality, surreality, sub-reality, hyper-reality, virtual-reality, and unreality
7. erase, absent, present, represent, reproduce, re-enact, legitimate, and counter
8. position, supposition, disposition, composition, superposition, opposition, exposition, and imposition
9. silence, distort, fabricate, exaggerate, implicate, explicate, delineate, propagate, and voice

The Chronological Concepts

1. historicism and historicity
2. linear-chronological and event-sequential
3. historical, ahistorical, prehistorical, and transhistorical

INTRODUCTION

The Pneumatological Concepts

1. demonise and transfigure

2. divine, vampyre, and devil

3. elemental, environmental, and universal

4. foresight, insight, and hindsight

5. *Sebi*, *Nebi*, and *Obi*

6. astral, astral body, astral force, and astral plane

7. *Hakim, Karim, Rahim*, and Allah

8. Horu construct, Hethor construct, Ausar conscious, and Auset conscious

9. existent, pre-existent, co-existent, de-existent, and re-existent

10. resurrected, incorporated, *phantomised*, internalised, and exorcised

11. empathic, psychopathic, sociopathic, *monopathic, duopathic, polypathic*, and *panopathic*

12. empath, dark empath, supernova empath, true empath, quiet empath, psychic empath, super empath, sigma empath, and Heyoka empath

INTRODUCTION

The Psychological Concepts

1. conscious and unconscious
2. libido and superego
3. inhibition, prohibition, and exhibitionism
4. object, selfobject, and objectify
5. subject, subjective, and intersubjective
6. trauma, complex, and therapy
7. power, empower, internalise, incorporate, and concretise
8. spectre, drive, constraint, ideal, and somatic

The Ideological Concepts

1. seduction, perverse seduction, and seductionism
2. sexualise, racialise, and criminalise
3. White superiority, White supremacy, and White privilege
4. acculturate, assimilate, integrate, and institutionalise
5. gaze, oppress, problematise, and deviate
6. shackling, unshackling, deshackling, and reshackling
7. typical, atypical, prototypical, and archetypal

8. institution, destitution, restitution, constitution, deconstitution, and reconstitution

9. sexual, asexual, heterosexual, homosexual, transsexual, intersexual, and hypersexual

10. modern, premodern, postmodern, late modern (liquid modern), anti-modern, and demodernise

11. colony, market-colony, industrial-colony, military-colony, penal-colony, settler-colony, spatial-colony, cultural-colony, corporeal-colony, mental-colony, epistemic-colony, counter-colony, neo-colony, and the Great United States Empire (GUSE)

The Sociological Concepts

1. embodied displacement (exile, migration, trans-migration, or tourism) and disembodied displacement (phantasy, fantasy, wish, dream, vision, imagination, or astral journey)

2. aetiology, teleology, and eschatology

3. locality, globality, and communality

4. ordination, subordination, and superordination

5. gnosis, prognosis, diagnosis, and epignosis

6. inertia, action, interaction (force), and act-species

7. interior, exterior, anterior, posterior, and ulterior

INTRODUCTION

8. mechanic, elastic, static, kinetic, and dynamic

9. politics, geopolitics, biopolitics, necropolitics, transpolitics, hyper-politics, body-politics, racial-politics, and sexual-politics

The Sociological Axioms

1. The Axioms of Social Mechanics

a) $x > 1$

b) $v < 670{,}616{,}629$ mph

c) $v = \dfrac{d}{t}$

2. The Axioms of Social Force

a) $v\left(\dfrac{x^n}{x^n}\right) = \alpha$

b) $x_1 + R = Lm$ and $x_2 + S = Lm$

c) $\alpha > x^{10}$

3. The Axioms of Social Movements

a) $x_1 > x_2 \leftrightarrow x_2 \alpha \searrow o$

b) $g \propto \alpha$

c) $g_1(pa) \to g_2(na)$ and $g_1(na) \to g_2(pa)$

INTRODUCTION

d) $d = (2\pi) \times \left(\frac{2\lambda + 2A}{2}\right)$

4. The Axioms of Social Kinetics

a) $x_1 + x_2 \to na$

b) $x_1 + x_2 \to pa \leftrightarrow Lm \searrow$

c) $pa > Lm \to D \leftrightarrow pa \searrow$

5. The Axioms of Social Statics

a) $g(Lm) \leftrightarrow \alpha \searrow o$

b) $\exists \alpha \searrow o \to x^u \geq g$

6. The Axioms of Social kinetics

a) $Lm > g$

b) $\exists (\alpha > Lm) \to g \nearrow$

c) $\exists Lm \to \alpha \searrow + g \searrow$

PART I
ECCLESIOLOGY

ECCLESIOLOGY

Following I will be exploring what I consider to be just concerning the name of Paul, even as the misuse and twisting of his teachings and very revolutionary ideas by that which is called the Pauline school has led to his current notoriety in the world as of capitalistic sensitivities. Choosing instead to consider what in Paul's life and work contains the kernel of his reality and avoiding all mystifying and otherworldly debates, I will be, in essence, trying to recapture that social theory that Paul implanted, or tried to implant, into his early followers and associates. It is my hope that in doing this, I may return us to the core reality of the apostle Paul's very revolutionary vision for social change. Indeed, whether intentionally or unintentionally, the apostle Paul brought into the heart of mainstream society a kind of subaltern ethics whereby the colonised subjects of his time could identify themselves. It is through this prism of subalternity that we can trace the silences, the hidden truths and ideas that go unsaid, whether due to common comprehension or governmental regulation, that unlock the true ideals that the apostle Paul envisaged.

Many Christians today, especially among evangelicals and Charismatics, use the apostle Paul as an excuse to justify their greed. Of all the apostles, he has been considered the most liberal, and certainly he needed business affairs to run smoothly as he was also a tentmaker (Acts 18: 1-3). But was the apostle

Paul's vision really for a capitalist world system as so many prosperity preachers claim it was, or is there in fact, hidden in the depths, the subterranean dungeons of this incessant political prisoner, an anarchic and anti-colonialist vision for social change. Herein, I shall be exposing classical Roman colonialism throughout Part I in order to allow you to understand and familiarise yourselves with the reality of Paul's hope to produce within the readers of his letters a mental and bodily decolonisation from the then form of Western imperialism.

In its current form, the world cannot afford to maintain the Western empire of implacable wealth creation. Competition inevitably turns into conflict, now open, now hidden conflict. It cannot but cause ruin because it is so disorderly and filled with contradictions. As István Mészáros pointed out, one of the contradictions which will prove to be, and has proven to be in the past, one of capital's absolute limits (capital being the means of production and exchange); is the contradiction between capital's national protectionism and its need to create transnational markets. Capital is of necessity private, personal, and nationalistic, yet it needs to become international to maintain a prosperous existence. The imperialistic tendencies within capital cause its national manifestation to seek the overpowering of other national capitals; yet it must itself maintain this international dominance to keep from competitive obsolescence.

This contradiction existed during the times of mid-modern colonialism. In those times, capital's nationalist tendencies triumphed over its internationalist tendencies to a certain extent; which caused the liberation movements to fight for national sovereignty instead of international anarchy. But this internationalist tendency within capitalism has not gone away; instead it has re-emerged as globalised capital; a globalisation that has provided fuel for the fire of its critics hostility.

Modern Western imperialism in the twenty-first century currently has had only two substantial opponents: (i) the anti-imperialists and (ii) the Islamists. The anti-imperialists are usually post-colonialists as they were at one time subject to the mid-modern West in the form of colonialism. For the most part they now fear a neo-colonial advance from the West as they hear them preaching globalisation, but practicing the subjugation of smaller countries under the national capital, rules, and power structure of more modernised countries. Based on the practice of the West, and not their preaching, these countries, having nationalised their governments, would go on to nationalise a number of big properties for the native population of their location.

These countries, again, mostly post-colonialist, usually believe that all national capital should be held within the nation and shared out among the people of that nation. They are unfortunately too small or weak to fight a substantial war with the neoliberal neo-colonial powers, so as potential profit margins and the possibility of gaining some desired resource could always cause the West to fight if diplomacy ceases to work, threats of overthrow or assassination are usually more than enough to keep them in line or from going too far against the wishes of their Western overlords.

With Islamism it is a different story. First of all, Islamism is not, and should not be considered, a pejorative term for terrorism – most Islamists are anti-terrorist, it is only the Jihadists that usually resort to terrorism, but I will discuss more on this subject in a later chapter – most Muslims simply define Islamism as: revolutionary Islam. So, considering now, therefore, the expansion of Western legal and political dominance around the world, and the globalisation of consumerism and commodification into Islamic countries. Plus, the extreme lack of morality in the articulated doctrines of modernism, especially by the standards held within those

Muslim countries. These have all coalesced to cause the religious communities of those Muslim countries to rise up in rebellion. So far this has led to religious wars between America, the bearers of modernism, and certain of those Muslim nations, as the keepers of religious purity. They war with America mainly due to Western oppressive tendencies and extreme lack of moral purity, whereas America fights back in the name of anti-terrorism.

This may explode into world war in the current clash of ideologies – especially considering the genocidal and imperialistic tendencies of Zionism towards its surrounding Muslim neighbours – and even though America (the key supporters of Zionism) may be the current global superpower, in a battle with a morally superior opponent they cannot win. The immorality of their neo-colonisation and White supremacy, which they maintain with the force of both weaponry and technology, will one day have to give way to a new morality. The so-called "gods" of the current system are lost in an ideological struggle with each other. Western modernisation must snatch up as much of the world in an imperialistic scrabble for territory as it can before these territories begin their own fight back in the form of global war. It is from here that we are able to see the apostle Paul as representing the intersection of both anti-modern views.

The Ghetto Saviour and the Game of Life

In order to understand the truth about the apostle Paul in his historical context, there is a fundamental issue that is extremely important for us to recognise first: this issue is that the Judeans of the apostle Paul's day were not like the Jews we have today. Virtually all Muslims and some enlightened Black people know that the original Judeans were themselves Black. That is, kind of dusky bronze (Black) in colour, as was said by the prophet Ezekiel, "In visions of God brought he me into the land of Israel, and set me upon a very high mountain, by which was as the frame of a city on the south. And he brought me thither, and, behold, there was a man, whose appearance was like the appearance of brass, with a line of flax in his hand, and a measuring reed; and he stood in the gate" (Ezekiel 40: 2, 3). Now the word translated here as brass is *nekhosheth*, which actually means copper, thus being in similitude to mahogany, and nowhere near the olive colour most Israelis have today. The implication from this Scripture is that the man is either a man of Israel or an angel of the God of Israel, either way he would have been the most likely colour of the historical people of Israel.

Yet if that is the case then why are the current Jews White? If we honestly wish to learn the truth we must begin by tracing the steps of Jose Malcioln, who himself found, "In 1941 Abraham

N. Poliak, an eminent Jewish scholar, born in Kiev in 1910, arrived in Palestine with his family determined to make a valuable contribution to Eretz Israel. Poliak was appointed professor of Medieval Jewish History at Tel Aviv University. He had read the true history of the origins and amalgamations of the original Hebrews and other tribes who lived in that area after the Flood. Qualified, secure, honest, and dignified as a scholar pursuing evidence to publish truth, Poliak read the books in Sabean, Cushitic, Aramaic, Arabic, and Hebrew. He then began publishing his findings in many books. In 1941, Professor Poliak wrote a book titled *The Khazar Conversion to Judaism!* His work appeared in a Hebrew publication called Zion."

So now, who were these Khazars he spoke of and why are they even important? According to Malcioln, "The Khazars ... were of Turkish-Caucasoid origin. Germany, Poland and Russia are replete with the descendants of these people whose forefathers converted to Judaism for political expediency rather than because of religious fervor. The Khazars did not speak Hebrew during the time of their conversion. They visited the Turks requesting to be taught Hebrew. The Turks advised them to visit the Greeks because they did not know the language either. ... The Greeks, who had been visiting and studying in Africa, and transporting information to Greece, taught the Khazars Hebrew and Torah" (Malcioln 1996: 90).

In continuing the narrative, eminent anthropologist Roland Dixon had this to say, "The Khazar being converted to Judaism in the eighth century, thereafter seem to have spread far and wide to the west and northwest, their modern descendants probably forming the preponderant element among the east European Jews." Malcioln further contributed that at their origins, "The Khazars [themselves] were interconnected through a confederation of tribes controlled by the Khagan or leader." Yet as of the eighth century he realised that his people would need to accept a monotheistic tradition, "The Khagan and his ruling class were clear on the issue. He and the top echelon knew the military power of the Caliph of Baghdad. If they chose Islam, they would be subjugated by the Caliphate according to the Islamic laws. If the Khazars chose Christianity, they would be equally subjugated by the Roman Emperor and dominated by his laws through the cross. So the majority of Khazar pagans followed their leader and the nobility, who selected Judaism to avoid subordination."

At this point, it could now be asked: What does all this have to do with anything? Well, according to Malcioln the "products of the Khazaric, Slavic, Turkish, Teutonic admixtures with even Magyars, commonly called Ashkenazim or European Jews," "went on to Western Germany, with some groups continuing on to Austria, through, and to, Bohemia, Hungary, Poland, Lithuania, Belorussia, and the Ukraine." But as we have already noted, these Ashkenazim were not authentic Jews and thereby never had the right to call themselves Semitic, even as we find written in the biblical Scriptures: "Now these are the generations of the sons of Noah, Shem, Ham, and Japheth: and unto them were sons born after the flood. The sons of Japheth; Gomer, and Magog, and Madai, and Javan, and Tubal, and Meshech, and Tiras. And the sons of Gomer; Ashkenaz, and Riphath, and Togarmah" (Genesis 10:1-3). Ashkenaz was always Japhethic.

Moreover, Malcioln further explicated the theory of Salmon Reinach that, "'The Hebrews [actually] made their first appearance in History as nomads.' Abraham, their patriarch, is said to have crossed the Jordan every Friday night – the Sabbath eve – to preach monotheism to the people of Canaan." Furthermore, this was all at a time "when Babylonia, Ethiopia, and Arabia were ruled by Africans." (Now obviously, the Arabs themselves, as descendants of Abraham, could not possibly have dominated Arabia, Egypt, or Babylonia in those days like they currently do today so the most likely inhabitants of all those lands was actually Black Africans). He further continued that it was around about that time that those who were "converted (including Abraham himself), went to Egypt, in Africa, abandoning Palestine and looking farther south. When they reached Ethiopia, the Egyptians and other Africans called them 'Falashim,' meaning strangers or foreigners."

Malcioln further went on to articulate how, "Several men [from among them that were] able to read and translate the Egyptian hieroglyphics and Ethiopic alphabet began writing contemporary history. Some copied the predictions of the sages from the walls of tombs, shrines, obelisks, and pyramids. Others wrote prophecies and laws. These writers were called prophets. Their collection of short and long stories copied from Egyptians and Babylonians was called the Bible … Before that, a part of it was called *Torah*. Their compilation of history, myths, predictions, laws, and admonitions became chapters or 'books.' … Thus, the Falashas [effectively] became known as 'the People of the Book.'" Here, ultimately revealing effectively that the original and authentic Hebrews of Canaan, Egypt, Arabia, Ethiopia, and Babylonia during its ancient history, and even deep into its early Islamic history, were most decisively a Black people.

Based on further deep research into the subject, Malcioln explained how, after the Falashas returned to the land of Canaan with Moses, a lot of them chose to remain behind in Egypt and Ethiopia. They became known throughout East Africa as the Agaw (the original Ge'ez Falashim that can be traced back to Abraham). Some tribes, however, began to migrate again out of Canaan land to further destinations. As noted, some "black-skinned members of the priesthood ran back to Egypt where they had gained the knowledge of religion and the key to the mystery system. Others ran to Tehemu, or Libya, where masonry was practiced, and eastern Cyrenaica, Mumidia, or Algiers, and Tunisia." Most of these became either Tuareg or Sephardic tribes; some travelling as far as Turkey, Sicily, France,

Spain, and Portugal, and after various, in some cases, forced intermarriages with the Europeans, formed the more lighter-skinned Sephardi in the world today.

Some of them, however, migrated to East Africa from Canaan forming the Kyla (said to have descended from the tribe of Ephraim) and the Amhara (said to have descended from the lineage of Solomon). Some of them went down south to Arabia and Yemen, and from there went even further south to southern Africa and Mozambique. Most of these became either Zagwe (said to have descended from Moses and his Ethiopian – most likely Oromo – wife) or the Lemba (said to have descended from the Levitical priesthood) tribes. Finally, some migrated as far west as Senegal and Mauritania founding and governing several great empires in West Africa including, but not limited to, the Ghana Empire, the Mali Empire, and the Songhai Empire. Within the last of these were included: the Fulani ethnicity, the Ashanti kingdom, the Judan kingdom, the Wenchi kingdom, the Dahomey kingdom, the Yoruba kingdom, and the Igbo kingdom.

Nevertheless, Malcioln also took note that, "In 1870 a French Jew named Joseph Halevy visited the Falashas. He was studying the languages of the various African tribes when he met this unusual group observing Hebrew customs and religious practices. The Falashas informed Halevy that they were the only Hebrews left in the world. They had not come in contact with any other Hebrews or Jews for centuries. The Falashim's Torah was [also] written in Ge'ez. This sociolinguistic find was announced by Halevy as the 'discovery of the Falashas.'" However, something far more diabolical was at play. Due to the high volume of intermarriages among the European Jews, both Ashkenazi and Sephardi, many Jews of the nineteenth century understood the precarious position their Judaism was in. For this cause, in order to authenticate themselves as Jews they had no further recourse but to return to their traditions. As most

Jews were well informed, sometime after the Neo-Babylonian Empire many of the ancient Falashic Hebrews were scattered to the four winds of heaven, though some of them were chosen by the Persian Emperor Cyrus to rebuild their fallen temple and re-establish their lost traditions.

That said, according to Islamic tradition, by the time those Hebrews returned to do so the Amorites had already destroyed most of the authentic copies of the Tawrat. It was therefore up to those scholars and lawyers, who had committed the Tawrat to memory to accomplish the task. However, unbeknownst to them at the time, copies of the true and authentic Tawrat had been kept preserved in Ethiopia and Saba for centuries. Herein we find that Halevy's intentions may not have been so noble as to simply find, or even preserve, African traditional cultures. Moreover, according to the Jewish Encyclopedia of 1959, Halevy "taught at schools of the Alliance Israelite Universelle in Turkey and Rumania and in 1868, went at the request of the Alliance to Ethiopia where he visited the Falashas. Subsequently, the Academic des Inscriptions et Belles Lettres sent him to Yemen where, disguised as a native rabbi, he succeeded in collecting 686 Sabean inscriptions (1869-70)."

What this shows is, basically, at the request of those "credible academic bodies" Halevy, through deception and dishonesty, was instructed to smuggle and steal various Sabean documents and thereby to learn and teach various true and authentic Hebrew customs and traditions. Indeed, these Sabean documents were obviously urgently needed by the European Jews in order to learn the authentic liturgy, customs, and rituals of the Sabean Hebrews. But this also, at the same time, undermines the authenticity of their own Hebraism. For if they truly considered their own Hebraism to have been authentic there would have been no need for all the subterfuge. Thereby proving that the true and authentic Hebrews were actually the Falashism.

None of this means we Black people should hate the Ashkenazim for appropriating one of our religions. It does, however, mean the Ashkenazim must acknowledge what their ancestors did and stop denying it as merely anti-Semitic propaganda. It also means the apostle Paul's journey to self-discovery must have been a very interesting and even complex one, with all the racial minefields he must have traversed. We can even get glimpses of its depths scattered throughout his letters in the biblical tradition. From this biblical account the little information we gather about his life before joining the messianic movement are such: Paul was born Saul in the city of Tarsus in modern-day Turkey. He was a Benjamite Judean, and still most likely a Black man, however, he was also tellingly born a citizen of the city of Rome.

From this little information we can gather that Paul was bought up in a middle class family from two places; the fact that he was born a citizen of Rome even though he was Judean by race and the fact that Tarsus was famed by early authors such as Strabo for being a very wealthy place filled with intellectuals as well as aristocrats. Saul then obviously went on to learn Judaism as well as philosophy as an apprentice, a truth we can gather from his letters' almost Platonian style. Saul was bought up a Pharisee. And although he was born in Tarsus, the accounts in Acts say he was bought up in Jerusalem and was mentored in the way of the Torah by Rabbi Gamaliel. So Saul apparently had a good Judaic upbringing from Tarsus to Jerusalem. And from Paul's own testimony we find that he also persecuted the messianic communities when they first began popping up.

This same Saul, as most Christians would know, was converted because while he was on his way to Damascus to persecute the messianic communities there, he received a vision of the risen Messiah and was blinded. Then, it was a follower of the messianic tradition who opened his eyes to see again, converting and baptising him into the messianic movement.

Saul, from that moment, went through a real humbling. It is very reminiscent of the conversion of Malcolm X, a pimp, a hustler, and a thief, who went on to found several Muslim temples in America for the Nation of Islam.

Malcolm X's conversion story is a little less well known than that of the apostle Paul's. Malcolm Little was arrested in Boston for theft and was given a ten year sentence. During the majority of his time, of which he served seven years before being paroled to his brother, his family was able to convince him they could get him out of prison. At this time Malcolm had become so depraved that the other inmates called him Satan. He would argue with the correction officers and chaplains and would pretend he forgot his prison number to get put into solitary. Malcolm's Damascus experience is when his brother told him he knew a man, a Black man, who had 360° of knowledge. Soon, in a vision Malcolm would see this man as Master Fard Muhammad, the founder of the Nation of Islam. Like with Saul Malcolm was humbled and devoted the rest of his time in prison to studying and learning about the Nation of Islam. By the time he was released he was still not ready yet to preach, but, just like Saul, when the time was right Malcolm could not be stopped.

Malcolm Little was given the name Malcolm X by the Nation of Islam just as Saul was given the name Paul by the messianic movement. This messianic movement, predominantly being filled with Black Judeans, predominantly being filled with peasant farmers and non-industrialised workers, shared many similarities with the early Nation of Islam. Messianism as a movement started out among the lower classes, then grew to gain aristocrats and merchants, and soon people from all walks of life. Thus, Paul became a poor righteous teacher in the early messianic movement even as Malcolm X would become in the Islamic nationalist movement. But none of Paul's teachings say the kind of social system he believed God would approve of. To him the kingdom of God (or Nation of God) was imminent –

even Malcolm X shared a similar feeling of imminence about the Nation of Islam – but unlike most of his messianic contemporaries, his form of anti-imperialism was not through violent sedition but through ethical progression.

At the height of his influence he wrote to the messianic communities of Rome, saying, "I am not ashamed of the gospel of Christ: for it is the power of God unto salvation to everyone that believeth; to the Jew first, and also to the Greek" (Romans 1: 16). As, in the apostle Paul's time, these Jews he spoke of were still predominantly Black, when Paul said things like, "to the Jew first, and also to the Greek", he was actually saying to the Black first and also to the White, he was naming the full spectrum of racial orientation. The apostle Paul was a Black man and as a Black man he understood the realities of the Black struggle. The sufferings he experienced as a Judean in imperial Rome were the sufferings of a Black man in a White world system.

Malcolm X's understanding of the racial dichotomy was relatively different. Though Malcolm X accepted that in the struggle of the races, the Black was first, in his consideration of the White man he felt more sure of their overthrow and judgment. Malcolm X wrote, "The Honorable Elijah Muhammad teaches us that since Western society is deteriorating, it has become overrun with immorality, and God is going to judge it, and destroy it. And the only way the black people caught up in this society can be saved is not to *integrate* into this corrupt society, but to *separate* from it, to a land of our own, where we can reform ourselves, lift up our moral standards, and try to be godly." Thus, the kingdom of God, for him, as a separatist, was in a separated land where Black people could practice Islam freely, with justice and ethics.

The apostle Paul's own insistence on justice and ethics was also based on his understanding that with an imminent kingdom of God, judgment was going to rain down on the enemies of God. In perilous determination he pointed out that not only salvation but also tribulation began with the Jews and continued on to the Greeks. "For the Jews require a sign, and the Greeks seek after wisdom: But we preach Christ crucified, unto the Jews a stumblingblock, and unto the Greeks foolishness; But unto them which are called, both Jews and Greeks, Christ the power of God, and the wisdom of God." Again, where it said wisdom the word used was *sophia*, as in philo*sophia* and the word he used for power was *dynamis*, as in dynamism. The judgment given to each would be based on their own interpretation of the actuality of God, particularly in his manifestation as the crucified Messiah. Still, this tells us nothing of the desired social programme God, from the apostle Paul's perspective, sought for.

Justice and ethics can obviously be discerned in his doctrine. However, that is not to say there was no contradiction, though we also read in the apostle Paul, "The just shall live by faith. And the law is not of faith: but, The man that doeth them shall live in them", justice by faith also proves to be a vain standard to fear without knowing that in which you are placing your faith. For if you place your faith in vanity to walk after that, the corruption of "sin is at the door" and it will master you. And if you put your faith in the flesh (that is, the material world) to walk after that, "the end thereof is death" and there is no coming back from that.

Malcolm X's own predilection toward justice and ethics was due to him realising, "The black man in the ghettoes ... has to start self-correcting his own material, moral and spiritual defects and evils. The black man needs to start his own program to get rid of drunkenness, drug addiction, prostitution. The black man in America has to lift up his own sense of values." He also recognised that it would be the extent of our self-awareness that would allow us to come to the full conclusion of our place in society: "My black brothers and sisters – *no* one will know *who* we are ... until *we* know who we are! We never will be able to *go* anywhere until we know *where* we are! The Honorable Elijah Muhammad is giving us a true identity, and a true position – the first time they have ever been *known* to the American black man!" Thus the consideration of the Black predicament is, and was to people like the apostle Paul and Malcolm X, based on the self-awareness of Black people as to their condition.

When Her Poker Face Destroys His Flush

"For as many of you as have been baptized into Christ have put on Christ. There is neither Jew nor Greek, there is neither bond nor free, there is neither male nor female: for ye are all one in Christ Jesus." This exclamation of the apostle Paul's, at one time undermined, but also distorted, the social fields of contest and socio-political embodiment that existed for decades in imperial Rome. On the other hand, it was also a contextual mantra that eliminated all the ideological oppositions of the world: the ever faithful Manichaean conflicts. The first social field of contest that we shall explore following will be the gender conflict. Here the apostle Paul is not believed by most people, misogynist or feminist alike, to have really contributed anything towards the empowerment of women; but in fact to have actively encouraged their subjugation and subordination within both the messianic movement and within society at large.

However, the truths of positions and opinions can also, more definitively be discovered in the silences of history; those records and presentations not memorialised or contested. It is in these kinds of records that we can find the apostle Paul's true opinions about women in the messianic movement. For example, the apostle Paul wrote to the messianic community at Corinth, "Nevertheless neither is the man without the woman, neither the woman without the man, in the Lord. For as the woman is of the man [in regard to the need for spermatisation], even so is the man also by the woman [in regard to the need for gestation and deliverance]; but all things of God" (1Corinthians 11: 11, 12). Such is a different picture entirely to the one painted historically by the definitively misogynistic Western leaders, or even the feminists who have accepted their interpretations as fact and simply sought to invert or subvert them.

True, even this sexual egalitarianism can be problematised, especially in that it is said concerning the apostle Paul, that he essentially sought to control women's body politics and sexual politics, as the apostle Paul wrote to the messianic communities of Rome, "For this cause God gave them up unto vile affections: for even their women did change the natural use into that which is against nature" (Romans 1: 26). These ideas, especially in the imperial metropolis, had an air of the moralistic, and even the legalistic, about them. Obviously, the apostle Paul's homophobia is legendary, yet perhaps it is also overstated. The translators of the Bible played a much larger role in this apparent truth than anything else. For example, the word translated here as natural was the Greek word *physikos* which could also translate as instinctual, and "against nature" (*paraphysis*) can translate to sterile or to something more contextual like: inhibit the instincts.

Paul is, nevertheless, continually critiqued on his thirst to control women's body politics and bodily performances, particularly with regard to their mode of dress, which is viewed as to highlight and demarcate their subordinate position. Indeed, the apostle Paul did write, "Every man praying or prophesying, having his head covered, dishonoureth his head. But every woman that prayeth or prophesieth with her head uncovered dishonoureth her head: for that is even all one as if she were shaven. For if the woman be not covered, let her also be shorn: but if it be a shame for a woman to be shorn or shaven, let her be covered".

Conversely, what was being implied in the subtext of this verse was the apostle Paul's acknowledgment that women *could actually* lead prayer and *could actually* prophesy. Moreover, these kinds of regulatory practices and ideas were not unique to the apostle Paul or to first century behaviour. Even the Prophet said in the Quran, "Say to the believing men that they lower their gaze and restrain their sexual passions. That is purer for them. Surely Allah is Aware of what they do. And say to the believing women that they lower their gaze and restrain their sexual passions and do not display their adornment except what appears thereof. And let them wear their head-coverings over their bosoms. And they should not display their adornment except to their husbands or their fathers, or the fathers of their husbands, or their sons, or the sons of their husbands, or their brothers, or their brothers' sons, or their sisters' sons, or their women, or those who their right hands possess, or guileless male servants, or the children who know not women's nakedness. And let them not strike their feet so that the adornment that they hide may be known. And turn to Allah all, O believers, so that you may be successful" (Quran 24: 30, 31).

Furthermore, contrast these readings with the fabled, "Moreover the Lord saith, Because the daughters of Zion are haughty, and walk with stretched forth necks and wanton eyes, walking and mincing as they go, and making a tinkling with their feet: Therefore the Lord will smite with a scab the crown of the head of the daughters of Zion, and the Lord will discover their secret parts." But "Fear not; for thou shalt not be ashamed: neither be thou confounded; for thou shalt not be put to shame: for thou shalt forget the shame of thy youth, and shalt not remember the reproach of thy widowhood any more. For thy Maker is thine husband; the Lord of hosts is his name; and thy Redeemer the Holy One of Israel; The God of the whole earth shall he be called." So, "Let us be glad and rejoice, and give honour to him: for the marriage of the Lamb is come, and his wife hath made herself ready. And to her was granted that she should be arrayed in fine linen, clean and white: for the fine linen is the righteousness of saints" (Revelations 19: 7, 8).

Again, as the Messiah said also,

> *"The kingdom of heaven is like unto a certain king, which made a marriage for his son, And sent forth his servants to call them that were bidden to the wedding: and they would not come. Again, he sent forth other servants, saying Tell them which are bidden, Behold. I have prepared my dinner: my oxen and my fatlings are killed, and all things are ready: come unto the marriage. But they made light of it, and went their ways, one to his farm, another to his merchandise: and the remnant took his servants, and entreated them spitefully, and slew them. But when the king heard thereof, he was wroth: and he sent forth his armies, and destroyed those murderers, and burned up their city. Then saith he to his servants, The wedding is ready, but they which were bidden were not worthy. Go ye therefore into the highways, and as many as ye shall find, bid to the marriage. So those servants went out into the highways, and gathered together all as many as they found, both bad and good: and the wedding was furnished with guests. And when the king came in to see the guests, he saw there a man which had not on a wedding garment: And he saith unto him, Friend, how camest thou in hither not having a wedding garment? And he was speechless. Then said the king to the servants, Bind him hand and foot, and take him away, and cast him into outer darkness: there shall be weeping and gnashing of teeth"* (Matthew 22: 2-13).

There is clearly hidden meaning in these cultural articulations and dress-codes, meanings lost in the colonial appropriation of the dominant culture. Yet these codes, meanings, and their embodiments can be rediscovered through an identification of the hidden silences of history. Thus in the apostle John's saying, "And to her was granted that she should be arrayed in fine linen, clean and white: for the fine linen is the righteousness of saints" we see his use of the word *byssinos*, which was actually what classical Greek people called, transparent linen: something that was worn very frequently by the ancient Egyptians, and classical Greeks and Romans. In the early messianic movement manifestly encouraging this wearing of fine spun linen they thereby demonstrated a kind of embodied eroticism, a sensual effrontery, indeed, a transfigured deviance (a theme that shall be returned to throughout this book as it is its underlying theme), that was as much a sexy act as it was a holy. This can be seen as all the more true in that it is very likely they wore no underwear in the early messianic movement and so were completely naked underneath.

Indeed, the light exhibitionism of not wearing underwear would have also been considered in those days a form of what we in our day would call Afrosensuality; even Barbara Watterson said it was practiced very often by the people of ancient Egypt when she exclaimed that the "Ancient Egyptian women wore their revealing dresses without much in the way of underwear". Moreover, the same could have also been said concerning the ancient Kushites. Even the ancient Hebrews would have performed various Afrosensual act-species, as can also be viewed by fathoming the depths of the Hebraic concept of *qodesh*, which meant holy, though mainly in the sexual sense of the word.

Effectively, the Hebraic words *qadesh* and *qadeshah* were, respectively, the male and female equivalents of refined one, holy disciple, and saint; and were also the equivalents of sexual one, shrine prostitute, and seducer. Basically, the holy men and holy women of the ancient Hebraic culture were like our modern Tantrics, understanding the spiritual value of their sexuality. And though the translators in the days of King James I translated the word *qadesh* as sodomite, such a mistranslation was an expression of the times. Its proper translation as sexual one helps us to understand why the only Scripture in the Bible to translate it as sodomite, Deuteronomy 23: 17, condemned its practice in Israel: due to the excessive practice of sexuality in Judea just before its fall, as can be read in Jeremiah. (As noted, most of the sexism and heterosexism we read in the Bible today came mainly from Renaissance and Reformation translators and not from the actual intentions of the early writers).

True, this idea of an Afrosensual early messianism may seem surprising, even spurious, to some readers; but that is only due to the modern Western mindset. We have been raised to view our bodies from a purely profane, even vulgar, perspective. However, there are other traces that can be discovered here in bodily performance and presentation. Indeed, this kind of embodied cultural performative was not lost on people like Frantz Fanon in their own consideration of the several colonial appropriations, and the decolonisation of the body. Fanon wrote, "The way people clothe themselves, together with the traditions of dress and finery that custom implies, constitutes the most distinctive form of a society's uniqueness, that is to say the one that is the most immediately perceptible. Within the general pattern of a given costume, there are of course always modifications of detail, innovations which in highly developed societies are the mark of fashion. But the effect as a whole remains homogeneous and great areas of civilization, immense cultural regions, can be grouped together on the basis of original, specific techniques of men's and women's dress."

Herein we see that control of clothing patterns, dress-codes, and sartorial fashions were more than just some patriarchal desires enforced by various religious leaders but a contribution to reaffirming a fractured identity. Fanon went on to say concerning the process of decolonising the body, "Tradition is no longer scoffed at by the group. The group no longer runs away from itself. The sense of the past is rediscovered, the worship of ancestors resumed…" Here, when the Messiah, the

Prophet, and the apostle Paul, set out to impose sartorial demarcations within their movements, it was not with the intent of controlling or delimiting female spatial and bodily expressions. What they were actually attempting to do was re-member their ancient signs of belonging and recognition, re-establish their traditional forms of cultural representation and manifestation, and re-appropriate those communal customs and practices that would be capable of decolonising both body and mind.

It is thereby, in the apostle Paul's understanding, for women to be bodily decolonised they also had to first be mentally decolonised. It is further, for this cause, that he wrote to the predominantly female messianic community of Philippi, saying: "Let this mind be in you, which was also in Christ Jesus: Who, being in the form of God, thought it not robbery to be equal with God: But made himself of no reputation, and took upon him the form of a servant, and was made in the likeness of men: And being found in fashion as a man, he humbled himself, and became obedient unto death, even the death of the cross." Essentially, what the apostle Paul was trying to say was that his female followers in Philippi should develop in themselves the same mind as the Messiah; and seek that better part that comes only from God. As the apostle Paul's main following among the Philippians was female I feel he saw this mentality as necessary to their bodily decolonisation.

It would be through these sorts of instances of bodily resistance that the act of maintaining one's own cultural practices and identity would become, in themselves, a performance of transfigured deviance. The apostle Paul therefore strategically wrote in his letter to Rome, the then seat of imperialism, "For as many as have sinned without law shall also perish without law: and as many as have sinned in the law shall be judged by the law; (For not the hearers of the law are just before God, but the doers of the law shall be justified. For when the Gentiles, which have not the law, do by nature the things contained in the law, these, having not the law, are a law unto themselves: Which shew the work of the law written in their hearts, their conscience also bearing witness, and their thoughts the mean while accusing or else excusing one another;) In the day when God shall judge the secrets of men by Jesus Christ according to my gospel" (Romans 2: 12-16). If we historicise and demystify this Scripture we can see that the apostle Paul, in this transfiguration of deviance, was through these remarks challenging all the political superstructures upon which Roman imperialism was built.

Still, it is my hope that you will not be too discouraged by this continual reference to transfiguration, particularly to that of the deviant, for, inasmuch as we all carry within us the Spirit and presence of Allah, we also manifest his divine nature, as it was written by the apostle Peter: "Whereby are given unto us exceeding great and precious promises: that by these you might be partakers of the divine nature, having escaped the corruption that is in the world through lust" (2Peter 1: 4). For the mystery of the divine nature was revealed when "Jesus answered them, Is it not written in your law, I said, Ye are gods? If he called them gods, unto whom the word of God came, and the scripture cannot be broken; Say ye of him, whom the Father hath sanctified and sent into the world, Thou blasphemest; because I said, I am the Son of God?"

Consequently, in the resurrecting of this kind of Black divinity we need to understand that there were in the ancient Egyptian traditions two chief gods of all: the sungod Ra and the nightgod Ausar. That which the West called worship of the sun or of the dead ancestors was, in actual fact, the honouring of these two concepts, respectively. Again, Hethor (who in ancient Egypt represented the goddess concept), in her form as the divine cow that carried and married Ra, represented both lover to Ra and mother and sister to Ausar and Auset. And being goddess of love, joy, pleasure, sex, dance, music, sensuality, wisdom, intelligence, and virtually every other good thing, Hethor also passed a lot of these attributes on to her daughter Auset.

It is from here that we are able to see how the resurrection of the father is in the son and of the mother is in the daughter. And as knowledge and sexuality both represented male and female divinity, respectively; so Ra and Hethor embodied these two concepts symbolically. For though Hethor was the second thing Tum created (the first being himself as Ra Atum), as the skygoddess Nut (who in ancient Egypt was the Nature concept) Hethor was mother, daughter, and lover to Ra. Yet this was not to justify incest – which was a lot less practiced in ancient Egypt than most Egyptologists appreciate – or any Oedipal ideas; but merely to represent the interconnection of the Black family. In similar vein, Ausar and Auset were the male and female equivalent of the ancient Egyptian concept of the Black: *Asr* and *Ast*. However, these words meant Black in a far more divine manifestation, as in Black god and Black goddess. Here they conveyed to the ancient Egyptians a sense of Black divinity, Black perfection, Black prosperity, Black beauty, Black sensuality, Black intelligence, Black strength, Black soul, Black magic, Black rapture, Black power, Black erotica, and Black love.

Black divinity, for both male and female, was nevertheless rooted in love, even the apostle Peter had this to say about it, "Seeing ye have purified your souls in obeying the truth through the Spirit unto unfeigned love of the brethren, see that ye love one another with a pure heart fervently: Being born again, not of corruptible seed, but of incorruptible, by the word of God" (1Peter 1: 22, 23). To which the apostle Paul also continued: "And though I have the gift of prophecy, and understand all mysteries, and all knowledge; and though I have all faith, so that I could remove mountains, and have no charity, I am nothing. And though I bestow all my goods to feed the poor, and though

I give my body to be burned, and have not charity, it profiteth me nothing. Charity suffereth long, and is kind"; and this charity he spoke of, being the Greek word *agape* (pronounced aw-gaw-pae) is thus our key to thearchism, and by extension, to divinity. It also manifests the Black divinity of the Black family, inasmuch as we all have suffered long and suffered hard.

True, we all are very familiar with that oft-quoted Scripture of the gospel of John, "For God so loved the world, that he gave his only begotten Son, *that whosoever believeth in him* should not perish, but have everlasting life" (John 3: 16; emphasis mine). Yet this kind of agapic message is a very similar message to one spoken in the Quran, "Say: *If you love Allah, follow me*: Allah will love you, and grant you protection from your sins. And Allah is Forgiving, Merciful" (Quran 3: 31; emphasis mine). The soteriology of these statements being undeniable, because Allah, who definitely loves us, also desires to boast over us; as was written, "And the Lord said unto Satan, Hast thou considered my servant Job, that there is none like him in the earth, a perfect and upright man, one that feareth God, and escheweth evil? and still he holdeth fast his integrity, although thou movedst me against him, to destroy him without cause" (Job 2: 3). Hereby, it is always necessary to remember the power of Allah, for he said again through his prophet Isaiah:

> *"Behold, I have created the smith that bloweth the coals in the fire, and that bringeth forth an instrument for his work; and I have created the waster to destroy." "When thou passest through the waters, I will be with thee; and through the rivers, they shall not overflow thee: when thou walkest through the fire, thou shalt not be burned; neither shall the flame kindle upon thee. For I am the Lord thy God, the Holy One of Israel, thy Saviour: I gave Egypt for thy ransom, Ethiopia and Seba for thee. Since thou wast precious in my sight, thou hast been honourable, and I have loved thee" (Isaiah 54: 16; 43: 2-4).*

The obvious question to ask at this point would be: what then is Allah's core essence? As we have already hinted at earlier, it could therefore be assumed that his essential nature is actually Romantic (*Ashiq*) or Erotic (*Shawq*). ... Though, it is true that such may not be false: yet to say his essence is Sexuality, Sensuality, or Eros is too hot, too emotive, and too affective. Then again, if we were to say that Allah's essential nature was actually Agapic (Rahman) or Empathic (Rahim); it is true that such also may not be false either. Truly, Allah's essence is Compassion, Benevolence, or Pathos, yet such a vision and perception of Allah is incomplete too. It is too cold, too thoughtful, and too nice. Such is like the brain and the heart. The two work together to fully integrate love into what I call the libido. In that sense, Allah's essence could be called Libidinal, or to use, again, the Arabic language Muhibb.

In this sense, libido (*habba*) proves to be greater than purity as any purity without libido leads to internal uncleanness or blind obedience. Libido proves to be greater than faith as any faith without libido breeds superstition, paranoia, and open idolatry. Libido proves to be greater than justice as any justice without libido leaves all of us sinners under the judgment of Allah. Libido proves to be greater than sensitivity as any sensitivity without libido lacks discipline, correction, and even honesty. Libido proves to be greater than wisdom as any wisdom without libido is trickery, deception, and delusional arrogance. Libido proves to be greater than truth as any truth without libido is a self-serving lie or a self-loathing fear. Libido proves to be greater than peace as any peace without libido is hypocritical, fake, and doomed to be broken. Libido further proves to be greater than grace as any grace without libido leads to weak self-oppression or vain self-righteousness. Libido even proves to be greater than hell as it can turn even the worst of hells into the most beautiful of heavens.

Undoubtedly, most Muslims will at this point question this particular perception of Allah. To these Muslims Allah has ninety-nine names and attributes, each used specifically by the Prophet in the Quran, and of all these names most Muslims have agreed, whether due to tradition or to the fear of going beyond tradition, or beyond all bounds, that the greatest name of God will always be Allah. The reason they give for this is that this name encompasses all the other names written in the Quran. However, this theory only ends up turning Allah into a pick and choose with regard to his true mentality. This name therefore basically answers every problem, becoming a tool to be used to promote or defend whatever cause we have. But ultimately this is putting a band aid on a broken arm. Allah needs a clear focus, central aim, and key definition. That is, Allah, like humanity, must have a clear intent, reason, meaning for being. If Allah works in mysterious ways, what is the aim, goal, and overall motivation that drives him?

For the record, this is based more so on my search to find Allah's essence or nature, because one thing we know for sure: Allah may change his covenant, he may change his laws, he may change his prophetic word, he may even change his mind. Indeed, it is said of Allah that he is both slow to anger and his wrath flares in an instant. However, the nature of Allah, his very essence, is without either change or variability. He is the same yesterday, today, and forever. So again, the essence of Allah is important. Saying the name Allah encompasses his entire being may sound good and well, but again it lacks focus. Consequently, Allah not only needs a focal point; a single dominant focus; but he needs it to outweigh all other foci, attributes, and names so thoroughly that the imbalance can be measured like the 80/20 scale. Here, it would more likely be that 20 percent of the names/attributes – though actually closer to one percent, as it is only one specific name – making up 80 percent of his personhood and personality, and within the Black thearchy this name/attribute is Muhibb/*habba*.

The concept and personhood of Muhibb is *the* central aspect of Black thearchism: conveying the essence of Allah as the Love Triad of the agapic, empathic, and erotic energy that permeates the universe inspiring and motivating all interactivity. Yet this does not contradict godbody theory, even though to most godbodies Allah is one, and we identify him as knowledge, science, or intelligence. Still, to us Allah manifests himself and discloses himself, not only through the sciences, or in fact through being the Grand Science, but by adding on to his knowledge so that it eventually becomes understanding.

Herein lies the genius of the godbody theory, we all say, believe, and appreciate that understanding is the greatest – and thereby the most important – we then take that a step further by acknowledging that the highest form of understanding is love. All Black thearchism does is it takes that a step further still, and say that the most refined form of love is libido (*habba*). Furthermore, to us, as understanding is the greatest, the greatest aspect and property of Allah, who is himself manifested as a Universal Intelligence, must thereby be none other than libido itself. Effectively, the greatest attribute and the most essential aspect of Allah is therefore Libido.

Based on this definition of Allah at his essence, it is not impossible – indeed, it may even be commendable – for us Gods to acknowledge the Black woman's power and right to reach these same levels of Back divinity. Essentially, we Gods must learn to appreciate our Black women as Goddesses, as well as their souls, lest we forfeit our own divinity and the divinity of our people. In these sorts of areas we Black males have proven to be more religious than the religious, especially when it comes to what Allah said. While I may agree that we do need to become more dogmatic with regard to some things like our core ideology; I still say, we should try not to be too dogmatic about what Allah said while he was in the physical. Thereby we can embrace the general philosophy of what he tried to impart. There is actually a formula behind his philosophy and it applies just as much to women as it does to us Gods.

At the same time, one of the biggest bonuses that can come from us Gods actually considering Black women as Goddesses is that we will have effectively begun the process of transfiguring them. Transfiguration itself is a Tantric art that allows one to see their sexual partner as divine. Indeed, according to Tantric expert Dr. Ashby, "During Tantric training, each individual is instructed to regard the other as a divinity (which all humans are innately) and to worship each other as such and to alternate roles (each partner sees themselves as male or female) as they visualize the Life Force growing. During [any] 'physical' sexual intercourse between a man and a woman, it is the male who 'gives' and the female who 'receives'. Sexual intercourse [can accordingly, therefore, be] used to heighten the ecstatic feelings and to develop psychic energy for spiritual attainment." Not only so, but transfiguring Black women also psychologically conditions us to give her more pleasure during the sexual encounter, which in turn gives us a better reason than thinking of death or sad dogs or something ugly to prolong the sexual experience.

Moreover, as a result of these practices, we Black men can literally have multiple orgasms with the women we have thus transfigured. Indeed, by prolonging a sexual experience due to how amazing we think she is and how beautiful and divine we appreciate her to be, it is even possible, with time and practice, for us Black men to have literally hundreds of orgasms in our sexual encounters. Basically, by practicing what we in our day call "edging," we godbodies can experience heights of sexual ecstasy unimaginable. I can say myself, from my own experience: there actually comes a point in sexual congress when a man no longer wants, or even needs, to ejaculate as the level and extent of non-delusional ecstasy and pure sexual pleasure he has reached, through the simple process of transfiguring the Black woman into a Goddess.

In order to reach this state at will a man must, firstly, start practicing the art of letting the person he is having sex with enter *deep* into his heart through the process of transfiguration. Secondly, he must start practicing, for her sake, the self-discipline of not ejaculating. Such a practice is based on fully understanding the Tantric drive to attain a unification with the deity through sexual intimacy. Dr. Ashby further explained how in Tantric sexual experiences, "[The] participants are not allowed to reach climax … in order to channel all energies towards concentrating on the goal: development of their Life Force and its union with the Transcendental – Absolute divine through ever increasing ecstasy and devotion … Through repeated stimulation and concentration of the energies to the higher energy centers, the sublimation of the primal sexual and mental energy is possible."

From here it is also possible to understand the value and progress of what Tantric masters call: bindu sublimation. According to Swami Saraswati, a Tantric master in his own right, "Bindu means a point or a drop. … The source of bindu is actually in the higher centres of the brain, but due to the development of emotions and passions, bindu falls down to the lower region where it is transformed into sperm and ova." It is this concept of bindu that contains the secret as to why "edging" is currently acknowledged in the West as a form of transcendental meditation. It keeps sexual energy at a highly charged and explosive state.

Moreover, as Swami Saraswati continued on, "According to tantra, the preservation of the bindu is absolutely necessary for two reasons. Firstly, the process of regeneration can only be carried out with the help of bindu. Secondly, all the spiritual experiences take place when there is an explosion of bindu. This explosion can result in the creation of a thought or of anything. Therefore, in tantra, certain practices are recommended by which the male partner can stop ejaculation and retain the bindu." At the same time, this is mainly encouraged, "not so much to preserve the semen, but because it causes a depression in the level of energy."

Thereby we can see and understand that the practice of prolonging the sexual experience (edging), keeps the sexual energy at peak levels and ultimately allows for maximum pleasure to be experienced by us male figures. The same is also true for the women, as Swami Saraswati further noted, "In the female body, the point of concentration is at mooladhara chakra, which is situated at the cervix, just behind the opening of the uterus. This is the point where space and time unite and explode in the form of an experience. In ordinary language of tantra it is called an awakening. In order to maintain the continuity of that experience, it is necessary for a build up of energy to take place at that particular bindu or point."

Essentially, by allowing a love object to enter into the inner chambers of our heart and take deep root, that is, by transfiguring them, we essentially give ourselves access to receiving multiple orgasms. Conversely, I also recognise how difficult it can be for us men, particularly us Black men, to open our hearts to anybody, let alone a romantic interest. There is an unspoken fear that any displays of vulnerability will lead to emasculation and future pain/trauma. There is also the obvious humiliation of being called by our friends, or even by our love objects themselves, a simp, a bitch, or a chump who all up in their feelings, i.e., too emotional. "Never let anyone in your heart or they will either break it, abuse it, or take your kindness for weakness," so they say.

Though I am somewhat sympathetic to this advice, and I get the reasoning behind it, as someone who famously opens his heart regularly, and also gets disappointed regularly, I can say: I have no desire to ever stop opening my heart regardless of the name calling or mistreatment. First of all, I am confident enough in my own manhood to not care about name calling. Second, the rewards I get from opening my heart far exceed any pain I may have to endure as a result. To be sure, I never open my heart easily, and if someone breaks it I will never trust them again, even if we stay friends afterward. But that whole Stoic, cold, and closed off shit is dead. If such a person confronted me and called me a chump, I would very likely say, "You probably right," but deep in my heart I would be feeling sorry for them; knowing that they are not only missing out on the beauties, wonders, and joys of an emotionally intimate relationship, but also missing out on the orgasmic pleasures of sheer ecstasy that can only be reached by opening your heart to a love object and transfiguring them into a deity.

That notwithstanding, it is only natural, after experiencing a few of these kinds of sexual encounters, especially when the amount of sexual orgasms reach into the double digits, for both parties to assume it will only ever improve from there. While I am not saying such is impossible, it is nonetheless definitely improbable. That means there *will* be days and moments that you orgasm back into the single digits, or even worse, ejaculate/discharge. Do not worry too much about that, it is just a matter of getting back to transfiguration. Further, so long as both the God and Goddess practice, both the transfiguration of their lover and the holding back of their sexual discharge, they can open themselves up, in time, to storing enough sexual energy to gain supersensory abilities, or what the Tantrics call *siddhis*. These abilities will, in turn, provide us with all the more reason to transfigure them and them with all the more reason to transfigure us, but I might be getting a bit ahead of myself.

All these are Tantric concepts that are taught within the Tantric arts. Conversely, Tantric training has three prominent schools of thought that share their basic disciplines: the dakshina marga, the vama marga, and the kaula marga. To further explain the traditions of these three schools Dr. Ashby expertly continued, saying, "The first path is the conservative mainline of Tantrism including mandala meditations and worship of the Divine in the form of the Mother Goddess. The second includes traditionally forbidden elements, especially sexual intercourse (with detachment and non-ejaculation). The third is practiced by the Kula sect and is equivalent to Kundalini Yoga (Serpent Power)."

Furthermore, to provide a greater clarification of these schools: First note, the dakshina marga is the right hand path. They teach a celibate, sensorial, devotional, and vegetarian lifestyle. Second, the vama marga is the left hand path. They teach polyamory, sorcery, sacrilegiousness, drunkenness, and eating meats (like beef). This path is not for the weak minded and is very dangerous for most people. It can even be related to mental illness if an unstable mind practices it. Finally, the kaula marga is the united path. They teach sexual, supersensorial, religious, pharmacological, and dietary union with the Creator and Creatrix (Shiva and Shakti). Having myself learned from the kaula school I will say their lessons on transfiguring the Black woman have improved my sex life dramatically.

Nevertheless Malcolm X also lost none of these idea when he considered the divine positioning of the Black woman. Indeed, his understanding was based more on the pathology (sickness) of Black men toward disparaging and disregarding Black women than showing them the love they deserve. We have not protected them, we have not cared for them, we have not honoured them; for this cause, Malcolm X basically felt that such behaviours would only produce for us a direct course to our own enfeeblement, "The Honorable Elijah Muhammad teaches us that the black man is going around saying he wants respect; well, the black man never will get anybody's respect until he first learns to respect his own woman! The black man needs *today* to stand up and throw off the weaknesses imposed upon him by the slavemaster white man! The black man needs to start today to shelter and protect and *respect* his black woman!" When we Gods can do this we will really reach that divine nature we understand to be our birthright.

Playing With the Cards We Were Dealt

With regard to the question of bond and free we find lurking beneath the surface, in both silenced and echoed voices, the obvious question of the enslaving of human bodies. This is where the apostle Paul *appears* to differ substantially from Malcolm X; but upon closer examination, the two are not that far apart. Although in the Scriptures the apostle Paul said: "Servants, be obedient to them that are your masters according to the flesh, with fear and trembling, in singleness of your heart, as unto Christ; Not with eyeservice, as menpleasers; but as the servants of Christ, doing the will of God from the heart; With good will doing service, as to the Lord, and not to men: Knowing that whatsoever good thing any man doeth, the same shall he receive of the Lord, whether he be bond or free." He also said, "And we beseech you, brethren, to know them which labour among you, and are over you in the Lord, and admonish you; And to esteem them very highly in love for their work's sake. And be at peace among yourselves."

The apostle Paul was not there encouraging slavery, he was actually encouraging work. The imminence of the kingdom of God to him was not cause enough to stop with their secular lives. Such a prescience for what became the Western work ethic, again, speaks volumes by its silences. Fanon in fact helps us uncover the hidden meanings and subtexts behind why the apostle Paul was so concerned with promoting and encouraging these anti-imperialist communities to maintain their secular jobs, positions, and class placements in society: "colonialism is not simply content to impose its rule upon the present and the future of the dominated country. Colonialism is not satisfied merely with holding a people in its grip and emptying the native's brain of all form and content. By a kind of perverted logic, it turns to the past of the oppressed people, and distorts, disfigures and destroys it."

Basically, what the apostle Paul was uncomfortably trying to do was negotiate being the leader of what, for all intents and purposes, was a subaltern movement of lowlifes, outlaws, bandits, thugs, revolutionaries, commoners, artisans, slaves, indentured workers, and women, with actually very few landowners, businessowners, and professionals. To be sure, according to all Roman records of the time, the first century messianic movement was a socially and publicly disreputable movement to belong to, on a par with being a member of a super-gang today. In this situation, the actions and act-species one used, not to mention the panoptical surveillance of the then imperial government, could determine life or death. He understood that his teachings either could be used as a vital resource for the community or get him executed for inflammatory and seditious speech.

The apostle Paul exemplified this uncomfortable tension in his second letter to the Thessalonian messianic communities, saying, "Now we command you, brethren, in the name of our Lord Jesus Christ, that ye withdraw yourselves from every brother that walketh disorderly, and not after the tradition which he received of us. For yourselves know how ye ought to follow us … For even when we were with you, this we commanded you, that if any would not work, neither should he eat." Again, although this message could theoretically be expressed as the apostle Paul's unceremonious attempt to organise the messianic movement into a class structure. It could, moreover, be asked from this if there is any idea more impressed upon a person than this within the current capitalist system?

To answer this question we must instead ask a new question: how would the apostle Paul feel about the work ethic within our capitalistic model? It is obvious that the apostle Paul had no intension of denying all non-workers the right to ever eat at all, but to make work itself a domain within which the anti-colonial and messianic struggles could also be fought. This strategic acculturation and amelioration of Paul's, what I call his "Anansian bargain," really came into sharp relief, especially in his letters to the messianic communities of Thessalonica, as can be seen when he wrote a little further down, "For we hear that there are some which walk among you disorderly, working not at all, but are busybodies. Now them that are such we command and exhort by our Lord Jesus Christ, that with quietness they work, and eat their own bread." Even emphasising this point in his first letter to them, saying, "And that ye study to be quiet, and to do your own business, and to work with your own hands, as we commanded you; That ye may walk honestly toward them that are without, and that ye may have lack of nothing."

Again, these kinds of statements are also familiar references within the prophetic tradition, where can be found statements such as, "These are the things that ye shall do; Speak ye every man the truth to his neighbour; execute the judgment of truth and peace in your gates: And let none of you imagine evil in your hearts against his neighbour; and love no false oath:" "Wash you, make you clean; put away the evil of your doings from before mine eyes; cease to do evil; Learn to do well; seek judgment, relieve the oppressed, judge the fatherless, plead for the widow." For the same Allah of ancient Hebraism and the same Allah of early messianism is the same Allah of social pragmatism. He even went on to say through his prophet Zechariah, "Thus speaketh the Lord of hosts, saying, Execute true judgment, and shew mercy and compassions every man to his brother: And oppress not the widow, nor the fatherless, the stranger, nor the poor; and let none of you imagine evil against his brother in your heart."

Thereby attempting to reveal justice and compassion to the earth; and to the widow and the fatherless, and the stranger and the poor, with a *completely partial* identification with them; and against the sinister hand of corrupting and oppressing individuals. All effectively highlighting Allah's determinative partiality towards certain subaltern groups, that the value, the "subterranean wealth" of these "worthless" groups, may not be absented from the record. Furthermore, the apostle Paul's Anansian bargain with the imperial state we should not assume to have been collusion, as he clearly had no problem with these subaltern groups among non-workers receiving daily bread and services from those who had the power to give. We know this because when he was given his commission from the other apostles; as he said later in a letter to the messianic communities of Galatia, "Only they would that we should remember the poor; the same which I also was forward to do." He even said to the Ephesian messianic communities, "Let him that stole steal no more: but rather let him labour, working with his hands the thing which is good, *that he may have to give to him that needeth*" (emphasis mine); thereby plainly showing his concern for the genuinely poor and needy, while still promoting a work ethic.

The defiant, indeed, deviant, bodies of God's people have throughout time been a message to the principalities and powers that have existed historically. Effectively, the expectation of social justice and ethics among the ancient Falashim was far more undeniable as their prophets fought and spoke against any oppressive or self-gratifying practices among the people. Yet during the time of the Neo-Persian Empire, the Falashim of the time colluded with imperialism thereby becoming rich through these same corrupted and oppressive practices. It is for this cause that Allah spoke to them through his prophet Malachi, saying, "And I will come near to you to judgment; and I will be a swift witness against the sorcerers, and against the adulterers, and against false swearers, and against those that oppress the hireling in his wages, the widow, and the fatherless, and that turn aside the stranger from his right, and fear not me, saith the Lord of hosts." In fact, in those days what marked out a prophet or the prophetic was this central theme: the calling of the people from the fear and worship of vanities and idols towards monism; that is, belief in the oneness of the family, the community, the society, the world, the environment, the universe, the astral, and the divine.

It is for this cause that the prophets cried out against destabilising actions like defrauding workers of their wages or oppressing strangers, the widow, and the fatherless; all practices continued in much sharper relief within modern Western societies, which have taken the mercantile mentality of the Near East and turned it into a moralised, indeed, a valorised, principle. But what did the prophet Amos have to say on this, "Hear this, O ye that swallow up the needy, even to make the poor of the land to fail, Saying, When will the new moon be gone, that we may sell corn? And the sabbath, that we may set forth wheat, making the ephah small, and the shekel great, and falsifying the balances by deceit? That we may buy the poor for silver, and the needy for a pair of shoes; yea, and sell the refuse of the wheat? The Lord hath sworn by the excellency of Jacob, Surely I will never forget any of their works." Again, this was written at a time when the Falashim were colluding with imperialism, only in this case it was the Syrian Empire.

Indeed, in late modernity these four groups would be called: the single parent and single parent families, foreign exiles, and the jobless non-workers. These four groups make up the current underclass, and have been the most marginalised class in all imperial geographies. These glaring inconsistencies in the imperial state eventually become clear to everybody, even as Fanon further informed us, "sooner or later, colonialism sees that it is not within its power to put into practice a project of economic and social reforms which will satisfy the aspirations of colonized people. Even where food supplies are concerned, colonialism gives proof of its inherent incapability. The colonialist state quickly discovers that if it wishes to disarm the nationalist parties on strictly economic questions then it will have to do in the colonies exactly what it has refused to do in its own country" (Fanon 1969: 166).

Moreover, it could be said, based on what we know of the apostle Paul's message, that he spoke directly against the vanity of placing your faith in good works, as he wrote to the messianic community of Rome, saying, "if Abraham were justified by works, he hath whereof to glory; but not before God. For what saith the scripture? Abraham believed God, and it was counted unto him for righteousness." (Romans 4: 2, 3). Nevertheless, this saying was written with the intention of building commitment and loyalty against passivity; not of abolishing the total practice of just works, let alone of those unto God; in the hopes of allowing the cultural reproduction of messianic practices as against Hebraic. Again, so as to show the subterranean representations he actually felt to be of importance he further explained that "by grace are ye saved through faith; and that not of yourselves: it is the gift of God: Not of works, lest any man should boast. For we are his workmanship, created in Christ Jesus *unto good works*, which God hath before ordained that we should walk in them" (emphasis mine).

However, Malcolm X was also in agreement concerning the work ethic, saying, "No Muslim who followed Elijah Muhammad could dance, gamble, date, attend movies, or sports, or take long vacations from work. Muslims slept no more than health required. Any domestic quarreling, any discourtesy, especially to women, was not allowed. No lying or stealing, and no insubordination to civil authority, except on the grounds of religious obligation." As the American Black people of his days were lost in a sea of confusion having no means of achieving success in a world designed against them. Malcolm X felt that these struggling Black people just needed to learn the right course. It is for this cause, he further continued, "The America Black man should be focusing his every effort toward building his own businesses, and decent homes for himself. As other ethnic groups have done, let the black people, wherever possible, however possible, patronize their own kind, hire their own kind, and start in those ways to build up the black race's ability to do for itself."

The obvious correlation here between these hopes and work ethics in the Nation of Islam and the apostle Paul's conviction that those claiming to be in the kingdom of God should admire those guided by their own work ethic is intriguing. In the late modern era, however, it is a very different story. Here it is political ideologues who fight for such ideals. Among them Rosa Luxemburg felt particularly compelled to promote these kinds of issues, stating, "A general requirement to work for all who are able to do so, from which small children, the aged and sick are exempted, is a matter of course in a socialist economy", but still, "The public at large must provide forthwith for those unable to work – not like now with paltry alms but with generous provision, socialized child-raising, enjoyable care for the elderly, public health care for the sick, etc." This general requirement to work, being not too dissimilar from the apostle Paul's and Malcolm X's work ethics, shows that the idea of people having to work is not simply a religious ideal but existed within a Leftist framework too.

This work ethic is and will also be necessary within godbodyism too, as to us work is itself a battleground through which we decolonise our minds and bodies. We must also encourage each other to make a reasonable contribution to our societies and our communities and thereby work for their improvement. For the grace manifested by Allah to the sinner is of his own doing, in that he loves them and desires to save them. Moreover, as the apostle Paul continued in his letter to the messianic communities of Rome, "What then? shall we sin, because we are not under the law, but under grace? God forbid. Know ye not, that to whom ye yield yourselves servants to obey, his servants ye are to whom ye obey; whether of sin unto death, or of obedience unto righteousness?" (Romans 6: 15, 16).

This statement takes on even newer bounds when one replaces the apostle Paul's use of the word sin with the word crime – which is how the first century readers would have interpreted it. However, when he used the word righteousness, the apostle Paul was here speaking specifically of the righteousness of Allah, and not that of colonial legality nor based on the standards of colonial legality. So if thereby the apostle Paul understood that Allah, in his righteousness, could judge as criminal that which he deemed to be criminal according to his own ethical interpretation, then the apostle Paul clearly saw him as all the more able to redeem from the colonial standards of criminality those whom he found to be of genuine spirit.

Malcolm X also agreed with such a sentiment, feeling himself that, in like manner, the Nation of Islam should be, and had to be, the agglomeration of Black people into a creditable community. "Our businesses sought to demonstrate to Black people what black people could do for themselves – if they would only unite, trade with each other – exclusively where possible – and hire each other, and in so doing, keep black money within the black communities, just as other minorities did." These Black communities, formulated as an expression not of instinctual aggression, self-interest, or some internal need for conquest and power; but in response to the depreciation of the Black population in the United States, were to uplift the people and allow us to become a decolonised race.

As to the apostle Paul's social theory for the colonised people of his time, it did bear some similarities to these, but his vision was primarily for the messianic communities to take care of themselves. His statement to the messianic communities of Corinth articulates this idea, "Who goeth a warfare any time at his own charges? who planteth a vineyard, and eateth not of the fruit thereof? ... he that ploweth should plow in hope; ... he that thresheth in hope should be partaker of his hope. If we have sown unto you spiritual things, is it a great thing if we shall reap your carnal things?" Here the apostle Paul was stating very plainly that the early messianic movement, which was still at the time predominantly a Black movement, should take care of its own. He was also showing and proving, like Malcolm X, that it was quite respectable for the people of God to provide for their own ministers instead of waiting on some other people to provide for them. And one thing is definitely sure, if the messianic movement raised any funds, those funds were reaped and shared out only among the brothers and sisters.

Effectively, the apostle Paul spoke all his arguments in favour of workers not in favour of capitalistic non-workers. We can see this by the statement following, "Now to him that worketh is the reward not reckoned of grace, but of debt." Here showing that when somebody works they deserve to reap the benefits thereof. Then again, we must not forget some of the more feudalistic ideas he espoused in the above, "who planteth a vineyard, and eateth not of the fruit thereof?" Surely, it was the capitalists and the feudal lords who owned the vineyard and the workers who merely worked it?

When the apostle Paul said, "he that ploweth should plow in hope;" he was saying in essence that the worker, the one who worked the plow, should receive of what he had worked. The feudal lord was not considered for as he said in a letter to Timothy, "The husbandman that *laboureth* must be first partaker of the fruits" (emphasis mine). I see the apostle Paul as talking here about those who plant *and* work the vineyard, because somewhere else he said "every man shall bear his own burden." So he was essentially saying that the person who works the vineyard is worthy of its fruits.

The importunity of the initial question also opens up a general insistence by the preachers of prosperity: there is a seed time and a harvest time. Those who wish to harvest must sow the right seeds. One who sows into financial success through their tithes and offerings will reap financial success in their lives and businesses. This is an obvious vulgarisation of what the apostle Paul said to the messianic communities of Galatia, "Be not deceived; God is not mocked: for whatsoever a man soweth, that shall he also reap." The trouble is these preachers fail to read further on, where it says; "For he that soweth to his flesh shall of the flesh reap corruption; but he that soweth to the Spirit shall of the Spirit reap life everlasting."

Even so, the apostle Paul said regarding his struggles to decolonise minds and bodies in the imperial underclass, that "we have this treasure in earthen vessels, that the excellency of the power may be of God, and not of us. We are troubled on every side, yet not distressed; we are perplexed, but not in despair; Persecuted, but not forsaken; cast down, but not destroyed; Always bearing about in the body the dying of the Lord Jesus, that the life also of Jesus might be made manifest in our body." Furthermore, as these inter-embodied interactions and confrontations transpired they would cause colonialists' spaces, and thereby the colonialists' right to power, to be problematised. Such problematisations even potentially triggering rebellion and sparking revolution.

What we see therefore is as Fanon also said, "Decolonization is the meeting of two forces, opposed to each other by their very nature, which results from and is nourished by the situation in the colonies. Their first encounter was marked by violence and their existence together – that is to say the exploitation of the native by the settler – was carried on by dint of a great array of bayonets and cannon." For this cause, the apostle Paul wrote again to the messianic communities of Rome, saying, "There is therefore now no condemnation to them which are in Christ Jesus, who walk not after the flesh, but after the Spirit. For the law of the Spirit of life in Christ Jesus hath made me free from the law of sin and death. For what the law could not do, in that it was weak through the flesh, God sending his own Son in the likeness of sinful flesh, and for sin, condemned sin in the flesh: That the righteousness of the law might be fulfilled in us, who walk not after the flesh, but after the Spirit." (Romans 8: 1-4). Again, while the Spirit hereby frees us from the legal requirement, according to the gospel the apostle Paul taught, it still does not free us completely from the responsibility to do righteous works; for we find the prophet Ezekiel crying out for Allah:

> *"Therefore, thou son of man, say unto the children of thy people, The righteousness of the righteous shall not deliver him in the day of his transgression: as for the wickedness of the wicked, he shall not fall thereby in the day that he turneth from his wickedness; neither shall the righteous be able to live for his righteousness in the day that he sinneth. When I shall say to the righteous, that he shall surely live; if he trust to his own righteousness, and commit iniquity, all his righteousness shall not be remembered; but for his iniquity that he hath committed, he shall die for it. Again, when I say unto the wicked, Thou shalt surely die; if he turn from his sin, and do that which is lawful and right; If the wicked restore the pledge, give again that he had robbed, walk in the statutes of life, without committing iniquity; he shall surely live, he shall not die. None of his sins that he hath committed shall be mentioned unto him: he hath done that which is lawful and right; he shall surely live. Yet the children of thy people say, The way of the Lord is not equal: but as for them, their way is not equal" (Ezekiel 33: 12-17).*

This form of justice and ethics, this very realistic form of justice and ethics; is Allah's form of justice and ethics. That Allah held justice and righteousness as so essential effectively showed that Allah himself was and is beyond anything we have thus far assumed of him. Still, as we know, modern Western society has no formal conception of ethical orientation. Modernity sees justice and ethics purely in the liberal and in the popular. In fact, popular opinion is the main standard of justice and ethics in most modern societies. Here it is society that keeps itself from its own redemption, but we poor righteous teachers, taking our stand, will ultimately bring to society a powerful liberation through our own iron determination.

Pulling the Race Card and Other Absurdities

The final social field of contest we shall consider in relation to the apostle Paul here is race. It is here that the apostle Paul is unfortunately usually believed to be anti-Semitic and bigoted. However, as he wrote again in his letter to the messianic communities of Rome, "For I could wish that myself were accursed from Christ for my brethren, my kinsmen according to the flesh: Who are Israelites; to whom pertaineth the adoption, and the glory, and the covenants, and the giving of the law, and the service of God, and the promises; Whose are the fathers, and of whom as concerning the flesh Christ came, who is over all, God blessed for ever. Amen" (Romans 9: 3-5). Malcolm X also saw this kind of divine calling on the Black people of his time, saying, "We believe that the miserable plight of America's twenty million black people is the fulfillment of divine prophecy. We also believe the presence today in America of The Honorable Elijah Muhammad, his teachings among the so-called Negroes, and his naked warning to America concerning her treatment of these so-called Negroes, is all the fulfillment of divine prophecy."

We Black people of the world have historically been lost in a system designed against us. Here Fanon, in his own attempts to encourage the decolonisation of mind and body, articulated what we could take to be a new prospect for us struggling Black people to aspire to, reminding us how "decolonization is quite simply the replacing of certain 'species' of men [and women] by [other] 'species' of men [and women]. Without any period of transition, there is a total, complete and absolute substitution." The apostle Paul's revolutionary theory also contained certain similarities, as he wrote to the messianic fellowships of Corinth, "Therefore if any man be in Christ, he is a new creature: old things are passed away; behold, all things are become new. And all things are of God, who hath reconciled us to himself by Jesus Christ, and hath given to us the ministry of reconciliation. To wit, that God was in Christ, reconciling the world unto himself, not imputing their trespasses unto them; and hath committed unto us the word of reconciliation. Now then we are ambassadors for Christ, as though God did beseech you by us: we pray you in Christ's stead, be ye reconciled to God" (2Corinthians 5: 17-20).

This Scripture contains herein something of the elemental, the environmental, even the primal, about it. Whereas with Fanon the new humanity comes about by armed struggle and resistance, with the apostle Paul the new creature comes about by accepting the Lordship and Messiahship of Jesus. Indeed, the Black thearchy posits the idea that every creature in the universe, animate and inanimate, is entitled to give and receive love, peace, and happiness in life, for as long as they shall live. These rights should also be protected by the Gods and Goddesses of their various jurisdictions, to the beautifying of the creation. Now while such an ask may seem innocent enough in our current world of decoupled Church from State, in the first century by identifying the representatives of the imperial government, and particularly the Caesar himself, as possessing the divine right to make, break, and judge the law as they saw fit, the people of society effectively avoided persecution from that very same imperial government.

Still, even though he only saw himself as an ambassador for the Messiah, the apostle Paul's own messianism was fundamentally one of political significance: "For we wrestle not against flesh and blood, but against principalities, against powers, against the rulers of the darkness of this world, against spiritual wickedness in high places." In this Scripture – which is usually taken for an otherworldly warfare – can be apprehended within its historical absences voices silenced yet historicised and embodied. The first thing we can identify is that a principality was considered any territory ruled over by a prince. The next thing we can identify is that the Greek word used here for powers was not *dynamis*, but was in fact the word *exousia*, which meant jurisdiction. Now, these two concepts possess spatiality, territoriality, and historicity. Again, the word used for world was cosmos, which can translate to world, universe, or even to system. Herein, the apostle Paul was stating that this dark system of socio-political governments and jurisdictions, and all their spiritual wickedness, was to be the messianic movement's true enemy and opponent.

Furthermore, the apostle Paul also explained how we were to fight against these enemies and opponents, stating, "For though we walk in the flesh, we do not war after the flesh: (For the weapons of our warfare are not carnal, but mighty through God to the pulling down of strong holds;) Casting down imaginations, and every high thing that exalteth itself against the knowledge of God, and bringing into captivity every thought to the obedience of Christ" (2Corinthians 10: 4, 5). Again, the word used here for imaginations was the word *logismos*, literally meaning logic or reasoning. The apostle Paul was basically encouraging his followers to cast down the vain logic of colonial princes and authorities, or said another way, cast down the vain ideology of imperialism. Here, debate was to be the central methodology the apostle Paul was encouraging. To him the messianic movement was to represent an ethical entity so righteous that it put the Roman Empire to shame.

To explain this methodology for pulling down logical and psychological strongholds, the apostle Paul said, "Beware lest any man spoil you through philosophy and vain deceit, after the tradition of men, after the rudiments of the world, and not after Christ. For in him dwelleth all the fulness of the Godhead bodily." But what made the messianic event so significant, at least to the apostle Paul? We actually get a glimpse of it as he continues on in this letter to the messianic communities of Colossae: "Blotting out the handwriting of ordinances that was against us, which was contrary to us, and took it out of the way, nailing it to his cross; And having spoiled principalities and powers, he made a shew of them openly, triumphing over them in it." While the apostle Paul was clearly speaking here about the laws of Moses, there was nonetheless, hidden in what was being silenced, a subterranean voice, whispered and absented, that we can detect through the prism of the apostle Paul's over-surveilled body, and his over-cautiousness due to his consciousness of that over-surveillance.

The apostle Paul's rhetoric calls for, demands, de-mystification; through which can be glimpsed the apostle Paul's antinomian, even anarchic, leanings. These leanings will have to be explored more fully later on, but for now simply acknowledge that the apostle Paul saw the goal of reconciling the world to Allah as more than merely a continuum of religious or spiritual act-species, he saw it as political, even as world historical. Herein, the apostle Paul was not blind to the suffering of his own race but sought all the more for their unification to Allah, saying, "Brethren, my heart's desire and prayer to God for Israel is, that they might be saved. For I bear them record that they have a zeal of God, but not according to knowledge" (Romans 10: 1, 2), which he wrote, again, to the messianic communities of Rome. Malcolm X also saw lack of knowledge in the Black communities of America as our greatest weakness, saying, "My homemade education gave me, with every additional book that I read, a little bit more sensitivity to the deafness, dumbness and blindness that was afflicting the black race in America."

Through this prism we can also see that what the apostle Paul was most likely trying to explain in all these verses was that through the understanding that he received from Allah he could see that what the state-sponsored lynching of the Messiah on the cross ultimately did was render the state utterly impotent, thereby removing all moral and ethical credibility from the Roman government. The injustice of the Messiah's death effectively exposed the Roman state implied in the conception of "pax Romana" instead as "violence incarnate," with no intention of bringing peace, protection, prosperity, or pride to the colonised masses, or subject nations.

As Fanon also said concerning colonial states, their only intention is to subjugate them and to break them. Yet, even though, "In the colonial context the settler only ends his work of breaking in the native when the latter admits loudly and intelligibly the supremacy of the white man's values. In the period of decolonization, the colonized masses mock at these very values, insult them and vomit them up." This is telling, as the apostle Paul, at least in his beginnings, and very likely for all his adult life, valued his Roman citizenship. Indeed, there is almost a hint of pride that passes through the ages and pages of time and sources when one reads Paul saying to the chief captain sent in to quiet a riot that was happening, "I was free born" (Acts 22: 28). Though these kinds of contradictions are not uncommon in freedom fighters and revolutionaries they are also telling in there uncomfortable absurdity.

Any Anansian negotiations on the part of the freedom fighter, any transfigured deviances in the social spheres of conflict, these Malcolm X considered to be merely birthing pangs as a result of a liberation struggle. Fanon had a similar understanding of the mass element, seeing the liberation struggle occurring in two phases. Of these, he recognised that it is "during the second period, which is characterized by the putting into operation of the enemy offensive. The colonial forces, once the explosion has taken place, regroup and reorganize, inaugurating methods of warfare which correspond to the nature of the rising. This offensive will call in question the ideal, Utopian atmosphere of the first phase. The enemy attacks, and concentrates large forces on certain definitive points. The local group is quickly overrun, all the more so because it tends to seek the forefront of the battle. ... But the losses are serious, and doubts spring up and begin to weigh heavily upon the rebels. [Here, the] group faces a local attack as if it were a decisive test."

These stages of systemic decolonisation, after decolonisation has occurred in mind and body, then it is about putting it into effect in the society. When this process begins the colonial regime will obviously declare all participants illegal, criminal, deviant, even seditious, and will thereby feel within their rights to prosecute or even execute all perpetrators. This may be true, but as Fanon further pointed out, "The oppressor's government can set up commissions of inquiry and of information daily if it wants to; in the eyes of the native, these commissions do not exist. The fact is that soon we shall have had seven years of crimes in Algeria and there has not yet been a single Frenchmen indicted before a French court of justice for the murder of an Algerian. In Indo-China, in Madagascar or in the colonies the native has always known that he need expect nothing from the other side. ... On the logical plane, the Manichaeism of the settler produces a Manichaeism of the native. To the theory of the 'absolute evil of the native' the theory of the 'absolute evil of the settler' replies."

It may feel strange to consider, but as Black people in the world today most of our minds, bodies, and cultures are deviant to White people, indeed, they are devilish. In this, Black divinity inverts the White gaze and imposes on it a counter-gaze; inverts their discourse and imposes on it a counter-discourse; inverts their narrative and imposes on it a counter-narrative; inverts their culture and imposes on it a counter-culture; and inverts their performances and imposes on them counter-performances. If to White people Black people must be the devil, then to Black people White people will also be the devil. If White people really believe they are a chosen or divine race, then Black people will counter that with a belief in our own divinity as a race. If, "in fact, my life is worth as much as the settler's, his glance no longer turns me into stone. I am no longer on tenderhooks in his presence; in fact, I don't give a damn for him."

Now let us not forget that Malcolm X was himself good friends with Frantz Fanon, who was himself a key figure in the Algerian Revolution; and was also friends with Ali Shari'ati, a key figure in the Iranian Revolution; and with Fidel Castro, the key figure in the Cuban Revolution; and with Kwame Nkrumah, the key figure in the Ghanaian Revolution; and with Patrice Lumumba, the key figure in the Congolese Revolution; and also travelled to Africa and Asia long before he left the Nation of Islam. As he went on himself to say, "[There was great] national publicity ... in the offing for the Nation of Islam [so] Mr Muhammad sent me on a three-week trip to Africa. Even as small as we then were, some of the African and Asian personages had sent Mr Muhammad private word that they liked his efforts to awaken and lift up the American black people. Sometimes, the messages had been sent through me. As Mr Muhammad's emissary, I went to Egypt, *Arabia*, to the Sudan, to Nigeria, and Ghana" (Malcolm X 2001: 339; emphasis mine).

Herein, the Elijah's method for decolonising the Black American mind and body, and all neo-colonialist spaces, real or imagined (that is, the public and semi-public locations where the spatial representation of neo-colonial power existed: indeed, the geography of domination); was to contest these sites of inter-embodied confrontation. Malcolm X also went on to note how, "[If an] addict is brought into the local Muslim restaurant, he may occasionally be exposed to some other social situations – among proud, clean Muslims who show each other mutual affection and respect instead of the familiar hostility of the ghetto streets. For the first time in years, the addict [will hear] himself called, genuinely, 'Brother', 'Sir' and 'Mr'." And, "That's a powerful combination for a man who has been existing in the mud of society."

In like manner the apostle Paul wrote to the messianic communities of Rome, "For I speak to you Gentiles, inasmuch as I am the apostle of the Gentiles, I magnify mine office: If by any means I may provoke to emulation them which are my flesh, and might save some of them. For if the casting away of them be the reconciling of the world, what shall the receiving of them be, but life from the dead?" (Romans 11: 13-15). Here, in declaring himself an apostle to the Gentiles (in Greek *ethnos*, meaning nations), the apostle Paul was literally identifying himself as the anti-racist *par excellence*. However, in saying that his message to the nations (*ethnos*) was for the purpose of stirring up his own Falashim people (Parashim, from where we get the word Pharisees, which meant set apart ones, consecrated ones, or separatists, was a corruption of the Ethiopic Falashim, which meant wanderer, nomad, or stranger – a culture very suited for a tentmaker) towards godliness by emulation, he could also be perceived to be justifying rivalry and competition. So what about competition?

It could be said at this point, surely, the apostle Paul viewed competition as a legitimate form of self-expression and self-identification, for he said, "And every man that striveth for the mastery is temperate in all things. Now they do it to obtain a corruptible crown; but we an incorruptible"? If the apostle Paul did not problematise competitive striving then why should we start doing so now? The answer, however, is that mental or bodily identification with competitiveness leads inexorably to carnality, even as the apostle Paul said again, "For ye are yet carnal: for whereas there is among you envying, and strife, and divisions, are ye not carnal, and walk as men?" Indeed, he also encouraged his followers in Galatia, saying, "If we live in the Spirit, let us also walk in the Spirit. Let us not be desirous of vain glory, provoking one another, envying one another." Again, he further wrote to the messianic communities of Corinth, saying, "God hath chosen the foolish things of the world to confound the wise; and God hath chosen the weak things of the world to confound the things which are mighty; And base things of the world, and things which are despised, hath God chosen, yea, and things which are not, to bring to nought things that are: That no flesh should glory in his presence" (1Corinthians 1: 27-29).

Effectively, while the apostle Paul admitted that he saw the purpose of his mission to the nations to be to provoke his own people to jealousy, such was not done to inspire competetiveness, so as to lead them to glory in their own righteousness, but based on an understanding that all living creatures learn by osmosis and emulation, and without seeing an incorruptible people how could his own people possibly learn to be incorruptible? It is here that the apostle Paul proved himself a true product of the world of Roman imperialism. But, whereas among most of the Falashim Judeans of his time the methodology of seditious militarism and armed insurrectionism were the chosen forms of bodily counter-performance against the Roman Empire, the apostle Paul incorporated a more socially viable form of engagement with Roman imperialism, based on re-educating and re-unifying the masses throughout the Roman world.

Using his own field of expertise, the nineteenth century Russian geographer and social scientist, Pyotr Kropotkin, speaking on Darwin's *The Descent of Man* also articulated how:

"He [further] pointed out how, in numberless animal societies, the struggle [of existence] is replaced by co-operation, and how that substitution results in the development of intellectual and moral faculties which secure to the species the best conditions for survival. He intimated that in such cases the fittest are not the physically strongest, nor the cunningest, but those who learn to combine so as mutually to support each other, strong and weak alike, for the welfare of the community."

This idea was also maintained in what could be considered a summary of Kropotkin's views of a human historiography of competition, "It is evident that it would be quite contrary to all that we know of nature ... if a creature so defenceless as man was at his beginnings should have found his protection and his way to progress, not in mutual support, like other animals, but in a reckless competition for personal advantages, with no regard to the interests of the species. To a mind accustomed to the idea of unity in nature, such a proposition appears utterly indefensible." Moreover, "Sociability and need of mutual aid and support are such inherent parts of human nature that at no time of history can we discover men living in small isolated families, fighting each other for the means of subsistence. On the contrary, modern research ... proves that since the very beginning of their prehistoric life men used to agglomerate into *gentes*, clans, or tribes, maintained by an idea of common descent and by worship of common ancestors."

Moreover, this idea of a co-operative, re-unification process was witnessed by Fanon in the adoption by the Black people of his time of the philosophy of what we in the Anglophone countries would call Negroism. He identified that, "This rush of Negro-ism against the white man's contempt showed itself in certain spheres to be the one idea capable of lifting interdictions and anathemas. Because the New Guinean or Kenyan intellectuals found themselves above all up against a general ostracism and delivered to the combined contempt of their overlords, their reaction was to sing praises in admiration of each other." Yet he could not, at the same time, fail to notice a contradiction. In spite of these intellectuals' praising and honouring their Black identity, they were still beholden to the system, the objective reality, of colonial morality and legality. "In Kenya, for example, during the Mau-Mau rebellion, not a single well-known nationalist declared his affiliation with the movement, or even tried to defend the men involved in it" (Fanon 1969: 171).

These kinds of contradictions did not elude the apostle Paul either, therefore, though his doctrine concerning the Gentiles (*ethnos*) may have been somewhat more lenient than his doctrine concerning his own Falashim people, such was not the same with regard to his doctrine concerning the elites within the movement, as we can see in his letter to the evangelist Timothy, "Charge them that are rich in this world, that they be not highminded, nor trust in uncertain riches, but in the living God, who giveth us richly all things to enjoy; That they do good, that they be rich in good works, ready to distribute, willing to communicate; Laying up in store for themselves a good foundation against the time to come" (1Timothy 6: 17-19). Malcolm X also had no tolerance, in his time, for the concept of a Black bourgeoisie (pronounced boo-jwa-zee), as he said "it is those few bourgeois Negroes, rushing to throw away their little money in the white man's luxury hotels, his swanky nightclubs, and big, fine, exclusive restaurants ... proving they're integrated." Such concerns were obviously far from Malcolm X.

Even Frantz Fanon stood up against what he would go on to call the "Negro bourgeoisie," believing himself only in the concept of decolonisation, saying, "This bourgeoisie, expressing its mediocrity in its profits, its achievements and in its thought, tries to hide this mediocrity by buildings which have prestige value at the individual level, by chromium plating on big American cars, by holidays on the Riviera and week-ends in neon-lit night-clubs." Yet Fanon was not here speaking against wealth in general or even the right to wealth. To calm his critics Fanon further explained concerning what could happen during the process of a political decolonisation, "The former colonial power increases its demands, accumulates concessions and guarantees and takes fewer and fewer pains to mask the hold it has over the national government. The people stagnate deplorably in unbearable poverty; slowly they awaken to the unutterable treason of their leaders. This awakening is all the more acute in that the bourgeoisie is incapable of learning its lesson. ... [This] bourgeois caste, that section of the nation which annexes for its own profit all the wealth of the country, by a kind of unexpected logic will pass disparaging judgements upon the other Negroes and the other Arabs that more often than not are reminiscent of the racist doctrines of the former representatives of the colonial power."

From here Malcolm X saw the problem faced by the Black community. Thereby he desperately sought to remind his people, "There are two types of Negroes in this country. There's the bourgeois type who blinds himself to the condition of his people, and who is satisfied with token solutions. He's in the minority. He's a handful. He's usually the handpicked Negro who benefits from token integration." See, "Most of the so-called Negroes that you listen to on the race problem usually ... are Negroes who have been put in that position by the white man himself. And when they speak they're not speaking for black people, they're saying exactly what they know the white man who put them in that position wants to hear them say." The social disintegration produced as a result of social forces beyond the control of the various Black leaders thereby has the potential to expose the true persona of those who purport to speak for us.

Herein, Malcolm X was very forthright. He said concerning the Black predicament of 1960s America, "you have two types of Negro. The old type and the new type. Most of you know the old type. When you read about him in history during slavery he was called 'Uncle Tom.' He was the house Negro. And during slavery you had two Negroes. You had the house Negro and the field Negro. The house Negro usually lived close to his master. He dressed like his master. He wore his master's second-hand clothes. He ate food that his master left on the table. And he lived in his master's house – probably in the basement or the attic – but he still lived in the master's house. So whenever that house Negro identified himself, he always identified himself in the same sense that his master identified himself." The example given by Malcolm X of this pathology is, "When the master would be sick, the house Negro identified himself so much with his master he'd say, 'What's the matter boss, we sick?' His master's pain was his pain."

Clearly, the stand-up call to fight for liberation with a willingness to use violence if necessary is a truly noble and efficacious pursuit for any enslaved people. Here Malcolm X noted the second class of Negro during the time of slavery. "But then you had another Negro out in the field. The house Negro was in the minority ... the field Negroes were the masses. They were in the majority. When the master got sick, they prayed that he'd die." Indeed, "If someone came to the house Negro and said, 'Let's go, let's separate,' naturally that Uncle Tom would say, 'Go where? What could I do without boss? Where would I live? How would I dress? Who would look out for me?' That's the house Negro. But if you went to the field Negro and said, 'Let's go, let's separate,' he wouldn't even ask you where or how. He'd say, 'Yes, let's go.'"

Fanon and Malcolm X were effectively seeking for the general improvement of their people, not for the creation of an elite among their people. Yet it could still be asked, where did the apostle Paul's heart lie in his own racial programme? Firstly, concerning the leaders in our community becoming elite or receiving a large amount of money for preaching the gospel, the apostle Paul does say you should give to preachers of the word, acknowledging, "Now ye Philippians know also, that in the beginning of the gospel, when I departed from Macedonia, no church communicated with me as concerning giving and receiving, but ye only. For even in Thessalonica ye sent once and again unto my necessity." So the apostle Paul felt that revolution leaders were worthy of pay, as any and all workers are worthy of pay.

There is nothing wrong with leaders receiving payment for administering leadership, but there are some who would prey on the gullible so as to beguile them out of their money. The apostle Paul said of such people they are lost, drowned in the "Perverse disputing of men of corrupt minds, and destitute of the truth, supposing that gain is godliness". To the apostle Paul godliness was not found in a measure of financial gain. Godliness was found in living by righteousness. How can working and underclass people possibly sow their way out of financial difficulty without any capital or assets of their own to sow into? God blesses what you have, but if you have no assets or capital then where will your blessing go?

Still, perhaps the most powerful argument most prosperity preachers use is this Scripture oft-quoted by them, "For ye know the grace of our Lord Jesus Christ, that, though he was rich, yet for your sakes he became poor, that ye through his poverty might be rich." What makes this Scripture so complicated is the fact that we know most of the people in the early messianic movement were poor. Whether he was talking about spiritual wealth or material we do not know for sure, but it is more likely, considering the context in which it was written, that he was talking about material. So, was this statement a bold-faced assertion by the apostle Paul in defence of material prosperity, and if so of a capitalist standard and capitalist class?

In order to grasp fully what the apostle Paul was trying to convey let us look at the verses preceding this one to make sense of its context. The apostle Paul said here, in his second letter to Corinth, "Moreover, brethren, we do you to wit of the grace of God bestowed on the churches of Macedonia; How that in a great trial of affliction the abundance of their joy and their deep poverty abounded unto the riches of their liberality." The apostle Paul was speaking here of the messianic communities of Macedon, which included Philippi, Berea, and Thessalonica. Although they were poor materially, and even in extreme poverty, they gave liberally to the apostle Paul. But why was he bringing this up? Because he wanted them to give liberally too, when Titus came to them.

The apostle Paul continued in the next verses of the same chapter, "Therefore, as ye abound in every thing, in faith, and utterance, and knowledge, and in all diligence, and in your love to us, see that ye abound in this grace also. I speak not by commandment, but by occasion of the forwardness of others, and to prove the sincerity of your love." But as we continue on we can find the true social opinions of the apostle Paul staring us right in the face: "For I mean not that other men be eased, and ye burdened: But by an equality, that now at this time your abundance may be a supply for their want, that their abundance also may be a supply for your want: that there may be an equality: As it is written, He that had gathered much had nothing over; and he that had gathered little had no lack." So that now we can see in a nutshell the apostle Paul's social philosophy, which absolutely rubbishes the capitalist philosophy. Furthermore, we see here the apostle Paul stating very plainly his desire for economic equality, and even using the Torah to back it up.

That is not to say that the apostle Paul necessarily sided with Roman economic policy. Evidently, he was not the biggest fan of how things operated throughout most of the empire. We can see this by the succeeding statement he made to the evangelist

Timothy, "But they that will be rich fall into temptation and a snare, and into many foolish and hurtful lusts, which drown men in destruction and perdition." So again, what would the apostle Paul think of elites and bourgeoisies? He clearly would see them as only useful for supporting the poor so that there could thereby be an equality, as the apostle Paul believed in equality.

The Great White Bluff ... Why Everyone Loses!

Ultimately, in the apostle Paul's understanding of reconciliation he sought all the more for his people's final deliverance, saying, "For I would not, brethren, that ye should be ignorant of this mystery, lest ye should be wise in your own conceits; that blindness in part is happened to Israel, until the fulness of the Gentiles be come in. And so all Israel shall be saved: as it is written, There shall come out of Sion the Deliverer, and shall turn away ungodliness from Jacob: For this is my covenant unto them, when I shall take away their sins" (Romans 11: 25-27), as the apostle Paul wrote to his followers in Rome. On this particular position Fanon and Paul were in partial agreement, for Fanon argued, "The leader, who has behind him a lifetime of political action and devoted patriotism, constitutes [only] a screen between the people and the rapacious bourgeoisie since he stands surely for the ventures of this caste and closes his eyes to their insolence, their mediocrity and their fundamental immorality." To be sure, there is nothing wrong with revolutionary leaders being honoured for their service in guiding and propagating the revolution, especially considering the devotion and peril they take on as frontispieces.

True indeed, however, to Fanon the revolutionary leadership will always be in a precarious situation with regard to the lengths to be taken to achieve revolutionary liberation. All their "hypnotic discursives," all their "Carthagean retreats," all their "Anansian bargains," and "ecstatic eye-wash;" from that point on will ultimately be for the lulling of the masses. Here Fanon took great care to explain the situation, "At the level of individuals, violence is a cleansing force. It frees the native from his inferiority complex and from his despair and inaction; it makes him fearless and restores his self-respect. Even if the armed struggle has been symbolic and the nation is demobilized through a rapid movement of decolonization, the people have the time to see that the liberation has been the business of each and all and that the leader has no special merit" (Fanon 1969: 74).

Malcolm X was even more vehement saying this concerning the Black leadership, "This tokenism ... was a program that was designed to protect the benefits of only a handful of handpicked Negroes. And these handpicked Negroes were given big positions, and then they were used to open up their mouths to tell the world, 'Look at how much progress we're making.' He should say, look at how much progress he is making. For while these handpicked Negroes were eating high on the hog, rubbing elbows with white folk, sitting in Washington, D.C., the masses of Black people in this country continued to live in the slum and in the ghetto." He even made very clear concerning these masses in the Black community, "The worst housing conditions in America always exist in the so-called Negro community. Yet the white liberals, who own these run-down houses, force us to pay the highest rent. Faced with this high overhead, we are forced to take in roomers in order to help make up our rent. Our apartments are filled with both relatives and strangers. Our communities soon become overcrowded."

Malcolm X continued that an interesting metamorphosis occurs as a result of this situation, "The overcrowded homes of our community force us to live under some of the worst sanitary conditions imaginable. It becomes almost impossible to practice the rules of good hygiene. And therefore tuberculosis, syphilis, gonorrhoea, and other destructive social diseases are on the rampage throughout our community." "And because there seems to be no hope or no other escape, we turn to wine, we turn to whiskey, and we turn to reefers, marijuana, and even to the dreaded needle – heroin, morphine, cocaine, opium – seeking an escape." Then again, "Unemployment and poverty [also force] many of our people into a life of crime. But the real criminal is in the City Hall downtown, in the State House, and in the White House in Washington, D.C. The real criminal is the white liberal, the political hypocrite."

Malcolm X further explained how White people use these realities experienced in the Black community to further oppress us, saying, "When[ever] they want to suppress and oppress the Black community, what do they do? They take the statistics, and through the press, they feed them to the public. They make it appear that the role of crime in the Black community is higher than it is anywhere else." But, "It's [all] imagery. They use their ability to create images, and then they use these images that they've created to mislead the people. To confuse the people and make the people ... actually think that the criminal is the victim and the victim is the criminal." In this situation, as Malcolm X said further, "instead of the sociologists analyzing [things as they actually are] they cover up the real issue, and they use the press to make it appear that [our] people are thieves, hoodlums. No! They are the victims of organized thievery, organized landlords who are nothing but thieves, merchants who are nothing but thieves, [and] politicians who [are] in cahoots with [these] landlords and merchants."

Yet, while he was still in the Nation of Islam, Malcolm X understood, or at least had a plan for, what to do about this particular situation, stating, "The Honorable Elijah Muhammad has the only permanent solution. Twenty million ex-slaves must be permanently separated from our former slavemaster and placed on some land that we can call our own. Then we can create our own jobs. Control our own economy. Solve our own problems instead of waiting on the American white man to solve our problems for us." Still, in delineating this separatist vision he was careful not to thereby endorse segregation, as he explained to his critics, "We reject *segregation* even more militantly than you say you do! We want *separation*, which is not the same! ... To *segregate* means to control. Segregation is that which is forced upon inferiors by superiors. But *separation* is that which is done voluntarily, by two equals – for the good of both! The Honorable Elijah Muhammad teaches us that as long as our people here in America are dependent upon the white man, we will always be begging him for jobs, food, clothing and housing. And he will always control our lives, regulate our lives, and have power to segregate us."

Malcolm X was effectively stating here a desire for the Black people of America to have self-determination; a right given to every nationality that has fought for it. For this cause, he championed the idea of Black separatism from the United States in their own struggle for national liberation. "America is a colonial power ... She's a twentieth-century colonial power; she's a modern colonial power, and she has colonized [us] African-Americans." "Since [we] were originally Africans, who are now in America not by choice but only by a cruel accident in our history, we strongly believe that African problems are our problems and our problems are African problems." Effectively, "The Honorable Elijah Muhammad teaches us that on our own land we can set up farms, factories, businesses. We can establish our own government and become an independent nation. And once we become separated from the jurisdiction of this white nation, we can then enter into trade and commerce for ourselves with other independent nations."

Nevertheless, Fanon also recognised a problem that arises with the independence of the nation: the bourgeois class begins to assume responsibility for the state, and in many cases is incapable, or at least inexperienced, and therefore re-establishes the conditions of the former colonial power. Here Fanon stated, "The national middle class which takes over power at the end of the colonial regime is an under-developed middle class. It has practically no economic power, and in any case it is in no way commensurate with the bourgeoisie of the mother country … [Effectively, in its] wilful narcissism, the national middle class is easily convinced that it can advantageously replace the middle class of the mother country." That is not to say our Black bourgeoisies are completely incapable, but that the class position without the cultural and economic capital to back it up, only leads inevitably to failure.

That said, a curious puzzle arises when deeply considering the apostle Paul's understanding of the class structure of the early revolutionary movement, we find that he himself identified a class hierarchy for the messianic communities to adhere to: "And God hath set some in the church, first apostles, secondarily prophets, thirdly teachers, after that miracles, then gifts of healings, helps, governments, diversities of tongues." If the apostle Paul acknowledged several different social classes within his own revolutionary vision for social change then who is to say that Allah himself does not identify, or even encourage, the existence of different social classes for different societies? Again, if there was a hierarchy in the early messianic movement then why should there not be hierarchies in society, and even Black society too?

The prosperity preachers will also cry in unison that the current capitalist system is only natural, in that classes have existed in the messianic movement from its inception and have existed in society since the origin of civilisation. Although these ideas will be challenged throughout this series, the understanding that the apostle Paul, being himself a moderately poor man, would not condone competition or permit his followers to be inequitable, shows that at least the idea of social justice was a part of the apostle Paul's revolutionary vision for social change.

Nevertheless, we are still confronted with this discrepancy; the influence of which could produce, and is already producing; various levels of mental, social, and racial complexes as a result. Fanon himself would even articulate how, "The doctrine of cultural hierarchy is thus but one aspect of a systemized hierarchization implacably pursued." Moreover, the cultural narrative, performative, and reproductive of these kinds of systems of unintended dissociation, effectively allow for a social kinetics of superiority and inferiority, thereby showing that those faithful to the apostle Paul's hierarchical structuring would still not undermine his, as important, vision for a socially and economically equal commonwealth.

Consequently, in his letter to the messianic communities of Rome the apostle Paul still chose to complicate the matter further, saying: "For as we have many members in one body, and all members have not the same office: So we, being many, are one body in Christ, and every one members one of another. Having then gifts differing according to the grace that is given to us, whether prophecy, let us prophesy according to the proportion of faith; Or ministry, let us wait on our ministering: or he that teacheth, on teaching; Or he that exhorteth, on exhortation: he that giveth, let him do it with simplicity; he that ruleth, with diligence; he that sheweth mercy, with cheerfulness" (Romans 12: 4-8). These two letters promoting structural hierarchy in the early messianic movement feel shrill, strident, and piercing. They echo throughout the many ages of Christian religious ordination and imperious domination.

However, as I have tried to point out, this was actually a system of unintended dissociation that the apostle Paul did not design disingenuously. In fact, this was not an endorsement of social classes at all, but an ordering and organising of the then disorganised messianic movement. Notwithstanding, while these hierarchical orderings could very well be considered classes, such in fact discounts their revolutionary potential. From a more anarchic perspective such could, by all rights, be considered something far more interesting. Herein, we can see the revolutionary potential of their social superstructure.

An anarchic hierarchy could be constructed either on a federalist structure or a syndicalist structure. A federalist hierarchical structure would be similar to a tribal or governmental structure. The federal bodies would thereby operate to promote and enforce the laws/rules of the social or global body. However, far more potential can be gleaned from the syndicalist hierarchical structure. This is to have in place workplace workers' meetings and neighbourhood consumers' meetings that interact, on one level; and that also hierarchically rise to district level (either village, town, city, or borough); and to regional level (either northwest, southwest, southeast, or northeast); then to national level (including 5 members from each region); then, finally, to international level. This syndicalist chain should essentially go up from the bottom, and not from the top down.

This, in our time, would be the best means of hierarchical structure we could possibly hope for. However, it does beg the question: should such a superstructure be organised on bureaucratic, meritocratic, or technocratic lines? Obviously, in our current "liberalised" institutions we see examples of all three. Yet, in truth, we see examples of none. Monopoly, oligarchy, nepotism, racism, orientalism, sexism, heterosexism, cis-sexism, and various other forms of discrimination pollute society today. In this case, though believing the technocratic option to be the best for us godbodies; I also recognise how hard it will be to implement. Technocracy, similar to meritocracy, is based on the concept of the most qualified rise within the hierarchy; yet, in a technocratic system it is a little more refined. The most technically qualified for a specific position should be the one to get that position. It should be thus regardless of age, class, race, gender, sexual orientation, or any other societal distinction. This is similar to Jim Collins' estimation to not only have the right people on the bus (meritocracy) but the right people in the right seats (technocracy).

However, if we consider again the structure of the later messianic movement we see that it was based primarily on the distortion and corruption of words used by the apostle Paul, nevertheless his actual intended hope was always to produce a system of interdependent offices and vocations within the messianic movement that would function similar to how the human body functions. Just as within the complete functioning of our own bodily composition there are many tasks and many operations, some invisible, some visible, some honourable, some embarrassing, some now co-ordinating with this group, some now co-ordinating with another; yet our entire bodily composition still works in conjunction with the whole to the benefit of all members.

Even so, the apostle Paul's actual vision for the messianic movement (and by extension for Black society as a whole), was that each member would work together for the benefit of all. Though some are skilled at production, others at leading, others at service, and some at manual work, some can operate various devices, some can sell anything, some can entertain, others have mastered a particular art, while still others can retain vast amounts of information and scientific knowledge. All these gifts and abilities were given by Allah to specific individuals. And just as the apostle Paul also said, "If the ear shall say, Because I am not the eye, I am not of the body; is it therefore not of the body? If the whole body were an eye, where were the hearing? If the whole were hearing, where were the smelling?" Even so we should not dismiss the apostle Paul's hierarchical structuring of the early messianic movement, as, in truth, it could not have been avoided. To continue the analogy: we actually do have body parts that are considered more valuable or more honourable than others. It is only when we lose these less valuable members, whether through mutilation or dysfunction, that we appreciate how valuable they really were.

We can see here, through this analogy of the body, certain aspects of the apostle Paul's sociological views about life and nature; that though the analogy actually dates back to Plato, the apostle Paul had an interdependence view of the functionings of society long before Durkheim made it popular. This view and understanding of the interconnection of one part of the body to all the others, and of their relation to how well the body functions as a whole, would effectively allow for those within the messianic movement to adopt traditions of solidarity and brotherhood that transcended *ethnos*, class, gender, and sexuality, and even transcended the ages. It is this holistic view of interconnection that would also lay the ground work for future social and biological theorists throughout Western history. Effectively, within the apostle Paul's revolutionary vision for social change our relation to each other is no longer based on *ethnos*, though *ethnos*, class, gender, and sexuality would ultimately still exist; but on mutual interaction and support. Thus the apostle Paul was trying, in essence, to build among his followers strong familial chords of relation. These chords of relation would effectively allow them to escape the excesses of ethnic, class, gender, and sexual politics to become one family in the Messiah.

The economic aspect of the apostle Paul's revolutionary vision for social change within the early messianic movement was clearly that goods, services, and information be distributed among the brothers and sisters based not on charge but on need. That if a follower within a messianic community had a need they would be able to make known their need to another follower, whether brother or sister, based on what was needed. Thus like an eye needing the help of a hand to see better, it could communicate this information to the hand, who in turn would provide the service. This service, for the sake of equality, would then be provided free of charge as the server would soon, or some other time, require a service from they whom they have just served, thereby maintaining equality.

This vision can further be seen in the following statement, which he made to the messianic communities of Rome, saying, "Be of the same mind one toward another. Mind not high things, but condescend to men of low estate. Be not wise in your own conceits. Recompense to no man evil for evil. Provide things honest in the sight of all men. If it be possible, as much as lieth in you, live peaceably with all men" (Romans 12: 16-18). Herein, Malcolm X asked the very pertinent question concerning the Black community, "What divided us? Our lack of pride. Our lack of racial identity. Our lack of racial pride. Our lack of cultural roots." Yet, he went on to explain why this was so: "Until 1959 [our] image of the African continent was created by the enemies of Africa. Africa was a land dominated by outside powers. A land dominated by Europeans. And as these Europeans dominated the continent of Africa, it was they who created the image of Africa that was projected abroad. And they projected Africa and the people of Africa in a negative image, a hateful image. They made us think that Africa was a land of jungles, a land of animals, a land of cannibals and savages."

Malcolm X further continued, "From [around 1960 onward] the flames of nationalism, independence on the African continent, became so bright and so furious, they were able to burn and sting anything that got in its path." The racial tensions this provoked were strong and Malcolm X understood that. According to Malcolm X this revolutionary spirit sparked by the African nationalists changed the Black people in the West's perception of Africa and thereby it changed their perception of themselves. In this situation, "the three major allies, the United States, Britain, and France, have a problem today that is a common problem. ... And that common problem is the new mood that is reflected in the overall division of the Black people within continental France, within the same sphere of England, and also here in the United States. So that – and this mood has been changing to the same degree that the mood on the African continent has been changing. So when you find the African revolution taking place, and by African revolution I mean the emergence of African nations into independence ... [it] has absolutely affected the mood of the Black people in the Western Hemisphere."

Malcolm X thereby noted, "You and I are living at a time when there's a revolution going on. A worldwide revolution. It goes beyond Mississippi. It goes beyond Alabama. It goes beyond Harlem. There's a worldwide revolution going on." He also noted that this revolution was a nationalist revolution, stating, "The spirit of nationalism on the African continent [has meant that] the powers, the colonial power, they couldn't stay there. The British got in trouble in Kenya, Nigeria, Tanganyika, Zanzibar, and other areas of the continent. The French got in trouble in the entire French Equatorial North Africa, including Algeria. ... The Congo wouldn't any longer permit the Belgians to stay there." At the same time, "when the Black revolution begins to roll on the African continent it effects the Black man in the United States [too] and affects the relationship between the Black man and the white man in the United States."

Deuces are Wild (With No Jokers)

Despite all that has been said so far an argument could still be made that even if we were to accept the idea that the apostle Paul actually was an anti-imperialist revolutionary, there is still hard evidence that he also was yet an apologist for the colonial regime, evidence that itself can be found in his letter to the messianic communities of Rome, where he said to the fellowship, "Wherefore ye must needs be subject, not only for wrath, but also for conscience sake. For for this cause pay you tribute also: for they are God's ministers, attending continually upon this very thing. Render therefore to all their dues: tribute to whom tribute is due; custom to whom customs; fear to whom fear; honour to whom honour. Owe no man any thing, but to love one another: for he that loveth another hath fulfilled the law" (Romans 13: 5-8).

Nonetheless, we also find here a general theme articulated by all the Falashim prophets: all of them crying out for justice in human dealings and interchange, and against the iniquities and inequities of unsociable behaviours and individuals. These prophets would say things like, "Woe to them that devise iniquity, and work evil upon their beds! when the morning is light, they practise it, because it is in the power of their hand. And they covet fields, and take them by violence; and houses, and take them away: so they oppress a man and his house, even a man and his heritage." "Woe to him that increaseth that which is not his! how long? and to him that ladeth himself with thick clay! Shall they not rise up suddenly that shall bite thee, and awake that shall vex thee, and thou shalt be for booties unto them?" "Woe to him that coveteth an evil covetousness to his house, that he may set his nest on high, that he may be delivered from the power of evil! Thou hast consulted shame to thy house by cutting off many people, and hast sinned against thy soul."

So how then do we confront the apostle Paul's assertion "Wherefore ye must needs be subject," and "they are God's ministers"? Let us not forget that the apostle Paul, an international riot-maker and rabble rouser in his own right, most definitely had spies and agents of the state watching him, and imperial police officers reading and examining his letters (as they did with all the apostles and early messianic writers). Remember also, the apostle Paul was a leader in a global revolutionary movement, therefore, any statements of governmental or imperial appeasement should be read as merely Anansian negotiation and strategic dissimulation. Yes, the apostle Paul taught and encouraged honesty and "speaking the truth in love," but imperial methods, historical records, historical context, and implied subtext, all tell a very different story. Therein the social relations and social kinetics of imperialism can be seen: political and cultural suffocation rendered all levels of challenge impotent.

It is for this cause that what we read from the apostle Paul was so easily used by the Roman Imperial officers of the time to say that movements such as the messianic had a duty to give due respect to the existing imperial state, even as it was later used by Roman Catholic clergy to say the same thing these millennia later. Allah was the one who ordained its power, so they say, so it is only ours to give them their due of submission and obedience. The condemnation for such nonsensical guidance was levelled against the imperial power structure of the twentieth century by Malcolm X in his own fiery anti-imperialist retorts: "the American racists know that they can rule ... the African American, only as long as we have a negative image of ourselves". And again, "The white man so guilty of white supremacy can't hide his guilt by trying to accuse The Honorable Elijah Muhammad of teaching black supremacy and hate! All Mr Muhammad is doing is trying to uplift the black man's mentality and the black man's social and economic condition in this country."

Accordingly, in spite of the apostle Paul's apparent deference to imperialism, in this very letter to his followers in Rome, there was still discernible certain invisible slippages, certain subterranean confessions, occultly lurking beneath the surface, and attempting their ascent. It is in fact these occult risings that reveal, or dare I say, expose, the apostle Paul's true intentions when he wrote to the Roman believers, "he that loveth another hath fulfilled the law. ...Love worketh no ill to his neighbour: therefore love is the fulfilling of the law" (Romans 13: 8, 10). What anarchic statements! In fact, they could even be considered the very basis of anarchism.

Moreover, this was not the first time he made such statements of antinomian (lawless) motivation. The apostle Paul wrote to the messianic communities of Galatia, saying: "For, brethren, ye have been called unto liberty; only use not liberty for an occasion to the flesh, but by love serve one another. For all the law is fulfilled in one word, even this; Thou shalt love thy neighbour as thyself" (Galatians 5: 13, 14). Herein remember, this fulfilling of *all the law* through loving our neighbour was written before the American Revolution and the idea of separating Church from State. Therefore, as stated before, the apostle Paul was not simply talking about all the laws of Moses; he meant *all* legal judgments and requirements.

Having himself an undeniable grasp of the words spoken by the Messiah, when he was confronted by the Herodians (Judean sympathisers with the Roman government) as to whether it was fitting for a Judean to pay taxes to Caesar, he answered, "Shew me the tribute money. And they brought unto him a penny. And he saith unto them, whose is this image and superscription? They say unto him, Cæsar's. Then said he unto them, Render therefore unto Cæsar the things which are Cæsar's; and unto God the things that are God's" (Matthew 22: 19-21). In this, neither the Messiah nor the apostle Paul were advocating the giving of tribute to Caesar or that such was to be instituted as a new Judean tradition from then on, forevermore. What they were really saying was, so long as that empire existed, so long as that power structure existed, they should pay their tribute. If the empire ever fell, however, there would no longer be any need to pay them further tribute (and on an even deeper level: though now Caesar's law exists, follow the law of love and if Caesar's law ever gets abolished we never followed it anyway).

The apostle Paul, therefore, saw the commonwealth of Israel being fulfilled politically in an anarchic system where people would be free to walk in love. So while he may have never instigated an actual revolution (though himself being undeniably a revolutionary), he definitely did not believe in Caesar, or his laws, or his state. He also continued this theme further on in his message to the messianic communities of Rome, saying, "So then every one of us shall give account of himself to God. Let us not therefore judge one another any more: but judge this rather, that no man put a stumblingblock or an occasion to fall in his brother's way. I know, and am persuaded by the Lord Jesus, that there is nothing unclean of itself: but to him that esteemeth any thing to be unclean, to him it is unclean" (Romans 14: 12-14). Thereby, saying, that the structural mechanisms of culture formation that essentially determined the practices, customs, and traditions of the culture, were neither static nor predetermined, but were even then flexible, contestable, and meaningful.

On the other hand, if we look at an institution like Black erotica, which is based substantially on concepts like Black love, free love, and plural love; while it may be a free expression of Black sexuality that has pneumatological potential, it is still heavily judged and stigmatised within society at large. Nevertheless, the main purpose of Black eroticism should centrally be to generate libidinal love, thus producing for the Black community a sensual resurrection. Ultimately, if the Bible intended for the first resurrection to be a mental resurrection, then it would have said that the *noia* or the *noema* was to be resurrected. Instead, it said the psyche was to be resurrected.

For those who do not know, however, the Greek word psyche, back in the classical era, actual meant something more along the lines of: the driving forces that produce our external behaviours/activities. In Freudian theory these drives are acknowledged as predominantly sensual drives inspired by the pleasure principle. Herein, we see why in the King James Bible they chose to translate the Greek word *psychikos* as the English word sensual, even if nowadays the word psychic has taken on a far more abstracted meaning. Based on the Freudian interpretation of a sensual, indeed, sexual psyche we can see how the first resurrection was always far more likely to have been considered to be a sensual resurrection.

Accordingly, the godbody prohibition of marriage helps us to fulfil this *eschaton*, or last days' thing, by allowing us to practice a form of free love, or even plural love, in our communities. The truth is, we godbodies need to address this issue of Black eroticism in our philosophy as to not do so would make us hypocrites, using all this language of caring for children and educating the masses in our public discourse while, at the same time, practicing in secret sexual liberality. We either need to add sexual liberality to our public discourse, that is, add the discourse of Black eroticism, or abandon what Allah was trying to teach us and where he was trying to lead us. It should be clear to anyone who gives any serious thought as to why the Father taught us not to marry according to the government that his goal was to promote among us free love practices, thereby sexually liberating us. The fullest expression of this sexual liberation thereby leading us to become sexual objects to the rest of the Black community.

Through this the God would become the sexual object of Black women and the Goddess would become the sexual object of Black men – and though I recognise that the word object has acquired certain negative connotations since Martin Buber (1927) that relate it to the "dehumanising" of human beings, I use it here in the Freudian sense of the word – making us like love objects that can be conduits of their transferences. As the godbody male and godbody female thus become the sexual objects of others they will thereby cause them to discharge sexual energy in the sexual act. Again, if we do not address this issue of sexuality and sexual liberation, we risk our word not being bond, claiming to only be about the family, while, at the same time, loving sex and behaving sexually without admitting that truth. At least if we publicly adopt a discourse of Black eroticism our word becomes bond to truth. Our word also stays *our* bond which others will be able to see in all our ways and actions toward our love objects.

That said, again, the sexual act must always be consensual between both: neither the male nor the female godbody should ever rape anybody, nor allow anybody to rape them. The godbody must therefore practice the use of seduction in their hypererotic behaviour to break down all resisting or reactionary behaviour. In this, there ultimate aim should be to generate within the sexual subject the most powerful force in the universe: sexual energy. That sexual energy will then either be discharged in the sexual act or sublimated into progressive acts – obviously it could also get inhibited once generated if the godbody does not guide them to a fruitful outcome. Therefore, the act of seduction must not be taken lightly. Though the key to Black eroticism must remain seduction it can be both positive and progressive (as it can instigate the liberation of a Black person's sexuality from inhibition or prohibition).

To further clarify, when I use the word seduction it is not here spoken of in the Freudian sense of the word but in the commonsense of the word. Freudian seduction shall henceforth be referred to as perverse seduction in that it takes for granted the idea that an adult, older sibling, or trusted authority will molest a child. Seduction as I use it is still Freudian to a degree, in that it produces within the sexual subject a wish, but it is not *the* Freudian theory of seduction as it has nothing to do with sexual molestation or betrayal. In this version of seduction, the sexual object becomes the sexual fantasy and thereby becomes fetishised – in the sense that they take on mystical attributes. The God becomes sex God to the Black woman thereby allowing her to recognise that the standards of society are, and have always been, artificial and illusory.

It is the central intent of this form of Black eroticism to liberate and empower Black minds, therefore the methodology the God should use to achieve this objective should remain seduction. Still, if one excuses the oversimplification, women will always be better seducers than men. Indeed, any woman can seduce any man she wants, simply by anchoring the constant and consistent exhibition of her body or sexuality to a positive experience he has had. These exhibitions will be like sharp goads on the man's heart, especially when he tries to resist them. Eventually, the pain will become so unbearable that he will be completely in her power. Therefore, a woman should never take anything a man says too seriously as she can easily break him by creating constant and consistent sexual associations and connections, in his mind, to a former positive experience. Obviously, a woman should not have to exhibit the private areas of her body or her sexuality just to seduce a man, however, if she does, it is the most potent form of eroticism she could perform.

True, feminist Jill Johnson did articulate back in the 1980s that, "Feminism at heart is a massive complaint, Lesbianism is the solution ... Until all women are lesbians there will be no true political revolution" (Johnson 1985; quoted in Kolawole 1997: 15); yet this was not as hopeless a call to action as it at first may seem. In my own experience, women tend to prefer things like masturbation and lesbianism to male sexual relationships. Herein homosexuality may not be as genetic in the case of women as it is in the case of men. The truth is, women are generally better at sexual expression than men, knowing in many cases instinctively how to sexually please both men and women. Add to that the emotional support, friendship, bonding, and compassion they are able to receive from other women, and the overall shittiness of men when they show or demonstrate the slightest bit of sexual independence or freedom and it makes it that much easier for women to leave the game entirely, either practicing lesbianism, or identifying as bisexual or pansexual. In certain cases, obviously, those women will continue to date or have relationships with men, however, in a lot of cases that will only be due to the stigma of self- or same-sex pleasure, or due to the wealth and power of men in the current world system.

Essentially, while what Johnson was hoping for may at first have seemed somewhat impossible, especially considering how far a cry it is from the "you don't choose to be gay" rhetoric, choosing instead the promotion of using love for political ends. Still, building on from her, a far more powerful war cry would be for *all* women to practice the lifestyle of free love and thus free themselves from the burden of marriage and the various other standards imposed on them by church and state. On the other hand, if we were to look deeper into the conception of Black eroticism, which is based fundamentally on Black love, free love, and plural love, it is definitely more than what marriage could ever be: it is a free expression of hypereroticism that possesses a high pneumatological potential.

We should also remember that according to Freud eroticism is the most powerful force in the universe. For this reason, I have been fighting so hard to allow Black women to express their own eroticism or hypereroticism. Imagine if you will that all Black men were suddenly to possess a superpower: the ability to transmit their thoughts to other Black men. Imagine that only Black men possessed this superpower and that they could use it to uplift the Black community. Now imagine that society continued to stigmatise and demonise this superpower as evil and ignorant. Imagine they also labelled those who used this superpower as corrupt and backward. Would any of this stop Black men from using their superpower to liberate Black people? Well, *all* women have a genuine superpower with eroticism, yet for some reason they despise their superpower unable to appreciate how great it is.

The truth is, men, even with all our political and social power, are unable to handle a very erotic woman, especially as women can stir up in us all the spiritual, social, cultural, martial, political, economic, scientific, and athletic genius we require in life through sublimation. As to the notion that *all men really despise and will never respect* these types of women: Napoleon Hill, one of the great heroes of this current alpha-male revival, had this to say in his most seminal, "One of America's most able businessmen frankly admitted that his attractive secretary was responsible for most of the plans he created. He confessed that her presence lifted him to heights of creative imagination, such as he could experience under no other stimulus" (Hill 2004: 217). Still, those determined to continue the argument may say that this was the man's secretary, with no placement at all in the so-called whorearchy; but sexual objectification is sexual objectification regardless of what position you hold in society.

Herein those at the lower levels of society, and of the whorearchical pyramid, may face great stigmatisation from those at the higher levels of both, but the men these higher level women assume despise them in many cases not only do not fall into these women's dehumanising stereotype of men, but actually *secretly adore* these women. As a man myself, a man who has done time in prison surrounded by a multitude of other men, I can attest: one of the most essential things that got us through our time in prison was not our wives or girlfriends as such. Although, obviously, they were extremely important, in every single case, they were also the cause of our biggest pain and difficulty, even when they gave us what we would call "naked flicks."

What really got us inmates through our time in prison, again, in every cis-hetero case, was what we called "pussy books", the softcore porno magazines featuring pictures of fully naked women. On the so-called whorearchy pyramid those types of women would represent the top (Cam Girls), but I guarantee this, during our time in prison – though I am obviously unable to speak for all of us – the vast majority of us cis-hetero males saw these same types of women as sacred, yes sacred, for their willingness to pose in those types of pictures. Why? Because without them prison would have been a more literal hell. We may change our tune when we get out and are among our N!gg@s, true indeed, but that is a different story altogether.

Again, these types of women, to us, had and have always had, a superpower. Yet rather than encouraging these types of women, and particularly those within the Black community, to use their superpower for their own liberation we join with White society, most likely jealous of the Black woman's predominance in this particular field; and condemn them whenever they do use it. Now some women may think that eroticism is not that great a superpower, but I disagree. It is an amazing, wonderful, and incredible superpower. The only real reason I can think of as to why so many women currently look down on such a force is because they have not yet learned to reject society's stigmatisation of it and use it to empower themselves.

Yet for any seductionist, *whether male or female*, the one overriding aim they desire is to give the greatest amount of erotic pleasure to those they are interacting with. Moreover, their seduction will always be deviant, though it should ultimately be a beneficial deviance, used to liberate and not to oppress. Their seduction must also be unoffendable, therefore it will not be discouraged by bad results but strengthened by them. Seduction by name means there is resistance. Indeed, with no resistance it is not seduction but arousal. They should not feel too discouraged because of these resistances though, as in their desire to produce in that person, male or female, the greatest amount of sexual pleasure they could possibly have, they will have effectively revealed to them the very face of Allah, which is al-Muhibb (the Libidinal One).

All these ideas take on a deeper meaning in the writings of the apostle Paul, who having his own transgressive doctrine, sought to re-educate the various ethnicities of the empire, saying, "Wherefore remember, that ye being in time past Gentiles in the flesh, who are called Uncircumcision by that which is called the Circumcision in the flesh made by hands; That at that time ye were without Christ, being aliens from the commonwealth of Israel, and strangers from the covenants of promise, having no hope, and without God in the world: But now in Christ Jesus ye who sometimes were far off are made nigh by the blood of Christ. For he is our peace, who hath made both one, and hath broken down the middle wall of partition between us" (Ephesians 2: 11-14). The kind of indoctrination the apostle Paul was here trying to impart to the messianic communities of Ephesus was with the sole aim of allowing them to see that they belonged to a separate kingdom or commonwealth from that of Imperial Rome: the very commonwealth of Israel itself.

What is quite telling in these statements is a hidden absence, one that is quite marked, though is rarely considered. The original message of both the Baptist and the Messiah was the message of the kingdom of God, yet the concept itself is noticeably and painfully rare outside of the gospels. More common are the ideas of: kingdom of Christ, kingdom of the Son, heavenly kingdom, etc. While it may be implied that they are all the same thing, it is clear that Paul's perception of the kingdom was of the imminent earthly rule of the Son of David over the commonwealth of Israel. Again, the apostle Paul was not hoping and fighting for a heavenly rule for the Messiah: in his view, as in that of the early messianic movement, the Messiah already ruled in a heavenly kingdom. What the apostle Paul was hoping and fighting to do was spread the Messiah's earthly kingdom among the various nations of the world.

Ultimately, such an interpretation, combined with all we have considered so far, opens up to us the deeper levels of the apostle Paul's ideological agenda. Firstly, the apostle Paul believed wholeheartedly in ethnic, gender, sexual, economic, and class equality. Secondly, his hope and desire for class equality did not necessarily mean to him the end of hierarchy altogether, just a redefinition of the social kinetics of hierarchy. To the apostle Paul hierarchy should be official (that is, based primarily on the office/positon the person occupied) and not personal (that is, based primarily on the calling, destiny, or charisma of the individual), so to him authority rested in the seat not the personality. Thirdly, the apostle Paul believed the function of society, and particularly of the messianic communities in society, was to operate like the human body, each part playing the role best suited to it similar to what we in our day would call a division of labour.

Here, we can understand that an honestly Pauline ideology would have to acknowledge a societal division of labour, however, one that is substantially different from our own in that it would not have its basis in the market forces of supply and demand, forces which ultimately commodify human beings (and everything else in existence); thereby placing our value and worth as human beings at the mercy of said forces. Herein also we see that the key ideological issues of the world today: hierarchisation, legitimisation, racialisation, sexualisation, heterosexualisation, cis-sexualisation, pornification, gendering, the division of labour, uneven social and industrial development, and the damaging of environmental integrity; are in fact not the real problem. The world can maintain all these divisions and the social kinetics they each entail and still be a just, fair, and perfect society. The problem is, and has been since modernity: commodification – that is, determining intrinsic value by market value. Though in feudal times value was determined by so-called divine right (another fallacy) in our time value, and thereby power, is determined only by market forces, which the apostle Paul would never have agreed to.

Even Malcolm X shared Paul's authentic views for most of his public career, while feeling, at the same time, that they could also be problematised, especially when it came to the issue of Black and White race-relations in America, saying, "Why, when all of my ancestors are snake-bitten, and I'm snake-bitten, and I warn my children to avoid snakes, what does that *snake* sound like accusing *me* of hate-teaching?" The apostle Paul in considering the Black and White races of the empire of Rome, felt that there was an opportunity to unify due to the Messiah's sacrifice, "For he is our peace, who hath made of both one, and hath broken down the middle wall of partition between us; Having abolished in his flesh the enmity, even the law of commandments contained in ordinances; for to make in himself of twain one new man, so making peace."

Ultimately, in walking this path of the anti-imperialist we must learn to supersede all legal articulation, and all the discourses used as their justification, so as to allow for their cultural valorisation. The apostle Paul said, "Not that we are sufficient of ourselves to think any thing as of ourselves; but our sufficiency is of God; Who also hath made us able ministers of the new testament; not of the letter, but of the spirit: for the letter killeth, but spirit giveth life" and such an outlook is the definition of revolutionary. Incidentally, Lenin made a point about most revolutionary movements that could be quite pertinent here: he said that their opportunist section have a tendency, at the height of their public acceptability, to deny the more utopian elements of their initial programme, even "as Christians, after their religion had been given the status of state religion, 'forgot' the 'naiveté' of primitive Christianity with its democratic, revolutionary spirit" (Lenin 2014: 81).

A further example of this revolutionary spirit is detectable in Fanon's heroic efforts, arguing that, "This rediscovery, this absolute valorization almost in defiance of reality, objectively indefensible, assumes an incomparable and subjective importance. On emerging from these passionate espousals, the native will have decided, 'with full knowledge of what is involved,' to fight all forms of exploitation and of alienation of man. At this same time, the occupant, on the other hand, multiplies appeals to assimilation, then to integration, to community" (Fanon 1964: 43). Fanon was here presenting a methodology for decolonising mind, body, and spaces, and for valorising the traditional narratives, performatives, and reproductives.

Yet even here the apostle Paul can help us, for inasmuch as he served and followed Allah, he was also willing to acknowledge "the working of his mighty power, Which he wrought in Christ, when he raised him from the dead, and set him at his own right hand in the heavenly places, Far above all principality, and power, and might, and dominion, and every name that is named, not only in this world, but also in that which is to come" (Ephesians 1: 19-21). What a valorisation! Yet remember, these were not simply spiritual (that is astral) principalities, powers, might, and dominions, these were earthly, corporeal, and imperial rulers. Moreover, each of these imperial rulers governed over their own small or large territory within the Roman Empire.

This idea is brought into even sharper focus by the words the apostle Paul said to the messianic communities in the city of Rome: "Now I say that Jesus Christ was a minister of the circumcision for the truth of God, to confirm the promises made unto the fathers: And that the Gentiles might glorify God for his mercy; as it is written, For this cause I will confess to thee among the Gentiles, and sing unto thy name. And again he saith, Rejoice, ye Gentiles, with his people. And again, Praise the Lord, all ye Gentiles; and laud him, all ye people. And again, Esaias saith, There shall be a root of Jesse, and he that shall rise to reign over the Gentiles; in him shall the Gentiles trust" (Romans 15: 8-12); this one is of particular interest to us here for, to give a more in-depth quotation:

> *"And there shall come forth a rod out of the stem of Jesse, and a Branch shall grow out of his roots: And the spirit of the Lord shall rest upon him ... And righteousness shall be the girdle of his loins, and faithfulness the girdle of his reins. The wolf also shall dwell with the lamb, and the leopard shall lie down with the kid; and the calf and the young lion and the fatling together; and a little child shall lead them. And the cow and the bear shall feed; their young ones shall lie down together: and the lion shall eat straw like the ox. And the sucking child shall play on the hole of the asp, and the weaned child shall put his hand on the cockatrice' den. They shall not hurt nor destroy in all my holy mountain; for the earth shall be full of the knowledge of the Lord, as the waters cover the sea. And in that day there shall be a root of Jesse, which shall stand for an ensign of the people; to it shall the Gentiles seek" (Isaiah 11: 1-10).*

This union of animals and people that anticipates the kingdom of God upon the earth is, in essence, a learning of empathic interconnection and communal support and interdependence. These figurative realities, however, are not that far from the truth of nature; for as the apostle James also said, "every kind of beasts, and of birds, and of serpents, and of things in the sea, is tamed, and hath been tamed of mankind" (James 3: 7). Pyotr Kropotkin also reminds us, "Association is found in the animal world at all degrees of evolution; … But, in proportion as we ascend the scale of evolution, we see association growing more and more conscious. It loses its purely physical character, it ceases to be simply instinctive, it becomes reasoned. With the higher vertebrates it is periodical, or is resorted to for the satisfaction of a given want – propagation of the species, migration, hunting, or mutual defence."

Moreover, a relation to such "liberation fauna" could potentially allow us to become a lot more zoopathic in our interchanges with nature. For example, as Kropotkin noted, in a "migration of fallow-deer which I witnessed on the Amur, and during which scores of thousands of these intelligent animals came together from an immense territory, flying before the coming deep snow, in order to cross passed before my eyes, I saw Mutual Aid and Mutual Support carried on to an extent which made me suspect in it a feature of the greatest importance for the maintenance of life, the preservation of each species, and its further evolution." This statement gives further credence to Mimi Sheller's understanding of how even nature "can take on quite widely differing symbolic meanings, can support highly varied social performances, and can become the material grounds for opposed 'productions of space' (Lefebvre 1991: 90)." It is therefore our empathy with nature, its flora and fauna, that gives us true connection.

Even nineteenth century social theorist and Marxist thinker Fredrick Engels confessed in his debates with the revisionist

Eugen Dühring concerning the Darwinian discussion that "the idea of the struggle for existence ... Darwin himself admitted, has to be sought in a generalization of the views of the economist and theoretician of population, [Thomas] Malthus, and that the idea therefore suffers from all the defects inherent in the priestly Malthusian ideas of over-population." But "the *fact* [that this struggle] exists also among plants can be demonstrated to him by every meadow, every cornfield, every wood; and the question at issue is not what it is to be called, whether 'struggle for existence' or 'lack of conditions of life and mechanical effects,' but how this fact influences the preservation or variation of species."

These kinds of "contested natures," ultimately reveal their subaltern identity, not only in the obvious fact of the struggles of cornfields and meadows, but also in the mutual aid and mutual interaction in cornfields and meadows. For it is impossible to look at these beautiful expressions of plant life and not see their sociable togetherness and unity, while their invisible struggles and fights for survival and maintenance, though real, are virtually insignificant to the senses. Indeed, Sheller took this concept even further, stating how "wild forests[,] as ciphers of subaltern historicity ... have an erotic force that transcends the scale of human lives and disrupts the ordering projects of states. Plants are protean, imperialistic, bent on reproduction by exercising a kind of agency from below that is both generative and destructive" (Sheller 2012: 193).

Moreover, as Engels further stated in a letter to his friend P. L. Lavron, "The whole Darwinist teaching of the struggle for existence is simply a transference from society to living nature of Hobbes's doctrine of *bellum omnium contra omnes* [war of all against all] and of the bourgeois-economic doctrine of competition together with Malthus's theory of population." Claiming, that even, "In recent times the idea of natural selection was extended ... and the variation of species conceived as a result of the mutual interaction of adaptation and heredity, in which process adaptation is taken as the factor which produces variations, and heredity as the preserving factor." Effectively, to him the Darwinian contribution was best summed in what he accomplished for science, "Darwin brought back from his scientific travels the view that plant and animal species are not constant but subject to variation." And this in itself was a remarkable achievement for his time. However, "It is true that in doing this Darwin attributed to his discovery too wide a field of action, made it the sole agent in the alteration of species and neglected the causes of the repeated individual variations, concentrating rather on the form in which these variations become general; but this is a mistake which he shares with most other people who make any real advance."

True indeed, "Animals [may] change the environment by their activities in the same way, even if not to the same extent, as man does, and these changes [may] in turn react upon and change those who made them. In nature nothing takes place in isolation. Everything affects and is affected by every other thing," so that, "Even the mere contemplation of previous history as a series of class struggles suffices to make clear the utter shallowness of the conception of this history as a feeble variety of the 'struggle for existence.'" For which cause, "In my opinion, the social instinct was one of the most essential levers of the evolution of man from the ape." (And though most Black people may not currently accept the idea that humanity evolved from apes, the fossil record itself is quite undeniable. The fossils of the earliest hominidae – humanlike beings – bear huge similarities to large primates, while the later ones come closer and closer to Homo sapiens people as we know them).

Kropotkin also agreed with Engels, showing how, "Association and mutual aid are the rule with mammals. We find social habits even among the carnivores, and we can only name the cat tribe (lions, tigers, leopards, etc.) as a division the members of which decidedly prefer isolation to society, and are but seldom met with even in small groups. And yet, even among lions 'this is a very common practice to hunt in company.' The two tribes of the civets (*Viverridæ*) and the weasels (*Mustelidæ*) might also be characterized by their isolated life, but it is a fact that during the last century [that is, the nineteenth century] the common weasel was more sociable than it is now". And, "apart from a few exceptions, those birds and mammals which are not gregarious now, were living in societies before man multiplied on the earth and waged a permanent war against them, or destroyed the sources from which they formerly derived food."

Furthermore, Kropotkin also had this to say concerning wildlife, "numberless are those which live in societies, either for mutual defence, or for hunting and storing up food, or for rearing their offspring, or simply for enjoying life in common … though a good deal of warfare goes on between different classes of animals, or different species, or even different tribes of the same species, peace and mutual support are the rule within the tribe or the species; and that those species which best know how to combine and to avoid competition, have the best chances of survival and of a further progressive development." These kinds of environments of recognition, these matrices of communication, will be essential for us Black people in our great pursuit of late modern unification.

He further stated on the subject, "When I explored the Vitim regions in the company of so accomplished a zoologist as my friend Polyakoff […] We both were under the fresh impression of the *Origin of Species*, but we vainly looked for the keen competition between animals of the same species which the reading of Darwin's work had prepared us to expect … We saw plenty of adaptations for struggling, very often in common, against the adverse circumstances of climate, or against various enemies, … but even in the Amur and Usuri regions, where animal life swarms in abundance, facts of real competition and struggle between higher animals of the same species came very seldom under my notice, though I eagerly searched for them."

To finalise the subject he then stated "mutual aid is as much a law of animal life as mutual struggle, but that, as a factor of evolution, it most probably has a far greater importance, inasmuch as it favors the development of such habits and characters as insure the maintenance and further development of the species," for "even in those few spots where animal life teemed in abundance, I failed to find – although I was eagerly looking for it – that bitter struggle for the means of existence, *among animals belonging to the same species*, which was considered by most Darwinists (though not always by Darwin himself) as the dominant characteristic of struggle for life, and the main factor of evolution."

As to the apostle Paul's doctrine of ethnicities, that is completely different from his doctrine concerning wealth. While he did tolerate the ethnic diversity of Imperial Rome he did not seem to tolerate wealth obsession. Though, at that time, far less oppressive than chattel slavery would prove to be in later years, ethnicity was not as important to the apostle Paul's anti-imperialism as the contradictions of wealth, for which cause he said in the same letter to the evangelist Timothy, "Charge them that are rich in this world, that they be not highminded, nor trust in uncertain riches, but in the living God, who giveth us richly all things to enjoy; That they do good, that they be rich in good works, ready to distribute, willing to communicate".

The apostle Paul was essentially saying here that in the Roman Empire those with wealth should share their wealth with a spirit of simplicity and humility. Also feeling the *ethnos* should learn to see each other as brothers and sisters in messianism. Malcolm X, on the other hand, did not believe ethnic brotherhood/sisterhood was really possible in the American Empire. To him this was not due to White racism as such, but due mostly to Black accommodation, trying desperately to please and suck-up to White people, "The *ignorance* we of the black race here in America have, and the *self-hatred* we have, they are fine examples of what the white slavemaster has seen fit to teach to us. Do we show the plain common sense, like every other people on this planet Earth, to *unite* among ourselves? No! We are humbling ourselves, sitting-in, and begging-in, trying to unite with the slavemaster!"

Again, that is not to say that Malcolm X had nothing but animosity towards White people, just that he knew from painful experience what they were capable of, "The North's liberals have been for so long pointing accusing fingers at the South and getting away with it that they have fits when they are exposed as the world's worst hypocrites." Indeed, with the "white Southerner, you can say one thing – he is honest. ... The advantage of this is the Southern black man never has been under any illusions about the opposition he is dealing with." Therefore, Malcolm X's general message was simple: "let us, the black people, *separate* ourselves from this white man slavemaster, who despises us so much! You are out here begging him for some so-called *'integration'!* But what is this slavemaster white, *rapist*, going about saying! He is saying *he* won't integrate because black blood will *mongrelize* his race!" Herein Malcolm X developed an anti-imperialism not of integration, like with Dr. King and the apostle Paul, but was much more of a separatist in seeking what he believed to be a true independence for Black Americans.

That said, to bring a close to this chapter, and to consolidate everything we have learned about the apostle Paul throughout so far, I wish to share with you what I believe to have effectively been, for all intents and purposes, the apostle Paul's Luthenian message of sacrifice; a message he shared with the messianic communities of Corinth for the purpose of inspiration. Hopefully it will give you strength just like it has given me all these years:

"I speak as concerning reproach, as though we had been weak. Howbeit whereinsoever any is bold, (I speak foolishly,) I am bold also. Are they Hebrews? so am I. Are they Israelites? so am I. Are they the seed of Abraham? so am I. Are they ministers of Christ? (I speak as a fool) I am more; in labours more abundant, in stripes above measure, in prisons more frequent, in deaths oft. Of the Jews five times received I forty stripes save one. Thrice was I beaten with rods, once was I stoned, thrice I suffered shipwreck; a night and a day I have been in the deep; In journeyings often, in perils of waters, in perils of robbers, in perils by mine own countrymen, in perils by the heathen, in perils in the city, in perils in the wilderness, in perils in the sea, in perils among false brethren; In weariness and painfulness, in watchings often, in hunger and thirst, in fastings often, in cold and nakedness. Beside those things that are without, that which cometh upon me daily, the care of all the churches. Who is weak, and I am not weak? who is offended, and I burn not?" (2Corinthians 11: 21-29).

As someone who has been a revolutionary for many years now I can say from a revolutionary perspective: this is what real revolution looks like.

Know When to Fold'em

Seeing now the true interrelation between the doctrine of the apostle Paul and the teachings we share within the godbody movement, it may be necessary, at this point, to state that though we godbodies are by personal definition practitioners of Islam, we are more so, in actual fact, a supra-religious culture, not dogmatically holding to the beliefs or ideas of any religion, or to the god of any religion. We choose instead to reserve any force of commitment to our own outlook, philosophy, beliefs, and practices.

For this cause, I feel that in most, if not all, points the godbody movement has been denied its constitutional rights under US — and most Western — laws, to freedom of peaceful assembly. Being ourselves practitioners of peaceful assembly, we do not feel, and have not felt, it necessary to tie ourselves down to any particular religion, but to attend whichever religious grouping we feel most connects with our spiritual and personal views. Here we are also most vehement, for we are unwilling to sacrifice our own right to freedom of assembly within our cipher. Our own religious connection is not based on formal institutions, but on how we practice our lessons culturally.

At the same time, the major thing that separates us godbodies from most of the mainstream of Black movements is not our radical views on race, sex, violence, deviance, or spirituality; but as Malcolm X said, that we "believe in one God, and [we] believe that that God had one religion, has one religion, always will have one religion. And that that God taught all of the prophets the same religion, so there is no argument about who was greater or who was better; Moses, Jesus, Muhammad, or some of the others. All of them were prophets who came from one God. They had one doctrine, and that doctrine was designed to give clarification of humanity" (Malcolm X 1989: 157). Godbodyism thereby embraces a supra-religious outlook and worldview; while also acknowledging that that which has been passing in our time as prophetic is, in actual fact, merely just utterance as given by Allah's grace, or delusion as given by personal vanity.

The current Christian prejudice against the Prophet Ali Muhammad is based primarily on ignorance, having its basis in the Crusades and not on any genuine antithesis in theoretics. Islam is actually, in essence, a messianic sect, and had it have come after the Reformation, it would have been seen as no different from the Adventists or the Jehovah's Witnesses. As to the three fundamental difficulties within Islamic Christology: that of his incarnation, death, and resurrection; these issues, though troublesome, are no reason at all for the tremendous abuse given to the Muslim world to try to choke them out of existence.

As to the central stone of contention, that of Muhammad's prophethood; in the early years of the messianic movement, it is well known and understood that several prophets and apostles arose among the faithful. These pre-Nicaean prophetic movements were unfortunately too dangerous to continue after Nicaea and so were altogether snuffed out by the religious establishment of the time. Those who chose to maintain this authentic legacy were thus forced to retreat into the wilderness of Egypt, the last vestige of spiritual expression, to join one of the monasteries there. Then, finally, at the fall of Rome, messianic spirituality and prophecy were eradicated completely from the culture, as was anything in any ways contrary to the orthodox Catholic views, as gnostic or potentially heretical and therefore illegal.

With prophecy thus outlawed and forbidden in both Western and Eastern Churches, and with the messianic movement by that time having decayed into an endless parade of useless doctrinal councils and nonsensical imperial tyre-kicking; Allah had no choice but to look outside of the Church to find one who he could speak to and work through. It is within this setting that we find the man Ali Muhammad. According to Malcioln, he was "an Arab of the Kuraish tribe of western Arabia. His grandmother was Ethiopian. His wife Amiva was also of the Kuraish tribe. His father Abdallah died shortly after the boy was born in 571 A.C.E. Therefore, Ali Muhammad was brought up by his uncle Abu Talib. This was six years after the reign of Justinian. Some scholars place Muhammad's birthplace at Mecca, others give Medina."

During that time, the vast majority of the lands of North and East Africa, and the Near Eastern Orient, were Christian: whether Orthodox, Nestorian, Arian, or Gnostic. Mecca, at that time, was one of the few islands of idolatry left in the world, having idols all housed in the Kabah. Yet if Mecca was one of the few islands of idolatry left in the world it was not due to ignorance. The Bedouin Arabs, who controlled trade along the Silk Road between Europe and the Far East, all had their own tribal deities and tribal superstitions: including the statues, amulets, talismans, and idols they believed in. These Bedouin Arabs, who came to the Kabah to visit their deities, gave to Mecca great wealth and prestige through trade.

At the age of 24, Muhammad married a rich Catholic widow much older than himself, named Khadija. He apparently loved Khadija deeply and took no other wives during her lifetime. For the next 12 years he became a shrewd and wealthy businessman and trader, travelling across the Syrian trade routes with his uncle Abu Talib and the two sons of Abu Talib. Malcioln further argued that Muhammad was described by those who knew him "as a likeable good-natured individual, and rather charismatic. He was also somewhat of a poet, but was not considered to be a learned man, even during those times. [Still,] he did practice writing religious verses in rhyming couplets with enough repetition to allow his semiliterate congregants to readily memorize his poems" (Malcioln 1996: 195).

It was also during his journeys that Muhammad clearly got acquainted with various Gnostic, Arian, and Kabalic traditions (most of them from non-canonical sources). These would have been what inspired him in his late 30s to retreat into the Arabian desert for the purpose of living an ascetic life. By the time he reached his 40s the life of a businessman had lost its charms and Muhammad could see the decadence of the Meccan elite, not to mention the fallen state of the Kabah, which was a shrine originally built by Abraham himself to honour the monistic principle the Muslims now call *al-tawhid*. At that point, Muhammad went into a cave on Mount Hirah to ask this monistic principle to send to his people a prophet like those of the ancient Falashim. It was then, according to legend, that Muhammad received a vision of the archangel Gabriel (Jibril), who told him that he would be that prophet he was praying for, and began to open up to him the Quran, a scroll known and hidden in the mind of Allah long before the creation of the universe began.

When Muhammad first announced to the people of Mecca that he was a prophet sent by Allah to restore them to the traditions and culture of their Abrahamic ancestors, they first began to taunt him, provoke him, slander him, and persecute him; then they stripped all his followers – of which after four years there were only 15 – of their titles and all their property. This response makes sense as his philosophy and message of political and religious monism was a threat to the political and religious elite of Mecca, and the established system that was in operation at that time, a system that allowed Mecca and its elites to become very wealthy. Indeed, Muhammad's only followers in those earlier years were slaves and women, for whom he was a champion. Still, after eleven years of prophesying he ended up with very little to show for his efforts but exclusion, poverty, and persecution. The very existence of the movement itself would not have been possible without several communal exiles. The final one, called by the Muslims the hegira (meaning migration, but also connoting exodus), was to Yathrib, a city populated by several Falashic, Arabic, and Sabean tribes.

Yet as Malcioln further explained, "It is written that when Muhammad fled his native Mecca in 622 A.C.E. (the hegira), he was much concerned about one reversal in particular. The Hebrew people from whom Muhammad had learned so much were expected to follow his new version of their old religion." It is for this cause that one of the Prophet's earlier messages while in the city of Yathrib, which he renamed Medina, was, "Say: We believe in Allah and (in) that which has been revealed to us, and (in) that which was revealed to Abraham, and Ishmael and Isaac and Jacob and the tribes, and (in) that which was given to Moses and Jesus, and (in) that which was given to the prophets from their Lord, we do not make any distinction between any of them and to Him do we submit" (Quran 2: 136). Indeed, the Prophet believed all prophecy represented a continuum, a line going all the way back to Abraham himself.

What is also interesting in this verse is the Prophet's reference to the historically silenced voice of Ishmael. The deafeningly loud absence of Ishmael's presence in all biblical accounts of the continuum actually speaks volumes. The Prophet's mention of Ishmael as within the prophetic tradition thereby identified his corporeal presence and valorised his embodied historicity. It also corrected the erasure of his sacramentality thereby giving sanctity to his deviant presence. As the Prophet saw himself as the confirmation and seal of prophecy (itself also a kind of transfigured deviance), he did not wish to exclude any he thought to be true prophets, within the Falashim prototype.

To carry this idea a little further the apostle John said in the epistle of Revelations that "the testimony of Jesus is the spirit of prophecy" (Revelation 19: 10); a basic idea that obviously had its roots in an incident that occurred when the Messiah was at his house teaching, "And John answered him, saying, Master, we saw one casting out devils in thy name, and he followeth not us: and we forbad him, because he followeth not us. But Jesus said, Forbid him not: for there is no man which shall do a miracle in my name, that can lightly speak evil of me. For he that is not against us is on our part. For whosoever shall give you a cup of water to drink in my name, because ye belong to Christ, verily I say unto you, he shall not lose his reward" (Mark 9: 38-41). A far cry from the words of former President Bush.

The question therefore becomes, what was the Prophet's view of Jesus? The Prophet said, "We gave Jesus, son of Mary, clear arguments and strengthened him with the Holy Spirit. Is it then that whenever there came to you a messenger with what your souls desired not, you were arrogant? And some you gave the lie to and others you would slay" (Quran 2: 87). Again, as the apostle John also said in his first general epistle, "I have not written unto you because ye know not the truth, but because ye know it, and that no lie is of the truth. Who is a liar but he that denieth that Jesus is the Christ? He is antichrist, that denieth the Father and the Son", to which the Quran answered, "When the angels said: O Mary, surely Allah gives thee good news with a word from Him (of one) whose name is the Messiah, Jesus, son of Mary, worthy of regard in this world and the Hereafter, and of those who are drawn nigh (to Allah)." Again, "The Messiah disdains not to be a servant of Allah, nor do the angels who are near to Him. And whoever disdains His service and is proud. He will gather them all together to Himself" (Quran 3: 45, 46; 4: 172).

Thus, in all this, we see the hand of Allah; for the apostle Paul also explained, "Wherefore I give you to understand, that no man speaking by the Spirit of God calleth Jesus accursed: and that no man can say that Jesus is the Lord, but by the Holy Ghost. Now there are diversities of gift, but the same Spirit. And there are differences of administrations, but the same Lord. And there are diversities of operations, but it is the same God which worketh all in all. But the manifestation of the Spirit is given to every man to profit withal. For to one is given by the Spirit the word of wisdom; to another the word of knowledge by the same Spirit; To another faith by the same Spirit; to another the gifts of healing by the same Spirit; To another the working of miracles; [and] to another prophecy;" all by the same Spirit and based on the same standard. Again, when he said, "no man can say that Jesus is the Lord, but by the Holy Ghost", he was showing that prophecy, one of the gifts of the Holy Ghost, is identifiable through acknowledging the Messiah's dominion.

Conversely, according to various sources, the Falashim of Medina, would challenge the Prophet Muhammad concerning his birth-right, saying, "You were born of Ishmael, but we are descendants of Isaac, Jacob, and Judah, who received the blessings of Abraham." To which the Prophet apparently answered, "Do not blessings (rather) follow the righteous, as they will dwell in Jannah enjoying that which their Lord has bestowed on them? For every child is born in innocence. It is his parents who turn him Judaic, messianic, or atheistic." Further, the Prophet also apparently spoke these words to them, saying, "O People of the Book, indeed Our Messenger has come to you, making clear to you much of that which you concealed of the Book and passing over much. Indeed, there has come to you from Allah, a Light and a clear Book, Whereby Allah guides such as follow His pleasure into the ways of peace, and brings them out of darkness into light by His will, and guides them to the right path" (Quran 5: 15, 16). However, according to

Malcioln, "They scorned 'the confused utterances of the Arab prophet in all that pertained to Judaism.'"

Essentially, "The Prophet allowed the Bene Israel to go unmolested for some time. He kept hoping that they would not have to be forced to join him. Muhammad, may Allah be gracious unto him, wished that the Hebrews would eventually become a segment of the Islamic community, but the years passed and the possibility faded. The Hebrews refused to give accreditation to the new religion. With no Hebrews among the Moslem chiefs of staff, and none in the Islamic hierarchy, with just a few in the lower echelons of the fighting forces, Muhammad said, 'We shall spread Islam with fire, and the sword.' Bekr, his disciple and commander-in-chief of the fighting forces, [also] suggested that Islam discard its Hebraic liturgical penchants" (Malcioln 1996: 197). From this point on the Prophet broke away from the Falashism, changed the qibla (focus and direction of prayer) from Jerusalem to the Kabah, changed the murad al-salat (expected number of prayers) from three to five, changed the yaum al-sawm (time of fasting) from the Yom Kippor to the month of Ramadan, and changed the hajj (focus of travel) from Jerusalem to Mecca. Around about that time he began to unify all the Christian and non-Christian Arabian tribes into one body.

It is then that Allah revealed to the Prophet, "You are the best nation raised up for men: you enjoin good and forbid evil and you believe in Allah. And if the People of the Book had believed, it would have been better for them. Some of them are believers but most of them are transgressors." Therefore, do not be afraid to "fight in the way of Allah against those who fight against you but be not aggressive. Surely Allah loves not the aggressors. And kill them wherever you find them, and drive them out from where they drove you out, [for] persecution is worse than slaughter. And fight not with them at the Sacred Mosque until they fight with you in it; so if they fight you (in it), slay them. Such is the recompense of the disbelievers. But if they desist, then surely Allah is Forgiving, Merciful. And fight them until there is no persecution, and religion is only for Allah. But if they desist, then there should be no hostility except against the oppressors" (Quran 3: 110; 2: 190-193).

True, this message may be a little too deviant for our oversensitive, "turn the other cheek" ears, yet we are still willing to let the police and the military use violence and slaughter for the preservation of this oppressive White supremacist system and for the cause of this White supremacist system. What the Prophet was basically saying was that instead we should be willing to fight and die to defend our own monistic system. Indeed, "Muhammad's strongest attraction in Islam, it is said, is the perfect brotherhood and equality before God of all his believers, regardless of color, origin, or status. Being himself dark-skinned, Ali Muhammad tried to protect the dark-skinned members of the faith." Even so, it has been incumbent upon all Muslims, from the time of the Prophet to this day, to fight against all forms of oppression and division, whatever form they actually come in.

Effectively, through these verses the Prophet was able to create a thearchic army willing to fight as a unified body, possessing a strong sense of destiny, and with the fear of nothing but Allah in their hearts. This martially embodied unit represents today a form of transfigured deviance, having a deep history of fighting against oppression that goes back for centuries. At the same time, let me bring back again the key determinant factor, "fight in the way of Allah against those who fight against you but be not aggressive." Those who fight against you but be not aggressive! The truth is, they are actually a lot further from the aggressive, religion by the edge of a sword, image most Westerners have of them.

Nevertheless, the apostle Paul still said concerning true messianism: "the righteousness which is of faith speaketh on this wise, Say not in thine heart, Who shall ascend into heaven? (that is, to bring Christ down from above:) Or, Who shall descend into the deep? (that is, to bring up Christ again from the dead.) But what saith it? The word is nigh thee, even in thy mouth, and in thy heart: that is, the word of faith, which we preach; That if thou shalt confess with thy mouth the Lord Jesus, and shalt believe in thine heart that God hath raised him from the dead, thou shalt be saved." To which the Prophet Muhammad said,

> *"The People of the Book ask thee to bring down to them a Book from heaven; indeed they demanded of Moses a greater thing than that, for they said: Show us Allah manifestly. So destructive punishment overtook them on account of their wrongdoing. Then they took the calf (for a god), after clear signs had come to them, but We pardoned this. And We gave Moses clear authority. And We raised the mountain above them at their covenant. And We said to them: Enter the door making obeisance. And We said to them: Violate not the Sabbath; and We took from them a firm covenant. Then for their breaking their covenant and their disbelief in the messages of Allah and their killing the prophets wrongfully and their saying, Our hearts are covered; nay, Allah has sealed them owing to their disbelief, so they believe not but a little. And for their disbelief and for their uttering against Mary a grievous calumny. And for their saying: We have killed the Messiah, Jesus, son of Mary, the messenger of Allah, and they killed him not, nor did they cause his death on the cross, but he was made to appear to them as such. And certainly those who differ therein are in doubt about it. They have no knowledge about it, but only follow a conjecture, and they killed him not for certain: Nay, Allah exalted him in His presence. And Allah is ever Mighty, Wise. And there is none of the People of the Book but will believe in this before his death; and on the day of Resurrection he will be a witness against them."*

These Quranic verses have troubled many Jews and Christians historically (obviously for different reasons); however, in the Maulana Muhammad Ali translation of the Quran is provided the beginnings of a reconciliation, at least with Christianity. According to Ali, "The words *ma salabu-hu* do not negative Jesus' being nailed to the cross; they negative his having expired on the cross as a result of being nailed to it." While this may be true and helpful, perhaps even more helpful in explaining the deeper meaning behind these verses is The Coptic Apocalypse of Peter, where it speaks of the apostle Peter's receiving an astral vision of the actual crucifixion of Jesus, yet at the same time, above the cross was a disembodied Jesus absolutely thrilled and laughing at the event.

Here is how the events were recounted by the apostle Peter,

> *"When he had said those things, I saw him apparently being seized by them. And I said, 'What am I seeing, O Lord? Is it you yourself whom they take? And are you holding on to me? Who is this one above the cross, who is glad and laughing? And is it another person whose feet and hands they are hammering?'*
>
> *The Savior said to me, 'He whom you see above the cross, glad and laughing, is the living Jesus. But he into whose hands and feet they are driving the nails is his physical part, which is the substitute. They are putting to shame that which is in his likeness. But look at him and me.'*
>
> *But I, when I had looked, said, 'Lord, no one is looking at you. Let us flee this place.' But he said to me, 'I have told you, "Leave the blind alone!" And notice how they do not know what they are saying. For the son of their glory, instead of my servant, they have put to shame.'" (Ehrman 2005: 80).*

What we can clearly see therefore is that the Prophet being most likely trained and guided in a gnostic tradition, as is also clear in several other gnostic references throughout the Quran that he could never have gotten without having been trained directly from the gnostic tradition (the books and writings themselves having been for the most part lost or buried). Moreover, it is only through and due to the discovery of the Nag Hammadi Library that we can see this gnostic influence in the Prophet's own development. It is for these reasons that I seriously doubt that this man, who clearly admired martyrdom and giving your life for Allah, could have had in mind anything less than the common Christian interpretation with his verses. And if he believed that Allah still exalted the Messiah after his death then he thereby also believed in the Messiah's resurrection.

Finally, the Prophet had this to say concerning Mary his mother, "She said: How can I have a son and no mortal has yet touched me, nor have I been unchaste? He said: So (it will be). Thy Lord says: It is easy to Me; and that We may make him a sign to men and a mercy from Us. And it is a matter decreed" (Quran 19: 20, 21). As to the question of the Messiah's incarnation the Prophet had this to say, "The likeness of Jesus with Allah is truly as the likeness of Adam. He created him from dust, then said to him, Be, and he was" (Quran 3: 59). Even so, concerning his ministry he also said, "I have come to you with a sign from your Lord, that I determine for you out of dust the form of a bird, then I breathe into it and it becomes a bird with Allah's permission, and I heal the blind and the leprous, and bring the dead to life with Allah's permission; and I inform you of what you should eat and what you should store in your houses. Surely there is a sign in this for you, if you are believers" (Quran 3: 49).

What we can gather from this brief history is that after the first 11 years of Muhammad's prophethood, he and his followers became nothing more than exiles and political refugees; however, after the second 11 years of Muhammad's prophethood he had effectively become the de facto ruler of Arabia, keeper and cleanser of the Kabah, and the founder of a movement that in time would stretch from India and Albania in the East, all the way to Senegal and Iberia in the West, and everywhere in between. "After the Prophet's death, Abu Bekr, also known as Bakr, became the first Caliph (632-634). His short reign dealt with homogenizing tribes who had never been accustomed to a central authority controlling them from a power base far away. … Bekr died in 634 A.C.E. Omar succeeded him and reigned until he was stopped in 644. He wrested Egypt and Syria from the Byzantine, Persia, and Iraq. He [essentially] died one year before his armies reached the borders of India and China."

In all, we can here see, not only the genuine prophethood of Muhammad, but also our right to claim Muhammad as one of our own prophets. In fact, the only reason why Muhammad was rejected from the body of Catholic prophets and saints was due to the historical foundations of Catholicism itself. Here the doctrine of Irenaeus of Lyon was adopted into the body of saintly doctrines. Still, Irenaeus incorporated the ideas of a centralised hierarchy, ideological supremacy, Christian patriotism, and intellectual authoritarianism into Catholic Christianity; while Muhammad incorporated the ideas of an informal structure, ideological assimilation, ultra-monotheism, and intellectual development into his vision for Orthodox Islam.

PART II
ESCHATOLOGY

ESCHATOLOGY

The epistle of Revelation is a very prophetic book. Written by the apostle John while on Patmos Island, it contains what most people believe to be the road map for the last days of the universe, or at least of humanity's existence in the universe. In order to understand some of the inherent symbologies behind these early traditions of messianism, and the mysticism of what physicists call phase-space, we will be venturing into a school of thought quite alien to most Westernised thinkers. Perhaps the best place to begin in this new school of thought is with the basic premise of all faith traditions: "It is by our faith that we know what we believe in will happen, being completely assured of a reality that is invisible" (Hebrews 11:1 my rewording).

Again, in ancient Egypt they had no problem with the idea of an invisible realm that only the third eye could tap into. A realm that we currently call the astral plane. Within this plane dwell as much of the deity's many manifold manifestations as within the physical, if not more. The obvious question from here then would be: if an invisible and basically astral realm exists where is the proof of its existence? Naturally, we godbodies understand that the symbolisms of the epistle of Revelation are just that: symbols. Yet we also see them as representing an interaction between astral, causal, and physical planes. With this understanding in mind we acknowledge that the epistle of Revelation has not yet been fulfilled, however, we also attempt to show and prove that the terrible plagues spoken of within it need never happen. To large sections within the godbody movement of the street life, judgment can be averted through respecting the life and teachings of Muhammad, Jesus, and the Prophets.

That said, Part II of the current book will not be dealing with everything written in the epistle of Revelation: that would take a book of far greater size to deal with. Part II intends to simply limit its range to the judgments spoken of at the opening of the seals of the great book of Allah. It shall also hopefully show the relation and correlation between the prophecies in the epistle of the Revelation and those in the book of the Prophets. This will thereby prove, not only a continuity, but even a remedy for the current complacency within the world of today towards ethical righteousness. Allah can change his mind, he can change his word, he can even change his laws; but Allah can never change his nature. He is the same yesterday, today, and forever. It is even written in Hebrews concerning him, "Thou, Lord, in the beginning hast laid the foundation of the earth; and the heavens are the works of thine hands: They shall perish; but thou remainest; and they shall wax old as doth a garment; And as a vesture shalt thou fold them up, and they shall be changed: but thou art the same, and thy years shall not fail."

Three things must be mentioned, however, from the outset of this expedition, each articulated by biblical Theologian Marcus Maxwell in his commentary on Revelation. First of all, "the book of Revelation would have been perfectly well understood by the first century readers, and therefore [was] not a detailed blueprint of the plan of God for the Second Coming. It primarily addresses the churches of the Roman province of Asia Minor," so it should not to be interpreted to mean that everything must or will happen exactly as was written by the apostle John, nor that their fulfilment was merely a last days thing and not a very current, in the moment thing.

Second, "John recounts the same events several times, expanding the detail and providing fresh viewpoints. For instance, there are three series of seven judgments: the seals (beginning in chapter 6), the trumpets (from chapter 8), and the bowls (chapter 16). At first sight these are successive events but on closer examination turn out to be different perspectives on the same thing, since all end at the last judgment." The epistle is basically telling the same story seven times and in seven different cycles (if one counts as cycles the seven opening messages and the seven later thunders); thus by studying any one of these cycles we should, generally speaking, be able to understand the whole Revelation.

The third thing we must understand about the epistle of Revelation before we proceed is that based on the eschatology of it. Maxwell said on this matter, "In recent years some scholars have begun to argue that the images of cataclysmic change in apocalyptic language are not really about 'the end of the world.' Instead, they should be seen as predicting, or even calling for, great changes in the social order." "It seems to me that to a great extent, both views can be held together."

Prior to the first advent of the Messiah the prophets taught the people about ethical living, crying out to the people of Israel, Judea, and of the whole of the Middle East, telling them to administer justice and practice ethics. The prophet Isaiah, who was called by many the Prince of the Prophets, was, in his own day, the leader of a Prophetic School in Judea. It was here that he prepared others to preach a message of justice and the fear of the Lord. The prophet Isaiah cried out in those days to these, at that time, corrupted Judean people, saying, "None calleth for justice, nor any pleadeth for truth: they trust in vanity, and speak lies; they conceive mischief, and bring forth iniquity." At the same time, other prophets and contemporaries of the prophet Isaiah, raised their own rallying cry against corruption, saying: If "He is a merchant, the balances of deceit are in his hand: he loveth to oppress. And Ephraim said, Yet I am become rich, I have found me out substance: in all my labours they shall find none iniquity in me that were sin". "And I said, Hear, I pray you, O heads of Jacob, and ye princes of the house of Israel; Is it not for you to know judgment? Who hate the good, and love the evil".

We can therefore understand from here and elsewhere that a Black astralism can reveal to the world the genuine righteousness of Allah; that Allah pleads the cause of the poor and vulnerable people of society. So we can see that, even from ancient times, they had a better understanding of the reality and cause for fear over the imminent "Day of the Lord" spoken of by all the ancient prophets with fear and trembling. For the wrath of Allah is manifested against humanity for all their corrupted ways and all their corrupted views and all their corrupted lies. Wherefore the imagery used in the epistle of Revelation was simply a graphic and symbolic depiction of social and astral realities: not the fantastic use of an illusionary narrative.

Obviously, other prophetic voices also spoke of this situation in a little bit more detail. The prophet Joel said during the time of the Neo-Persian Empire, "Blow ye the trumpet in Zion, and sound an alarm in my holy mountain: let all the inhabitants of the land tremble: for the day of the Lord cometh, for it is nigh at hand; A day of darkness and of gloominess, a day of clouds and of thick darkness, as the morning spread upon the mountains: a great people and a strong; there hath not been ever the like, neither shall be any more after it, even to the years of many generations." This army which was here gathered across the mountains had clearly gathered for the purpose of war. But what are they warring for and who are they warring against? From the Revelation we can get an idea: they were warring to, simply put, conquer; and they were warring against the people of Israel.

Yet the prophets said concerning their battle:

> *"And the remnant of Jacob shall be among the Gentiles in the midst of many peoples as a lion among the beasts of the forest, as a young lion among the flocks of sheep: who, if he go through, both treadeth down, and teareth in pieces, and none can deliver. Thine hand shall be lifted up upon thine adversaries, and all thine enemies shall be cut off."*

> And *"I will make Jerusalem a cup of trembling unto all the people round about, when they shall be in the siege both against Judah and against Jerusalem. And in that day will I make Jerusalem a burdensome stone for all people: all that burden themselves with it shall be cut in pieces, though all the people of the earth be gathered together against it. ... And the governors of Judah shall say in their heart, The inhabitants of Jerusalem shall be my strength in the Lord of hosts their God. In that day will I make the governors of Judah like an hearth of fire among the wood, and like a torch of fire in a sheaf; and they shall devour all the people round about, on the right hand and on the left: and Jerusalem shall be inhabited again in her own place, even in Jerusalem. The Lord also shall save the tents of Judah first, that the glory of the house of David and the glory of the inhabitants of Jerusalem do not magnify themselves against Judah."*

All this being a picture painted that gives the impression of a coming battle or warfare, one that, though appearing to be a political upheaval or conflict, may in actual fact be only a symbolic or figurative conflict. The reality of this view, though not yet very convincing, is given another thrashing by the prophet Ezekiel when he said quite plainly in his own astral journey: "And the word of the Lord came unto me, saying, Son of man, set thy face against Gog, the land of Magog, the chief prince of Meshech and Tubal, and prophesy against him, And say, Thus saith the Lord God; … After many days thou shalt be visited: in latter years thou shalt come into the land that is brought back from the sword, and is gathered out of many people, against the mountains of Israel, which have been always waste: but it is brought forth out of the nations, and they shall dwell safely all of them. Thou shalt ascend and come like a storm, thou shalt be like a cloud to cover the land, thou, and all thy bands, and many people with thee." All these words employed, essentially used the war imagery also employed by the prophet Joel, which themselves were employed so as to be an inspiration to his people.

From here we are also able to see the harsh realities of Allah bringing his thearchy to the earth, not the delusional fantasy of instant beauty and peace. Indeed, the Messiah himself said, "Think not that I am come to send peace on earth: I came not to send peace, but a sword." And again, "a mighty angel took up a stone like a great millstone, and cast it into the sea, saying, Thus with *violence* shall that great city Babylon be thrown down" (17: 21; emphasis mine). Whereby, just like with the "Day of the Lord" in most Judean minds, so with the "Second Coming" of the Messiah in most Gentile minds; heavily romanticised, whitewashed, and infantilised by its "prophets." For someone to come along and destroy every worldly power and authority is for someone to come along and viscerally destroy everything that the world stands for, believes in, and has held to be most sacred.

The ultimate triumph of the Black thearchist movement thus will not come as a result of godbodies saying the right words or being absolutely perfect in every way. The fact of the matter is, a person has a better chance of converting real people by being their real imperfect selves, not by trying to put on an over moral show. This lesson even goes doubly for those who eschew morality and just desire to engage in the sexual pleasures of having seduced the unseducible: the most perfect seductions are imperfect and invalidated. That is because it is in those moments that appear as though a person is unmoved and unwilling to yield that their memory system kicks in, through which the depths of Allah's essence can be revealed to them. Hence we here need to, of necessity, not necessarily relearn all the early messianic symbols, at least not yet anyway, but to explore the judgments expressed in the revealed drama concerning the execution of Allah's wrath, and our averting it.

All this is where the theological meets the thearchical. For in the fifth chapter of Revelation we find the unravelling of a heavenly crescendo of praise, in which the symbolic Lamb figure was found worthy of that which was found at the right hand of the heavenly throne, and in its Greek variation was given the name the *Biblion*. It was the opening (or unsealing) of this *Biblion* that brought about the manifestation or realisation of all the apocalyptic cataclysms that followed.

More Than Conquerors

At the opening of the first seal (6: 1, 2) a white horse and its horseman appeared before the apostle John and the four living creatures that stood before the twenty-four seats, each one seated with one of twenty-four elders (elders that we in the godbody call: twenty-four Scientists). This horseman, at the time, was holding a bow, and was then given a crown and told that he was to go out, conquer, and overcome the world. We find later on that this very one sent out to conquer and overcome, may in fact have been an allusion to the very Messiah who – in 19: 11-16 – leads the armies of heaven, also riding upon white horses. In order to fully explain this paradox Maxwell made clear concerning the epistle of Revelation that "there are repetitions, visions within visions, and themes that seem to disappear only to reemerge later." The truth is, the events written in the epistle of Revelation, like all events that transpire in the astral plane, did not actualise in any linear fashion from one event to the next. Or, as Koester said, "visionary time has no straightforward connection to chronological time".

Such things are also true within our current dream worlds. Time in a dream may not necessarily move forward, and events can occur or reverse as the dream progresses; this is especially the case with the epistle of Revelation. Still, I see the rider of the white horse as the messianic hope actualised as opposed to Maxwell's theory of him being an imperial conqueror. The main reason for this is that the heathen do not rage until a light has first come to them, and "the Lord God does nothing before first revealing his mysteries to his servants the prophets" (my rewording).

To get to the bottom of all this we might need to venture into one of the influences the apostle John probably considered when envisioning, or at least when writing, his epistle of Revelation, the apocalypse of 2Esdras:

> *"And it came to pass after seven days, I dreamed a dream by night: And, lo, there arose a wind from the sea, that it moved all the waves thereof. And I beheld, and, lo, that man waxed strong with the thousands of heaven: and when he turned his countenance to look, all the things trembled that were seen under him. And whensoever the voice went out of his mouth, all they burned that heard his voice, like as the earth faileth when it feeleth the fire. And after this I beheld, and, lo, there was gathered together a multitude of men, out of number, from the four winds of the heaven, to subdue the man that came out of the sea. ... And, lo, as he saw the violence of the multitude that came, he neither lifted up his hand, nor held sword, nor any instrument of war: But only I saw that he sent out of his mouth as it had been a blast of fire, and out of his lips a flaming breath, and out of his tongue he cast out sparks and tempests. And they were all mixed together; the blast of fire, the flaming breath, and the great tempest; and fell with violence upon the multitude which was prepared to fight, and burned them up every one, so that upon a sudden of an innumerable multitude nothing was to be perceived, but only dust and smell of smoke: when I saw this I was afraid" (2Esdras 13: 1-11).*

It is undeniable the influence this apocalyptic work had on the apostle John, for as he would go on to write in his own apocalyptic work: "And I will give power unto my two witnesses, and they shall prophesy a thousand two hundred and threescore days, clothed in sackcloth. These are the two olive trees and the two candlesticks standing before the God of the earth. And if any man will hurt them, fire proceedeth out of their mouth, and devoureth their enemies: and if any man will hurt them, he must in this manner be killed" (11: 3-5). And just in case you are unable to see here the relation between these two Scriptures and the rider on the white horse, the Messiah himself said concerning his message that "this gospel of the kingdom shall be preached in all the world for a witness unto all nations; and then shall the end come." Before the end can come Allah must first send out his witnesses to speak the message of thearchism; and when this begins to happens then know that judgment will soon follow.

To complete this very basic explication I will now turn to the prophet Zechariah, when he said, "then answered I, and said unto him, What are these two olive trees upon the right side of the candlestick and upon the left side thereof? And I said again, and said unto him, What be these two olive branches which through the two golden pipes empty the golden oil out of themselves? And he answered me and said, Knowest thou not what these be? And I said, No, my lord. Then said he, These are the two anointed ones, that stand by the Lord of the whole earth." All leading us to the interpretation that the two witnesses are in fact two messiahs who will be opposed by the people of this world when they share their witness of the thearchy. However, it may actually prove to be a little more complicated than that. The Hebrew word used by the prophet Zechariah in the above Scripture was not *mashiakh* (as in Messiah), but the word *yitshar*, which actually meant oil producers; yet I will here be translating it as little messiahs.

Thus, the rider of the white horse is not the Messiah as such, but is instead symbolic of the two witnesses, even as was said later on in the Revelation, "And the armies which were in heaven followed him upon white horses, clothed in fine linen, white and clean" (19: 14). Moreover, it also continued concerning the two witnesses, "these have power to shut heaven, that it rain not in the days of their prophecy: and have power over waters to turn them to blood, and to smite the earth with *all plagues*, as often as they will. And when they shall have finished their testimony, the beast that ascendeth out of the bottomless pit shall make war against them, and shall overcome them, and kill them" (11: 6, 7; emphasis mine).

Now for the record, the word used in this Scripture for witnesses was *martys*, which itself is rooted in the word *martyr*. Basically, the two witnesses are, or were supposed to be, two martyrs. What, however, is truly different about them is that they have the power to "smite the earth with all plagues as often as they will." As the Revelation was written to be predictive specifically of the *eschaton* (last things), the plagues called forth by the two witnesses must be understood to be the seven last plagues of the wrath of Allah (16: 1-21) – seven itself obviously being a symbolic number as the two witnesses may have a virtually limitless number of plagues they can call forth and bring forth upon the world. Therefore Revelation 16 provides a template of the kind of plagues the two witnesses may call forth – sores; turning seas into blood; turning rivers and fountains of water into blood; power over the sun; turning the Beast's kingdom to darkness; drying up the Euphrates to prepare the world for Armageddon; and earthquakes, thunderings, and great hail.

What is of extra interest is that there is also a relation between the seven last plagues and the seven trumpets. The first trumpet and the first plague affect the earth. The second trumpet and second plague affect the seas. The third trumpet and third plague affect the rivers and fountains of water. The fourth trumpet and fourth plague affect the sun. The fifth trumpet and fifth plague cause darkness to fill the land. The sixth trumpet and sixth plague affect the Euphrates. The seventh trumpet and seventh plague cause earthquakes, thunderings, voices, and great hail. In this instance, rather than look at all these plagues individually I shall simply say that the first five trumpets and first five plagues could be interpreted to coincide with, and result from, the first seal – and the coming of the two witnesses.

Conversely, it could now further be asked why these two witnesses or two martyrs are here considered to be two little messiahs and not in fact the Messiah and his bride? The answer is that the two witnesses are destined to die "where also our Lord was crucified" (11: 8). Again, "Wherefore they are no more twain, but one flesh. What therefore God hath joined together, let not man put asunder." What we see from these two Scriptures is that the two witnesses are very likely to not be symbolic of the true Messiah that was crucified, but of a little messiah: or in this case a Great Witness. Besides, it makes more sense if it is a little messiah and not the Divine Parousia (divine advent) itself, as that may turn out relatively different.

The witness that comes thereby carries within himself or herself, the last plagues of Allah, because in him or her is filled up the wrath of Allah. Moreover, when he or she has finished their testament he or she shall then be martyred (killed) for having martyred (testified) their message. So then, what will their message be? To be sure, it will not be "For God so loved the world," which carries neither wrath, nor plague, nor judgment. It will thereby be a message, not of salvation, but of redemptive vengeance. Again, why should we believe in and fight for redemptive vengeance? This is a good question: the answer is most likely that the blood of the prophets and of the righteous people of the earth who died unjustly, and all the suffering endured by the victims of any iniquity or inequity, has been crying out to Allah from the time of the Renaissance to this day. Basically, the days of vengeance come when the witness brings down the wrath of Allah on humanity, thus bringing down the great *eschaton*. Finally, this dramatic tale, or group of tales, will all lead inexorably to the great deliverance of the righteous when the Messiah comes again to destroy the mythical Beast character at the very end of the world.

Again, this Beast character – a borrowed symbol from the scroll of Daniel – who was himself personified in the Islamic traditions as the Great *Dajjal*; within the context of the vision and astral journey of the epistle of Revelation represented an opponent who was to fight against the Great Witness and ultimately bring about his or her actual death. Within certain Islamic sources it is even claimed that the Prophet said concerning the witness (who he considered to be a male), '"At that time a man who is the best of people – or from the best of people – will come and say to him, "I bear witness that you are indeed the Dajjaal, whom the Messenger of Allah ... spoke to us about." The Dajjaal will say, "Suppose I kill this (man) and then bring him back to life. Will you then doubt about the matter." The people present will say, "No." He will kill him and then revive him, and upon being revived the (righteous) man will say, "By Allah, I have never understood you (and your situation) more clearly than I do now." The Dajjaal will then want to kill him, but he will not be given power over him.' (*Muslim*) Abu Ishaaq said, 'It is said that that man is Khidr.'"

Effectively, the Witness, based on various Near Eastern traditions, particularly Islamic ones, was to be a man of al-Khidr (in Arabic, the Black one: or literally, the green one), an acknowledged guide to the prophet Moses during his time in Arabia, that was in time believed to be one that would bear witness against the Great *Dajjal* (the Imposter). Al-Khidr itself, in Arabic and Islamic sources, was considered to be a tribal grouping in Arabia. The Arabic word for tribe (*banu*, literally: the sons of) has for the most part been applied to al-Khidr in the Near East for centuries.

Herein it was also said concerning them, "The Khudr (of Banu) Muharib boasted of their black skin. The blacks are [indeed] called Khudr ... by the Arabs." Moreover, according to Riley, author of the *Historical and Cultural Dictionary of Saudi Arabia*, "The higher incidence of Negroid phenotypic features appear in Tihama [Yemen], while the Bedouin, especially in the Nejd tends to the more classic 'Mediterranean' type, though there is Negroid admixture in some areas. In a large band from Khaibur and the Shammar area to the Wadi Dawasir there are extensive Bedouin-Negro mixes, the Banu Khudair" (Riley 1972; quoted in M'bantu & Muller 2013: 48).

These truths are extremely important as it was originally understood that the early Arabs were, in fact, predominantly Black. To prove this idea M'bantu and Muller said, "In the 9th century there was an Arabic writer named Uthman al-Jahiz who had an African grandfather. Al-Jahiz was one of the most educated men in the world of his day and was attached to the royal court of the Abbasid dynasty in Iraq. ... Al-Jahiz also openly [talked] about how many Arab tribes have Black sections called *khudr*." He even declared of the Prophet's own grandfather, "The ten lordly sons of Abd al-Muttalib were very black in colour and large of body", and that the Abu Talib family, from whence the Prophet's cousin and son-in-law Ali came, "was more or less black-coloured."

Even so, it is acknowledged within Islam that the destiny of this Witness from the Banu al-Khidr is to bring and restore righteousness to the earth during the time of the great *eschaton*. He is, therefore, supposed to be the captain of the Messianic army to restore righteousness, and the witness of the Khidari tribe to remove wickedness. Moreover, it is also understood within Islam that he will be the main leader and rival standing against the Great *Dajjal*. At the same time, due to the corruption existing in the world during the days of *al-Dajjal*, it has also been understood that al-Khidr will face heavy opposition. However, this would not be before the *Dajjal* brings humanity to near ruin with his one-eyed mission to get revenge on humanity for his losses. Indeed, if we are perceptive we can see that actually he has in fact already done this. The world is currently, even right now, under the power of a villainous *Dajjal* (Imposter) and it will have to be one of al-Khidr that delivers us from the corruption he has brought to the world.

Still, when I use the word us in this statement, it is not to be taken as all-inclusive; the prophet Ezekiel wrote in his prophecies to the nations:

> *"The word of the Lord came again unto me, saying, Son of man, prophesy and say, Thus saith the Lord God; Howl ye, Woe worth the day! For the day is near, even the day of the Lord is near, a cloudy day; it shall be the time of the heathen. And the sword shall come upon Egypt, and great pain shall be in Ethiopia, when the slain shall fall in Egypt, and they shall take away her multitude, and her foundations shall be broken down. Ethiopia, and Libya, and Lydia, and all the mingled people, and Chub, and the men of the land that is in league, shall fall with them by the sword. Thus saith the Lord; They also that uphold Egypt shall fall; and the pride of her power shall come down: from the tower of Syene shall they fall in it by the sword, saith the Lord God. And they shall be desolate in the midst of the countries that are desolate, and her cities shall be in the midst of the cities that are wasted. And they shall know that I am the Lord, when I have set a fire in Egypt, and when all her helpers shall be destroyed. In that day shall messengers go forth from me in ships to make the careless Ethiopians afraid, and great pain shall come upon them, as in the day of Egypt for, lo, it cometh."*

To which the prophet Isaiah also continued, saying:

> *"In that day shall five cities in the land of Egypt speak the language of Canaan, and swear to the Lord of hosts; one shall be called, The city of destruction. In that day shall there be an altar to the Lord in the midst of the land of Egypt, and a pillar at the border thereof to the Lord. And it shall be for a sign and for a witness unto the Lord of host in the land of Egypt: for they shall cry unto the Lord because of the oppressors, and he shall send them a saviour, and a great one, and he shall deliver them. And the Lord shall be known to Egypt, and the Egyptians shall know the Lord in that day, and shall vow a vow unto the Lord, and perform it. And the Lord shall smite Egypt: he shall smite and heal it: and they shall return even to the Lord, and he shall be intreated of them, and shall heal them. In that day shall there be a highway out of Egypt to Assyria, and the Assyrian shall come into Egypt, and the Egyptian into Assyria, and the Egyptians shall serve with the Assyrians. In that day shall Israel be the third with Egypt and with Assyria, even a blessing in the midst of the land: Whom the Lord of host shall bless, saying, Blessed be Egypt my people, and Assyria the work of my hands, and Israel mine inheritance" (Ezekiel 30:1-9; Isaiah 19: 1-25).*

At this point some Black people may argue that with the original Egyptians being Black, especially considering these Scriptures just quoted, why should we concern ourselves with the Hebrew God, Allah, and with his prophecies at all. The reason is that we are currently in, or are coming out of, the time of the heathen (or Gentiles) that the prophet Ezekiel spoke of. Even as Allah promised ships to take the Egyptians and Ethiopians captive, even so in our own history ships came to take us captive. Furthermore, as it may actually be even more important for us to recognise, the true and original Hebrew people were themselves most likely also Black people. In this, when al-Khidr comes, being fated to bring about the Divine Parousia, *he* will ultimately put an end to the time of the Gentile (this is also likely to be the reason why in Revelation the narrative of the two witnesses is presented right after an allusive reference to the time of the Gentiles).

This ending of the time of the Gentiles was perhaps given its most accurate description in the writing of the prophet Zephaniah when he wrote, "Therefore wait ye upon me, saith the Lord, until the day that I rise up to the prey: for my determination is to gather the nations, that I may assemble the kingdoms, to pour upon them mine indignation, even all my fierce anger: for all the earth shall be devoured with the fire of my jealousy. For then will I turn to the people a pure language, that they may all call upon the name of the Lord, to serve him with one consent. From beyond the rivers of Ethiopia my suppliants, even the daughter of my dispersed, shall bring mine offering. In that day shalt thou not be ashamed for all thy doings, wherein thou hast transgressed against me" (Zephaniah 3: 8-11).

Herein, those same Egyptians and Ethiopians that the prophet Ezekiel doomed into bondage during the time of the Gentiles, were in fact therefore of the Hebrew people dispersed into those lands, and were always destined towards that path. At the same time, those who they were fated to be in bondage to were always supposed to be of the Grecian people, and were also always destined towards their path. But as Allah would go on to say by his prophets Joel and Zechariah, "The children also of Judah and the children of Jerusalem have ye sold unto the Grecians, that ye might remove them far from their border." Therefore, "Turn you to the strong hold, ye prisoners of hope: even to day do I declare that I will render double unto thee; When I have bent Judah for me, filled the bow with Ephraim, and raised up thy sons, O Zion, against thy sons, O Greece, and made thee as the sword of a mighty man" (Joel 3: 6; Zechariah 9: 12, 13).

Consequently, it was further prophesied:

"Therefore behold, the days come, saith the Lord, that they shall no more say, The Lord liveth, which brought up the children of Israel out of the land of Egypt; But, The Lord liveth, which brought up and which led the seed of the house of Israel out of the north country, and from all countries whither I had driven them; and they shall dwell in their own land." For, "As I live, saith the Lord God, surely with a mighty hand, and with a stretched out arm, and with fury poured out, will I rule over you: And I will bring you out from the people, and will gather you out of the countries wherein ye are scattered, with a mighty hand, and with a stretched out arm, and with fury poured out. And I will bring you into the wilderness of the people, and there will I plead with you face to face. Like as I pleaded with your fathers in the wilderness of the land of Egypt, so will I plead with you, saith the Lord God" (Jeremiah 23: 7, 8; Ezekiel 20: 33-36).

Although it will all take place in a manner of, as was noted by the apostle Paul, "every man in his own order: Christ the firstfruits; afterward they that are Christ's at his coming. Then cometh the end, when he shall have delivered up the kingdom to God, even the Father; when he shall have put down all rule and all authority and power. For he must reign, till he hath put all enemies under his feet." From all these images we get a clear idea of government, not by kingdom but by dictatorship, even as the classical Roman dictatorships were instituted by a general until order had been restored to the Roman provinces (of which all the apostles, including Paul and John, were observers); so it was acknowledged by their time that when the Messiah came he would have to seize and maintain power until every principality and power was crushed and order restored to the world. The idea of this seizing of power by Allah and his Messiah – with the Witness himself or herself probably being a chief captain – though foretold long before the first century, was never as graphically depicted except in the apostle John's Revelation.

Rosa Luxemburg also agreed that in a revolution the revolutionists "should and must at once undertake socialist measures in the most energetic, unyielding and unhesitant fashion, in other words, exercise a dictatorship, but a dictatorship of the *class*, not of a party or of a clique – dictatorship of the class, that means in the broadest public form on the basis of the most active, unlimited participation of the mass of the people". Conversely, whereas a modern economy – in the form of socialism or capitalism – sees dictatorship in the form of a class, a thearchic economy sees dictatorship in the form of the Messiah and his dominion of heaven: a dominion that is within us. Far from the dictatorship being that of a class over the rest of society, whether that class be a majority or a minority, the thearchy allows for self-government, trusting each to be ruled by the principles of justice and ethics as taught by the Messiah.

What makes the horseman of this white horse distinct from the other horsemen, however, is that he is given a crown and goes out to *nikao*, meaning to overcome, which happens to be the exact thing the Messiah encouraged the seven messianic communities to do in the opening cycle. Though there are many who consider this rider to be symbolic of 'Pestilence', there are no obvious clues to this in the actual description given of him *per se*. However, that is not to say there is absolutely no precedent for it. There is the possibility, due to his or her being destined to unleash plague and judgment upon the world, that this al-Khidr could very well be the embodiment and personification of Pestilence. Or some such theory could definitely be developed. While I cannot entirely deny these types of theories, it must still be appreciated that from the context of Revelation itself there is actually more proof of him or her being messianic than pestilent.

There are, however, some who would claim that the bow carried by this rider portends to something sinister. Yet most of these individuals somehow seem to have forgotten what David and Job said concerning Allah, "Yea, he sent out his arrows, and scattered them; and he shot out lightnings, and discomfited them." "For the arrows of the Almighty are within me, the poison whereof drinketh up my spirit: the terrors of God do set themselves in array against me." If even Allah has arrows and bow then it is quite fitting for his servants to also have such, even if only symbolically. In all this, what we can see here is that the first seal of the *Biblion* represented to the messianic communities of Asia Minor, both the first five trumpets and first five plagues of the later chapters. The next five seals, however, were clearly supposed to represent for them the sixth trumpet and sixth plague. Finally, the seventh seal, trumpet, and plague were all most likely supposed to represent the same end: what we Muslims call the *Yaum al-Din* or Day of Judgment.

The Unstoppable Rise of an Insatiable Beast

From here we can see not so much an actual warring, but more so a brewing and preparing; the rising of a new form of government to take the place of all former ones. We also find a deeper meaning to Ezekiel's astral drama: "Therefore, son of man, prophecy and say unto Gog, Thus saith the Lord God; In that day when my people of Israel dwelleth safely, shalt thou not know it? And thou shalt come from thy place out of the north parts, thou, and many people with thee, all of them riding upon horses, a great company, and a mighty army: And thou shalt come up against my people of Israel, as a cloud to cover the land; it shall be in the latter days, and I will bring thee against my land, that the heathen may know me, when I shall be sanctified in thee, O Gog, before their eyes. Thus saith the Lord God; Art thou he of whom I have spoken in old time by my servants the prophets of Israel, which prophesied in those days many years that I would bring thee against them?"

Even so, as the Israel of the prophet Ezekiel's vision met with huge opposition upon their returning back from conflict, so the tide of conquest began to turn as the Lamb opened the second seal (6: 3, 4). At this point a fiery red horse and its horseman came to stand before the apostle John and the four living creatures. This horseman was at this time given the express authority and power to take peace from the earth and to start wars. He was also given a large sword with which to drive men to slay one another. The usual name given to this angel by those lay Bible traditionalists is therefore 'War,' as it has been believed that this angel represents the violent inclination within the souls of humanity.

But war has existed from time immemorial, and though modernity has brought with it more wars than at any other period of human history, this manifestation is more a result of ideological programming than of any violent instinct within people's souls. Even during the time of the classical empires and their religious vanities there were less wars than have happened since the arrival of modernity; and all the great killings that have occurred as a result of even the smaller of modern battles exceeds those of most of the larger wars of pre-modernity. In considering the reality of this situation we must come to understand that modernity has mainly brought with it the intensification of wars, which have effectively been much deeper than at previous historical epochs.

In our time, neo-colonialism and imperialist globalisation have taken on the semblance of respectability by modern definitions. As Western elites pursue ever wider capitalistic visions of expansion and development, countries such as the US and the countries within the EU and UK are currently in the process of repackaging the brand of imperialism, at least in the enterprise sense. However, Vladimir Lenin, in his own day, sought to unmask the brutality and chicanery of these kinds of endeavours, saying, "The building of railways seems to be a simple, natural, democratic, cultural and civilising enterprise … But as a matter of fact the capitalist threads, which in thousands of different intercrossings bind these enterprises with private property in the means of production in general, have converted this work of construction into an instrument for oppressing a thousand million people (in the colonies and semi-colonies), that is, more than half the population of the globe" (Lenin 2010: 5). Thus the enterprise and commercial empires of the great Western powers with their unrepentant mission to reconquer and carve up the world, have been emboldened to continue these enterprises ever since the rise of the first private companies of King James I's Great Britain in the early 1600s.

Still, as Lenin further pointed out, it is incalculably necessary to "understand the fundamental economic question, viz., the question of the economic essence of imperialism, for unless this is studied, it will be impossible to understand and appraise modern war and modern politics." True, modern imperialism may have come about as a result of European missionaries' desire to spread Victorian values and standards in the colonies, but it also created a desire within many of them to make settlements in those very colonies in the first place. Accordingly, as arch-colonialist Cecil Rhodes said to a friend of his in 1895 (just a few years before the Boer Wars),

> *"I was in the East End of London yesterday and attended a meeting of the unemployed. I listened to the wild speeches, which were just a cry for 'bread,' 'bread,' 'bread,' and on my way home I pondered over the scene and I became more than ever convinced of the importance of imperialism. ... My cherished idea is a solution for the social problem, i.e., in order to save the 40,000,000 inhabitants of the United Kingdom from a bloody civil war, we colonial statesmen must acquire new lands [in other words, steal new lands] to settle the surplus population, to provide new markets for the goods produced by them in the factories and mines. The Empire, as I have always said, is a bread and butter question. If you want to avoid civil war, you must become imperialists."*

Obviously, we in our day, know the human cost of this vision Rhodes presented for the British working class; as Asante further explicated, "In the nineteenth century, Cecil John Rhodes sought to gain control of a large territory of southern Africa that was ruled by the Ndebele King Lobengula, and he sent emissaries to the powerful king in an effort to secure his consent. After many days of discussion with Lobengula, the white emissaries returned to Rhodes with the king's signature on a piece of paper. They told Rhodes that Lobengula had given him all of his territory, and Rhodes sent a column of soldiers into the area with the instruction to shoot any black on sight. Thus began the country of Rhodesia." Such an historically tragic occurrence gives a greater level of context as to the mind of Robert Mugabe, and his lack of trust or forgiveness for the White people of Zimbabwe (the decolonised name he gave to Rhodesia). When your people experience an historical tragedy like the murder of literally millions of their ancestors at the hands of a particular group, on the one hand, and you happen to lead a revolution against the descendants of that same group, on the other hand; surely you can be forgiven a level of hatred towards that said group, e.g. the Nazis – or was it the Palestinians(?).

Effectively, it is the spreading of propagations, and the narrations contained within those propagations, that allowed colonialism to also spread, as well as the ideas and values of colonialism. Modern colonialism thereby truly owes its development to the spreading of European propaganda. At the same time, it also owes a far larger amount of its progress to the development of capitalism. It further undeniably owes its continued maintenance to the naked brute force of aggressive militarism. Herein, as Fanon also said, "colonialism is not a thinking machine, nor a body endowed with reasoning faculties. It is violence in its natural state, and it will only yield when confronted with [an even] greater violence." Violence is how colonialism maintained itself, violence is how colonialism protected itself, and ultimately, violence brought colonialism to the brink of self-destruction; as Lenin would further explicate, "the war of 1914-18 was imperialistic (that is, an annexationist, predatory, plunderous war) on the part of both sides; it was a war for the division of the world, or the partition and repartition of colonies, 'spheres of influence' of finance capital, etc."

Thereby we can see that as the embodied development of finance capital – together with its active investment in the colonial project – continued it soon became clear, as Lenin further delineated, "Finance capital is not only interested in the already known sources of raw materials; it is also interested in potential sources of raw materials, because present-day technical development is extremely rapid, and because land which is useless today may be made fertile tomorrow if new methods are applied ... and large amounts of capital are invested. This also applies to prospecting for materials, to new methods of working up and utilising raw materials, etc., etc. Hence, the inevitable striving of finance capital to extend its economic territory and even its territory in general."

This statement reveals to us the influence that finance, and hence economics, had on the spread and reproduction of imperialism. As the Western powers sought to compete with each other for geographical locations and geopolitical territories, the banking and manufacturing industries began to consolidate into financial trusts able to open up and invest in markets all over the world. For this cause, Lenin also mentioned, "It is beyond doubt ... that capitalism's transition to the stage of monopoly capitalism, to finance capital, is *bound up* with the intensification of the struggle for the partition of the world." So, as what Lenin called, finance capital, began to consolidate, concentrating all wealth and resources into fewer and fewer hands, not only were they developing into monopoly industries, they were also exploiting and expanding into new global locations and territories.

In these situations, however, finance capital was more of an afterthought as most of the early and middle imperial powers of modern Europe already had a presence in the locations they were exploiting and sought later to influence. Nevertheless, the aftereffects of both the dislocation and relocation of the many resources (including the minerals, the wealth, and the human bodies and souls) of colonised territories – ultimately culminated in the abjectivity and impoverishment of those same colonised territories. Even Lenin was able to see how, "The growth of internal exchange, and particularly of international exchange, is [currently] the characteristic distinguishing feature of capitalism. The uneven and spasmodic character of the development of individual enterprises of individual branches of industry and individual countries, is [therefore] inevitable under the capitalist system." This insightful description and illustration of global conditions under the market tyranny of a capitalistic system allows us to appreciate that just as governments need checks and balances, so even the market needs checks and balances.

Concerning the further process of imperial development, Lenin went on to say, "When free competition in Great Britain was at its zenith, i.e., between 1840 and 1860, the leading British bourgeois politicians were opposed to colonial policy and were of the opinion that the liberation of the colonies and their complete separation from Britain was inevitable and desirable. … But [by] the end of the nineteenth century the heroes of the hour in England were Cecil Rhodes and Joseph Chamberlain, [both] open advocates of imperialism". Both these men would so outspokenly endorse the imperial project that, as leading socialist and editor, Chris Harman, later explained, "Those powers with empires sought to strengthen them by building up their military forces. Those without empires sought to take colonies and influence from those with. And, when it came to the crunch, they were prepared to wage world war against each other with Britain, France and Russia on the one side, and Germany and Austro-Hungary on the other."

That which would eventually lead up to World War I was originally conflicts and competitions over the carving up of the economic have-nots between the haves, and the political non-powers between the powers. Wars in 1898 between the US and Spain over Cuba and the Philippines. In 1899 between the British and the Boer settlers over southern Africa. In 1905 between Japan and Russia over Korea and northern China. In 1911 between Italy and Turkey over northern Africa (with a brief rivalry between France and Germany over Morocco in-between). And the war in 1912 between Russia and Austro-Hungary over the Balkans, which eventually led to World War I; were not national or even ideological wars as such, but were wars for ever broader economic and political spheres of influence.

With the global expansion of economic empires, arose the need to strengthen the military presence in such global territories so as to deter any abuses or mishandling of finances by said occupied territory or the capturing and annexing of the occupied territory by a rival empire. Economic-colonisation thereby led to military-colonisation; and with the missionary zeal of the Victorian era also added to the mix the end result was inevitably settler- and spatial-colonisation. Fanon also confirmed this reality, stating, "The colonial world is a Manichaean world. It is not enough for the settler to delimit physically, that is to say with the help of the army and the police force, the place of the native. As if to show the totalitarian character of colonial exploitation the settler [also] paints the native as a sort of quintessence of evil" (Fanon 1969: 32).

Though it could be said that this process of demonising the other began from the time of slavery, the process was improved, refined, modified, intensified, and even pathologised, during colonialism. Indeed, colonialism's brutality towards the native fed inexorably into the West's racist sentiments and ideas about the natives. "Racism stares one in the face for it so happens that it belongs in a characteristic whole: that of the shameless exploitation of one group of men by another which has reached a higher stage of technical development. This is why military and economic oppression generally precedes, makes possible, and legitimatizes racism." Basically, as Victorian morality and capitalist competition took Europeans to the lands of Africa, Asia, Australia, and the Americas to expand, exploit, and extract wealth, their interactions eventually led to colonial racism.

At the same time, we can also appreciate how both of the economic systems of modernity, capitalism and socialism, effectively came to crushed out all moral, economic, and military opposition within the territories thus conquered by colonialism. Thereby they appreciably made all past economic systems of those territories either *invisiblised* or appear obsolete. Kwame Nkrumah especially noted this reality in reference to pre-modern Africa, noting, "Under communalism … all land and means of production belonged to the community. When a certain piece of land was allocated to an individual for his personal use, he was not free to do as he liked with it since it still belonged to the community. Chiefs were strictly controlled by counsellors and were removable." The majority of Africans lived under this type of economic system for centuries (including King Lobengula), but it was unfortunately incapable of withstanding the enormous pressures of modernisation bought to bear by colonial violence.

Nkrumah said concerning Africa's historical progression towards the modernity forced upon it by colonialism, "Subsistence agriculture was gradually destroyed and Africans were compelled to sell their labour power to the colonialist, who turned their profits into capital". "With the growth of commodity production, mainly for export, single crop economies developed completely dependent on foreign capital. The colony became a sphere for investment and exploitation."

What we observe from here is that as modernity was imported into Africa from the West it substantially affected the continent causing it to not only surrender its raw materials, minerals, and Black bodies, minds, and souls to colonial powers but to be completely dependent on foreign capital for survival. Thereby Western capital became dominant in Africa through colonialism, and industrial development, along with railways, ports, engineering, construction, and, most importantly, fictitious capital, all these becoming dominant concerns for Africa.

Indeed, continents like Africa went through a rapid modernisation during colonialism that created the need for greater foreign investment and more foreign capital where it could be said that none formerly existed. Nkrumah further delineated on the subject: "the spread of private enterprise, together with the needs of the colonial administrative apparatus, resulted in the emergence of first a petty bourgeois class and then an urban bourgeois class of bureaucrats, reactionary intellectuals, traders, and others, who became increasingly part and parcel of the colonial economic and social structure" (Nkrumah 2006: 15). Yet investment in Africa would still continue, even after colonialism fell, as several countries sought partial import substitution.

An example of this is in that all of French Africa chose to come under the franc. Moreover, all "their currencies have been stabilized on a fixed parity with the French franc and have a total guarantee from the French Treasury. These States pay their receipts of French francs into operation accounts in the French Treasury. These accounts can be overdrawn and the States can draw on them against their own currencies to an unlimited extent. Obviously, however, whatever the theoretical-position, the international financial position of these countries is subject to control in that at any time their operation accounts in the French Treasury could be blocked, as was done in the case of Guinea" (Nkrumah 2022: 24).

Yet, all this took place before the US Treasury became dominant in Africa. Here, Nkrumah added that there was, even in his time, "increasing American investments in the continent's extractive industries and the growth of United States participation in financial establishments on this continent. American banking houses are making inroads into territories formerly catered for solely by European and British banks. The French banks still dominate in the former French countries and the Belgians in the Congo; but this is frequently a front for American participation." Interestingly enough, a new phenomenon was beginning to occur around about this time as the ex-colonies were going through the process of decolonisation.

Nkrumah called this new phenomenon neo-colonisation, explaining that the "neo-colonialism of today represents imperialism in its final and perhaps its most dangerous stage ... In place of colonialism as the main instrument of imperialism we have today neo-colonialism" (Nkrumah 2022: 1). In this current system the only neo-colonial power left in the world, and the one that is presently consuming most of the planet, is the Great United States Empire (GUSE). Nkrumah thereby continued, showing in particular, that America's foreign investments in Africa before World War II were only 3 percent, and that less than 5 percent of Africa's trade was with the US. But by the fall of 1949 certain British and American bankers colluded to establish American investments in the continent and other parts of the British Empire. He further affirmed that two months later, meetings were established in Africa between American and French bankers with a similar purpose in mind.

Ultimately, as Nkrumah made perfectly clear, "The essence of neo-colonialism is that the State which is Subject to it is, in theory, independent and has all the outward trappings of international sovereignty. In reality its economic system and thus its political policy is directed from outside." It is for this reason, he went on to say, "the African bourgeoisie, the class which thrived under colonialism, is the same class ... benefiting under the post-independence, neocolonial period." Hereby, even though Africa undeniably has conditions of abject poverty within it, urban Africa currently experiences what Engberg-Pedersen et al. called conjunctural poverty.

Within this situation, the formal sector, paid employment, and real wage decreases have been the major obstacle. At the same time, rural Africa experiences a huge differentiation with poverty being far more absolute. Here, poverty is measured in indicators such as: "food insecurity and malnutrition, lack of proper shelter, physical isolation in inaccessible rural areas, and vulnerability to external shocks, diseases etc. ... The rural/urban gap is also significant in regard to access to safe water, education and health services." This rural/urban gap could be considered a form of class warfare in practice between the majority African peasantry and the minority African bourgeoisie.

Within this particular class warfare, this biopolitical warfare, fighting mainly takes place in the subjectivities of the African people based on the idea that Africa is nothing more than these uninhabitable locations of immense and abject poverty. Essentially, biopolitics itself is when politics is used to control and discipline minds and bodies: when life becomes political and when the political, economic, and cultural "overlap" into everyday life. US capital has itself become biopolitical through the multimedia, multiculture, multi-religion, and politics itself, all becoming commodified and commercialised. The biopolitical nature of the GUSE thus causes those countries that rebel against the dollar to be drawn into a problematic situation. With the United States currently being the world banker, to need money at all places a country at a disadvantage to America. Thus American capital is not only biopolitical it is also globalised.

This was that "New World Order" spoken of by Bush Sr. at the end of the Cold War. War machines like NATO, though no longer necessary, were not abandoned, in actual fact, they were enlarged. The US after the ending of the Cold War actually spent more on arms and nuclear weapons up to September 11, 2001. Then with the incoming of 9/11 and the "War on Islam," they went on to spend a total of $379 billion in their military budget. And so the GUSE has become the current imperial power of the world. Going further still we can see one very obvious truth: the earnest manifestation of prophecy is not by the hand of humanity, nor will it be the duty of humanity to fulfil, it is only by the hand of Allah. Again, the many small battles, wars, and conflicts of global history have really just been preparation for Allah's big showdown. Lately, as we all can now see, there has been emerging one monopolistic superpower over all of global politics.

The Empire that Debt Built

At the opening of the next seal (6: 5, 6) there came to stand before the apostle John and the four living creatures a black horse and its horseman. This horseman himself carried a pair of scales in his hand, and there came a voice from the midst of the four living creatures that gave the impression of a scarcity of food and of near famine conditions. For this cause, this horseman is usually called by those who know of his existence, 'Famine.' This truth is a reality that is given an even broader explication in the prophet Ezekiel's astral vision, "Thus saith the Lord God; It shall also come to pass, that at the same time shall things come into thy mind, and thou shalt think an evil thought: And thou shalt say, I will go up to the land of unwalled villages; I will go to them that are at rest, that dwell safely, all of them dwelling without walls, and having neither bars nor gates, To take a spoil, and to take a prey; to turn thine hand upon the desolate places that are now inhabited, and upon the people that are gathered out of the nations, which have gotten cattle and goods, that dwell in the midst of the land."

Now by all modern economic interpretations a famine is a time of economic downturn when the demand for food is greater than the supply. However, such a phenomenon could never really happen in our times. What can happen is that the food that is available is too expensive for the poverty stricken inhabitants of a country to afford (in which case most of the food gets dumped out and wasted – or they may be given away to foodbanks as a corporation tax write-off); but ultimately there is food enough to feed the populations of the entire planet easily. So where is the problem then? There is not *money* enough in any particular country to feed its own inhabitants easily – and that is with both consumer shopping and state sponsorship in place. However the economic system of the apostle John's time looked there is one thing that is definitely undeniable, as a slavery- and market-based system it obviously had its own fluctuations and downturns. From this we can see that famine conditions themselves come about due to the fact that the purpose of food within every market economy is primarily to make a profit and not to feed or help the hungry.

Accordingly, modernity has seen various moments of economic downturns so great that it has called them Great Depressions or Great Recessions. In these times famine conditions affected not only a country but the entire planet. That is because the modern system has integrated all monies into a universal market system. Yet, as we just said, every market system, from their first formation in the ancient states of Africa and Asia, all go through their own cycles of famine and plenty. Then added to that is the fact that integrated money-capital, far from saving the system from the brunt of difficulty, only exacerbates the difficulty through what socialists have dubbed *the falling rate of profits*. Simply put, the increasing wealth of the few super-rich bourgeoisies inevitably takes money from the moderately rich or not as rich bourgeoisies. In sum, all monies are getting concentrated into the hands of fewer and fewer people, while those who were rich today become moderately affluent tomorrow, and those who were moderately affluent today become poor tomorrow, etc.

To go with this the devaluation of money through inflation and interest rates has meant that money by today's standards can do far less than money by the standards of five years ago, let alone ten or twenty years ago. Again, this is due to the rising of the profits and capital gains of the very few super-rich, which must be compensated for by taking profits and monies from the not as rich. These stolen funds, though increasing the wealth of the super-rich bourgeois individual, cause the average rate of profits for the *class* of the bourgeoisie to steadily decrease. In order to make up for this difficulty the national system of the country is forced to print more money to curve out this discrepancy. This solution may dupe the people, it may even dupe the struggling bourgeoisie, but it cannot dupe the system, which to balance out the losses devalues the excess money-capital produced. This devaluation of national currency in turn leads to rising prices, which is the by-product of inflation, which itself precedes recession.

To solve this problem of the falling rate of profits companies have done one or two of three things: (i) expand the market overseas, (ii) lengthen the hours of exploitation, or (iii) get more out of the workers in the time they have through improved technology. Lately, employers have been doing the third but as they have not confronted the central issue of market mechanisms the overall rate of profits for individual capitalists continues decreasing. Further, as competition between various Western powers also increases and the rush to open up new markets for the purpose of strengthening global hegemony grows, an obviously very familiar idea within the mechanisms of the system has ultimately been regaining legitimacy: imperialism.

In the 1870s and 1880s this situation existed with the great European powers, driving each to expand their individual spheres of influence; and thus causing overseas investment to rise substantially with land, labour, and other raw materials being cheap there and capital being scarce there. These opportunities to attain cheap resources (like diamonds and gold from Africa's vast quantity of diamond- and goldmines), plus the added opportunity to export their commercial products to the now opened up markets of their colonies, would all further allow the European powers to become fabulously wealthy. Effectively, by stealing wealth and prosperity from the colonies of Africa, Asia, Latin America, and Australia, Europe was able to make herself and her individual countries into the dominant powers of the world.

"Obviously, out of [their] enormous *super-profits* (since they [were] obtained over and above the profits which capitalists squeeze out of the workers of their 'home' country) it [was also] quite *possible to bribe* the labour leaders and the upper stratum of the labour aristocracy" (Lenin 2010: 9). Essentially, these corrupted European labour leaders soon became far more interested and concerned with maintaining the global legitimation and superordination of imperialism than with concretising or reproducing any just or ethical society – and this phenomenon was not unique to Europeans. As Fanon noted, "Colonialism hardly ever exploits the whole of a country. It contents itself with bringing to light the natural resources, which it extracts, and exports to meet the needs of the mother country's industries, thereby allowing certain sectors of the colony to [also] become relatively rich."

This issue is therefore one of extreme delicacy, as most people in this Western world system will be, and have been, willing to fight and die in order to preserve the system as it is, failing to appreciate that the system itself is a ticking time bomb of economic chaos and degeneration. Unfortunately, neither those relatively rich nor their relatively poor subordinates have been willing to question, challenge, or problematise, let alone counter, the Western compensation system; fearing that the loss of the market would mean the overall loss of incentive, and thus the social deviation and economic impoverishment of society. At the same time, they almost fanatically believe that the maintenance and reproduction of the system means the overall concretisation of prosperity. What they fail to appreciate is that the maintenance and reproduction of the system will concretise nothing but mass disorder and mass impoverishment on an ever grander scale.

The social aetiology of the GUSE's current neo-colonial expansion of market economics started from around the mid- to late-twentieth century. Prior to that, to all intents and purposes, Britain was the leading and largest empire of the world, taking the position of world manufacturer, world banker, and world marketer for the purpose of the maintenance and stability of the international dominance of British industry. The Sterling Area was thus the international storehouse of finance capital. Indeed, industrial-colonialism was purely a result of the collusion of finance capital and monopoly capital. Britain also established the "sanctity of debt" ideology within its debtor nations (the colonies) in order to keep them subservient and dependent.

In those days, the United States was a big banker but not "the World Banker." Moreover, the United States had no interest in becoming a world power, but mainly to stick to its own isolationist plan in economics, politics, and geopolitics. Things, however, would change after World War I as the world sank into an economic Depression. The US, at that time, began to build up its stock of gold reserves obsessively. By the end of World War II, the US was in control of almost 60 percent of the world's gold supply. This gave the US a very powerful and effective bargaining chip as, "Apart from metallic coinage, domestic currency is a form of debt, but one that nobody really expects to be [paid; as the futile attempting] by governments to repay their debts beyond a point would extinguish their [own national] monetary base" (Hudson 2021: 16).

Hereby, at the end of World War II, Europe, which was the chief colonising agent of the world, would also become the chief debtor to the United States in the world. America, at that time, had investments in banks all over Germany, Italy, France,

Belgium, Great Britain, etc. Thus, the US would enter the world stage and would enter it with force. Using its dominant position, as possessing the world's largest gold supply, it convinced Britain, and through Britain the rest of Europe, as well as the entire Sterling Area, to use the International Monetary Fund to stabilise each of their own currencies by the gold standard. Essentially, all currencies in the Sterling Area and Franc Area were, as a result, to measure their value at $35 an ounce of gold. Thereby, "foreign exchange rates were [effectively] linked to the dollar, which became the world's key currency, accepted in international reserves and used to pay foreign debts in lieu of gold."

On top of all that, the World Bank was also established in the United States, despite British protests that it be established in Europe (and, for the purpose of showing all cards on the table, it was established in Washington DC, as – according to their top officials – the Bank and Fund should never finance policies the United States believed went against their national interests). Indeed, the National Advisory Council on International Monetary and Financial Policies (NAC) was set up by the US government to oversee the Bank, the Fund, and all other inter-governmental lending institutions. According to Hudson, "The U.S. executive directors of the Bank and Fund were responsible directly to the NAC for their votes in these organizations."

As a result of all this manoeuvring, the system was able to sustain a somewhat stable economic growth period from the 1940s to the 1970s. Basically, before the 1970s all Western monies became measurable economic units. The system only began to fall apart in the 1970s when Richard Nixon took all the countries then in – what was by that time called – the dollar area off the gold standard. As money was needed to fund the Vietnam War, and as the workers and unions started getting greedy for revolution without actually being prepared to fight an actual revolution, or even knowing what they were fighting for, the economic system effectively took a downturn. That revolutionary spirit, which was a remnant of the 1960s, eventually turned to clouds of hostility and disillusionment as the world did not change nor become a better place. To make up for the discrepancy the people began to march and demonstrate, but not to actually fight. Thus the cities of the West ground to a halt, but with nobody seizing power crisis was inevitable.

Furthermore, with the diabolical development of fiat currency by the changes instituted by the Nixon administration, the dependent, and thus valueless, nature of global currency was thereby officially exposed to the world. Today all monies are merely numbers on a screen, bank notes and statements, or pieces of paper with fancy stuff in and on them. Money no longer exists in a substantial sense, hence why crypto was able to disrupt the banking system so easily. The truth is, at this time all currency is merely an IOU from a country's own central bank agreeing that the value of that piece of paper will be paid by the government if it should fail. This system becomes even more diabolical when we remember that all central banks themselves have no real power to determine the value of their own currency as, since the creation of the Bank and the Fund, all currencies in the dollar area are valued only through the dollar.

What all this therefore produces is a system whereby the stability and strength of all currencies within the dollar area (which by now is *virtually* the entire globe) are guaranteed merely by the strength of the US dollar. Nevertheless the US dollar, like all other currencies since 1971, has no value or strength of its own, all it is is paper with fancy shit in and on it. Ultimately, the US dollar is, and thereby all currencies within the dollar area are, basically guaranteed by an American IOU, i.e. debt, or better yet, a promise to pay us back. But again, with what? Currency(!) In other words, all the banks of the world, and all the currencies of the world, are held together by nothing more than numbers on a screen and pieces of paper with some shit in and on them. Worse still, this is not the only form of fictitious capital that exists within the current economic system: all stocks, shares, assets, bonds, options, equity, debt, credit, interest, and even wages, are themselves only forms of fictitious capital.

Imagine for a moment a wannabe investor going to a bank and depositing $5,000 cash. Apparently, for every dollar deposited the bank is to receive from their central bank, and thereby from a US promise, an additional interest based on their country's nationally agreed upon interest rate (all really just numbers on a group of screens). Then, now, the investor desires to purchase $20,000 worth of shares in a company, to get this she goes to the same bank and takes out a loan (just numbers in a bank account, and a piece of paper with both records and the bank's logo on it) for $20,000. Then she receives the loan and uses it to purchase the shares (which in turn are only just pieces of paper with a company's logo on them, and words and numbers on a digital screen). In time the company may go public so the shares become stocks or securities (both fictitious names to denote a change when nothing has really changed but words and numbers on several different screens).

Overall, all that really changes monetary-wise is the value *society* now gives to numbers as they become larger or enter into different word groupings and categories on those screens spoken of here so cynically. In other words, the entire edifice of finance capitalism is currently based on nothing more than numbers on screens. Herein also lies the central danger of finance capitalism, it deifies these numbers on screens giving them greater value than the lives, pains, and struggles of living, feeling beings, human and otherwise. Indeed, it even reduces living beings themselves to nothing more than numbers on a screen to be graphed and charted for the purpose of nothing more than to extract profits from them.

Reductions like this cause reactions from economists when chasms like economic crises occur, to consider such events nothing more than the system merely clearing the way to allow better businesses to consume smaller, less successful ones. Or to expand overseas or globally into new territory to disrupt the businesses of the local population of those territories. The acquired smaller businesses will either have to accept being consumed to save their lives or go completely bust during an economic downturn; while the survival of any indigenous people and their communal businesses become more and more tenuous due to the arrival of bigger Western businesses and cheaper Western products. Among the struggling workers in both cases, however, we find nothing but layoffs, wage decreases, or job depreciations all around, but hey, at least you got that BHAG(!).

All this inevitably leads to the concentration of wealth – again, just numbers on a screen and based entirely on an empty and unfulfillable promise – into fewer and fewer hands and thus to monopoly capital; and transnational monopoly capital is really just another form of imperial capital, as these corporate empires grow to take over the game even with their currencies of wind. Again, as capitalism gives way to corporate imperialism jobs and wages are not only at stake but are unsaveable. So, like it or not, the workers of today will be the underclass of tomorrow, even as the intellectuals of today, though usually unsuited to self-employment, in order to make ends-meet, will either have to take such or suffer complete joblessness.

This is all due to the process of what economists call *the business cycle of bust and boom*, or famine and plenty. To give the standard economist explanation of this process and why they say we go through it at all, to those who may have never heard of it; I shall now take you through *their* version of what it is. To start with booms are when businesses are doing well; profits are good; prices are reasonably set; wages are decent; companies are able to expand, make more branches, and invest in more productive property. With more companies expanding raw materials get scarce and their prices go up, which eventually leads to prices going up all around, thus to inflation. Inflation soon leads to bust or "recession", where unemployment rises along with bankruptcy; companies close down the new branches, lose millions, or get bought-out by larger companies.

Life in these times is pretty much miserable for everybody, and they seem to be unbeatable, but eventually there will come a time when smaller businesses will feel comfortable investing again and soon they will grow, and as they grow other companies will grow through them. A furniture store is doing well enough so they invest in more furniture. This gives work to more carpenters, who in turn give more work to loggers, who in turn give more work to truck manufacturers, who in turn help the steel and tire industries, who help other industries grow and eventually the whole system begins to grow again leading to another boom. So the *business cycle* is bust-boom-bust-boom.

This is the standard economist interpretation, however, another explanation for economic crises, and thereby famine, is that the current market system based on supply and demand seems overall to prioritise demand. That means, if the people/market (or your people/market) are not demanding or desiring your product, service, brand, or business, it will disappear in this Darwinian world of commerce. This market system therefore, of necessity, requires marketing and skills in marketing otherwise, again, instant death by irrelevance. This sort of system can and does work in the short term. However, in the long run, some companies, in order to stay relevant, popular, or even alive, will hawk to the public certain goods, services, and information that does nothing for them and only saves or fattens the pockets of the marketers and the businesses they are working for.

Unless we can create a co-ordinated operation to provide for the people, not what they currently demand, but more so what they genuinely need. One that, at the same time, also allows them the option of wider choices through a non-intrusive, non-bureaucratic, yet decentralised participatory methodology: one such as the programme I have outlined within my own conception of Black syndicalism (Islam 2024). Whatever programme is put in place will either limit the freedom of choice of the individual, in which case oppression, or limit the capacities of the system, in which case chaos. The two must work together, that is, limited market *and* limited state. To take power from the one without, at the same time, taking power from the other leaves an imbalance and inequality in the societal superstructure where power resides either in wealth or force.

Nevertheless, for the lack of this form of societal superstructure, and due to the inefficiency of the modern free market system, economists have been forced to resort to the now obsolete, now reviving, methods of their forebears, thus giving rise to neo-colonialism. From here the current and continuing war crises will remain the inevitable and persistent outcome. Moreover, we can now perceive that the imperialistic wars of 1914-18 and 1939-45 were merely a prelude of good things to come if we do not start looking harder for better solutions. The current global expansion of corporate enterprises are reminiscent of those of the late nineteenth and early twentieth centuries before the outbreak of global war. Here again, the stage appears to be being set for a very dramatic and climactic conclusion.

The Power of Absolute Power

With the opening of the fourth seal (6: 7, 8) the apostle John saw standing before him a pale horse whose horseman was called "Death," and Hades followed with him, probably riding on his own pale horse. Death was then given power over the fourth part of the earth, to kill by sword, famine, plague, and the wild beasts of the earth; and having a partner like Hades by his side he was completely prepared for what was about to take place. The mission set before him he had had in mind from the very beginning; he had been watching and waiting for the onslaught he would be sent out to inflict from his very creation. The pursuit of his vision and his destiny was declared all the more forcefully as the prophet Ezekiel's drama continued, "Therefore, thou son of man, prophesy against Gog, and say, Thus saith the Lord God; Behold, I am against thee, O Gog, the chief prince of Meshech and Tubal: And I will turn thee back, and leave but the sixth part of thee, and will cause thee to come up from the north parts, and will bring thee upon the mountain of Israel: And I will cause thine arrows to fall out of thy right hand."

While Death and Hades have definitely interfered in human lives, caused great and tragic loss, and brought with them an overabundance of suffering, this has all been within the remit of their sovereignty. Indeed, as Achille Mbembe also pointed out, "The ultimate expression of sovereignty largely resides in the power and capacity to dictate who is able to live and who must die." Herein Foucault's biopolitics becomes the defining of who gets to live and how they are to live, the defining of livelihoods and lifestyles. But as every light casts a shadow, so the shadow of biopolitics is Mbembe's necropolitics: the defining of who must die, how they are to die, and for what reason they must die.

In defining who dies and for what reason they must die, Death and Hades do not necessarily use only violence, or what could be called "hard power," to achieve this goal and objective. We have seen how the imperial forces of Europe eventually exploded into global war due to the expansive nature of capitalism. We have also seen how finance capital can turn into monopoly capital, and thus into imperial capital, simply by the investment into international projects ultimately leading to the extraction of resources from a colony in order to benefit a "mother country," whichever European country that happened to be. While the first, and the defining of who must die, may technically be seen as clear expressions of hard power, the second, and the defining of a reason for which they must die, could themselves be considered expressions of what is called in the political sphere "soft power."

In his book on the subject, Joseph Nye presented an effective definition of what he believed soft power to be, "It is the ability to get what you want through attraction rather than coercion or payments. It arises from the attractiveness of a country's culture, political ideals, and policies." Hereby, we can see that though Death and Hades definitely use coercion and aggressiveness to accomplish their tasks on one level, it is also clear that that is not the only means they use. They are very capable of also using seduction and attractiveness to accomplish their goals. Herein lies the genius of Allah, through his own use of soft power, he has been able to make their goals – those of Death and Hades – actually be the very goals and intentions he has always had for them, and even for the world.

Conversely, the hard power of Death and Hades has been explored by many authors, movies, and narratives throughout history. What I, however, intend to do is explain a little deeper how their soft power can be used effectively, and even devastatingly, to cause not only mass murder and death, but even the potential genocide of an entire race right under the noses of the international community. First, we have already seen how soft power is generally used by governments, cultures, and groupings to basically seduce, or at least inspire, others into following a path. Nye said again, "Seduction is always more effective than coercion, and many values like democracy, human rights, and individual opportunities are deeply seductive. As General Wesley Clark put it, soft power 'gave us an influence far beyond the hard edge of traditional balance-of-power politics.' But attraction can turn to repulsion if we act in an arrogant manner and destroy the real message of our deeper values."

Clearly, the idea that Death and Hades can or would use something so undervalued and underappreciated as soft power (even the name itself has an air of weakness about it) may leave something of a fowl taste in many of our mouths. Nevertheless, if we explore the tragic conflict between the Hutu and the Tutsi we will be able to see how soft power and representation could be used to create, both an aggressive genocidal attack, and an equally aggressive genocidal response, all while the international community looks on assuming both to simply be a case of rivalrous or tribal (that is, cultural/ideological) conflicts. Thereby outright genocidal activities can be masked through manipulating the public into sympathising with and toleration of those who perpetrate such genocidal activities.

Keen (2012) spoke on the usage of what he called the dangerous template of "ethnic war," and how it potentially blinds global populations as to the true, or at least desired, intentions of certain regimes. In this case, he spoke on, "A tragic example [being] Rwanda in 1994. Here, the world's media (and indeed the UN secretary-general) tended to present mass violence as a spontaneous 'Hutu versus Tutsi' conflict that was driven by senseless hatred – a damaging misrepresentation that helped to delay international recognition that this was actually a carefully planned genocide. In the crucial first four weeks of the Rwandan genocide, both the UN Security Council and the UN Secretariat focused their attention on the 'civil war' in Rwanda, virtually ignoring the genocide and the possibility of organising peacekeepers to prevent or reduce it."

In this particular instant, soft power – presenting the war as nothing more than a civil conflict or tribal war – blinded the masses as to what was really going on. The Tutsi were being systematically and purposively targeted for extermination and annihilation at the hands of various Hutu groupings so as to completely remove them from the Rwandan territory. The Hutu basically saw the Tutsi ethno-tribal grouping as only a hindrance to their own progression and mobility. Herein immigration and ethnocentric rhetoric were writ-large allowing xenophobic ambitions to cloud judgments on a tribal level. On the political and diplomatic level, however, ignorance and inability were being claimed by all governmental factions, in response to the various attacks being perpetrated against the Tutsi.

All realities very similar in our own time to that occurring in the current Israel/Palestine conflict. Governments can use their soft power to claim ignorance and impotence concerning the threat of an all-powerful monster beyond their control or can use it to hide the grand atrocities they themselves have been committing, without end, against their opponent. Effectively, throwing off or passing off as "innocent ethnic rivalries" any genocidal activities they themselves have been committing. Either way, soft power is being used to present something to the public; and either way, what is being presented to the public is a lie. Public presentation and representation are key assets of soft power, and both can be used to deadly effect. Here, Israeli historian Benny Morris painted a clear picture, explaining the tragic circumstances under which the Zionist forces invaded and seized Palestine in 1948. He explained, there was a much larger amount and extent of massacres than he expected, as well as far more cases of rape – many of which ending in murder – than he originally presumed.

Morris, himself an ardent and loyal Zionist, even to the point of excusing these horrors, when confronted on the idea that what really happened in 1948 was a Zionist attempt at systematic ethnic cleansing, said in their defence, "There are circumstances in history that justify ethnic cleansing. I know that this term is completely negative in the discourse of the twenty-first century, but when the choice is between ethnic cleansing and genocide – the annihilation of your people – I prefer ethnic cleansing." While such a logic – and I speak here with the deepest sarcasm – may have been excusable in the immediate aftermath of the Holocaust, the Palestinians were neither the perpetrators of the Holocaust nor did they have any connection to any of the sufferings Jewish people up to that point had ever endured. Moreover, if we look at the current *literal genocide* being perpetrated *by them* against the Palestinians, and the understanding that the Palestinians never had any intention of ever committing genocide against the Israelis, in spite of what had been, and even today still is, going on there, makes the whole Israeli cause in the current war somewhat laughable if it were not so tragic.

Instead, the Palestinians are painted as some horrific, villainous, and almost undefeatable monster that has it out for all the Jews in both "Israel" and the world over. Such rhetoric then couples with the showing of very strategic images, and the telling of very strategic stories, concerning only certain goings on in the actual war. Many times, they even mistranslate the Arabic or Israeli language to the public with no other intent but to spread the narrative that they want the West to hear. This is irresponsible journalism by, in many cases, non-journalists having no obligation to the journalist code of ethics, using Israel's soft power and global support to literally, not rhetorically – as is the case with their Muslim neighbours – wipe out an entire ethnic grouping.

Essentially, these types of individuals claim Islam has an historic hostility towards the Jews (usually Ashkenazi), as though we Muslims, Semites ourselves, are anti-Semitic, having anti-Semitism somehow built into the very fabric of our religion and traditions. But what does the Quran, the most authoritative book in the Islamic tradition, and the basis for all Islamic laws and principles, actually say concerning the Jews?

> *And certainly Allah made a covenant with the Children of Israel, and We raised up among them twelve chieftains. And Allah said: Surely I am with you. If you keep up prayer and pay the poor-rate and believe in My messengers and assist them and offer to Allah a goodly gift, I will certainly cover your evil deeds, and cause you to enter Gardens wherein rivers flow. But whoever among you disbelieves after that, he indeed strays from the right way. But on account of their breaking their covenant We cursed them and hardened their hearts. They alter the words from their places and neglect a portion of that whereof they were reminded. And thou wilt always discover treachery in them excepting a few of them – so pardon them and forgive. Surely Allah loves those who do good (to others).*

Firstly, take note that in Islam Allah is not impartial. He only loves those who do good. This idea is fundamentally different from the Western tradition that teaches the idea and concept of an unconditionally impartial God. Such a God, however, would thereby ignore corruption, deceit, injustice, and oppression. It is almost like, of course White people would promote such a God, they are currently in their position of power knowing that they only gained that power either through their own corruption and exploitation, or through the corruption and exploitation their ancestors inflicted on people of colour (POCs) around the world. What the Quran, and the God of the Quran, were saying here was that Allah has a preferential option – not for the poor, or for the majority, or for the oppressed, or for the victimised, or for the racialised, or for the gendered, or for even the religious, all representing groupings that could just as easily become unjust and corrupted if given the right opportunity – only for those who do good.

Secondly, and I want to make this very clear, this Scripture is a far cry from "an historic hostility towards the Jews." I must also here fervently remind you that when the Prophet here used the words, "Children of Israel" he was speaking specifically of a Falashic group, not the Ashkenazic, who at that time had not yet converted to Judaism. This Falashic group would have thereby been an authentic Black Hebrew grouping to match the time and location that all this took place in.

So then, what about the conclusion that Islam was spread "by the edge of the sword," i.e., that it is a religion of conquest and only by reason of conquest was ever accepted? Well, let us here return to the Quran to see the actual words the Prophet spoke concerning those who were, not only non-practitioners of Islam, but, themselves practitioners of the very pagan/polytheist religion Islam sought to replace: "And thus their associate-gods have made fair-seeming to many polytheists the killing of their children, that they may cause them to perish and obscure for them their religion. And if Allah had pleased, they would not have done it, so leave them alone with that which they forge" (Quran 6: 137).

Again, this is a far cry from the biblical tradition, particularly the Old Testament, which if misread or misinterpreted could just as easily be used to promote and justify *literal* genocidal practices, such as where it is written, "Thus saith the Lord of hosts, I remember that which Amalek did to Israel, how he laid wait for him in the way, when he came up from Egypt. Now go and smite Amalek, and utterly destroy all that they have, and spare them not; but slay both men and women, infant and suckling, ox and sheep, camel and ass" (1Samuel 15: 2, 3). And just in case there is any further doubt about it, the prophet Samuel cursed the Kish Dynasty of Saul because of King Saul's failure to actually go through with the complete and total genocide of the people of Amalek.

Indeed, this kind of mentality is very similar to that of those who attempted to inflict the Rwandan genocide. Herein, in order to get the full story of this situation we may have to start at the very beginning, in the aftermath of World War I. According to researcher and social media influencer, Lynae Vanee, after the Allied victory in World War I, the League of Nations gave possession of all German colonies in Africa, that is, of Rwanda and Burundi, to Belgium. On top of Belgium's already possessing the so-called Congo Free State, the new colonies now expanded their African colonial territory to three places. But Belgian rule, for the most part, was mainly through corporations, so as to extract Africa's many resources, and through missionary work. Add to this cocktail the popularity in Europe at the time of the doctrine of Eugenics, and particularly of Belgian Eugenics – a field that was built around a concept called anthropometry: in which a person's or racial group's capacity to learn and develop in science, ethics, rhetorics, aesthetics, hygienics, and advanced civilisation was determined by their bodily type, shape, and measurements.

Ultimately, what ended up happening was, using Belgian Eugenics, many of the Belgian authorities of Belgian East Africa assumed the Tutsi tribe were racially and biologically superior to the Hutu tribe. They therefore forcibly converted the Tutsi to Christianity; gave them positions of power in society and the labour force; gave them the power to inflict exploitative and punitive measures on the Hutu; and even made it so that education itself was only reserved for Tutsi children. All essentially leading to the poverty, famine, and oppression of the Hutu tribes. So now, by the time Rwanda regained its independence in 1962, the Hutu majority was thirsty for revenge, and so, in a burst of passion and destiny they burned down all Tutsi houses in numerous locations, sending some 300,000 of them into exile.

This was obviously only the beginning, however, as Keen further narrated quite expertly, "In 1994, militiamen from Rwanda's Hutu ethnic group had taken part in the murder of some 800,000 Rwandan citizens ... When Tutsi rebels seized power in Rwanda and put a stop to the 1994 genocide, Hutu militias (ably assisted by France) took refuge in eastern DRC [Democratic Republic of Congo], where they were planning to resume their murderous campaign inside Rwanda." In like manner, there is an overlooked relation between these Rwandan/Congolese genocides and the current Israeli genocide of the Palestinians – if not, then at least their forcing them into the most desperate of apartheid-like conditions. On top of this, them behaving surprised, even shocked and victimised, when they responded to this mistreatment with violence. In all, these events further demonstrate how Death and Hades are being very well present, using both soft power and hard power to accomplish their genocidal ends.

Moreover, to further explain the horrific conditions the Palestinians have been living through in the OPT (Occupied Palestinian Territory), Imseis spoke of the "massive influx of Israeli settlers into the OPT, causing their numbers to more than double, from some 200,000 to well over 400,000; the rapid construction of hundreds of kilometers of additional *settler-only* bypass roads connecting the settlements with Israel; the presence of some 200 Israeli *military bases/posts* throughout the OPT; the erection of the wall; the destruction of the Palestinian village-road network; and the imposition of a complex regime of closures, curfews, and a South-Africa style 'permit system' that severely limited Palestinian freedom of movement. As a result, the Palestinian inhabitants of the West Bank were confined in '227 non-contiguous islands,' and the Palestinians of the Gaza Strip were left to fester in one of the most densely populated and impoverished places on earth. According to the U.N. special rapporteur on human rights in the OPT, John Dugard, this situation led to the development of 'an apartheid regime worse than the one that existed in South Africa'" (Imseis 2010: 271; emphasis mine).

All this, to me, looks eerily close to the systematic erasure and removal of a people from their own land (or perhaps from the face of the earth), while claiming just and noble reasons for such a desire. The truth is, it is impossible to truly understand a people, a movement, or an insurgency until you consider its context. What most people have done, and in the case of Rwanda did, was throw these things off to ethnic squabblings. Indeed, to add a further justification the Israelis used the hugely emotive and demonising spectre of "Terrorist" to thereby cement what support they could gather from any potential stragglers. Hereby, to give a more comprehensive understanding to you, and to show the absolute bankruptcy of such a loaded and overused term, I will first detach it from its current relation and identification with Islam and Islamism; then I will hopefully be able to demystify its usage.

First, in order to detach the word "terrorist" from the word Islamist, or even fundamentalist, we must start by removing the blatant lie that Islamism is a late modern form of fascism. The following spectrum presented here is a non-biased and non-prejudiced spectrum of the various big ideological movements of the last three centuries. From left to right they are: anarchism (the furthest left), then ecologism (or the green movement), then communism, then socialism, then queerism, then feminism, then liberalism. These are the main left-wing movements. Moving on, again, from left to right: conservatism, *then fundamentalism*, then nationalism, then imperialism, then fascism, then Nazism. It is the most irresponsible of narrations and storytellings to equate and associate Islamism (a form of fundamentalism) with fascism (an oppressive, elitist, corporatist, brutalist, and imperialist form of police-statism), but that is what is currently done in many Western media, especially in the US.

To give further reference, virtually every one of those ideologies have, at some point in their history, a time when they themselves used or resorted to terrorism or to terroristic tactics in order to achieve their ideological vision. The anarchists post-Bakunin were known for using terrorist tactics to destabilise governments. The green movement has had a history of eco-terrorists and "green warriors" who have practiced what could be called "terrorism lite" as their attacks damaged property or freed wildlife but rarely killed anybody.

Communism's early history was one of terror, prior to Marx it was conspiratorial terrorism, attacking the governments of France and other Europeans locations, post-Marx communism was more about large masses led by Marxist or vanguard leaders. The early socialists could also be said to have used "terrorism lite" in that they bombed or disrupted factories, buildings, offices, derailed train tracks, and otherwise obstructed production, but very few people got hurt. And as I am not excessively familiar with all the ins-and-outs of either the queer or the feminist movements I will have to say that perhaps neither of them, of all these ideologies, ever engaged in any terrorist atrocities to get their message across, but I am fine with being proved wrong about that. As for the liberals, they have one of the most notorious histories of all with regard to terrorism, the Jacobin Great Terror, in which anyone showing any sign of monarchical attachment could literally get their head chopped off.

For the record, however, none of this means the Right has been excessively innocent in all this either. The history of conservative terrorism is a lot more nuanced. In English history the terrorism of Henry VIII against the Catholics and of Mary Tudor in response are legend. Then there was the further terrorism of King James I against the non-conformists (ultimately leading many of them to immigrate to Holland, and then from Holland to the New World). As to American conservative terrorists, I hopefully have no need to remind White America of the Salem Witch Trials, the existence of the Klan, and various other White supremacist groups, or of the terror inflicted by McVeigh and his like.

With regard to fundamentalist terror it is already well known from the side of the Islamist, however, what a lot of people in our time somehow fail to appreciate is that Zionism is also just as much a fundamentalist movement (cloaked and protected by European and American interests) as Islamism, mercilessly getting away with their numerous terrorist atrocities against the Palestinian people. Indeed, if we were now to consider "the question of Israel: how it was able to displace and obliterate the Palestinian presence and the fact that the Palestinians never stopped resisting their imposed fate or devising counter-strategies, of which the one-state solution was the one ... most strongly advocated ... Of course, [this] simple, largely agricultural people with poor education and modest political aspiration had been forced into close proximity with a formidable foe: European Jews allied to European imperialism, who were imbued with a 'yearning for Jewish political and religious self-determination ... to be exercised on the promised land." This has effectively all been accomplished through Israel's use and exploitation of both hard and soft power.

With regard to nationalism, we could, with no ill or undue malice intended, remember that many anti-colonial struggles used terrorism in the early parts of their liberation movements to fight against the settlers. Also, the IRA's (Irish Republican Army's) use of terrorist tactics to achieve their vision of a fully unified and independent Ireland is even to this day the stuff of legend. As to imperialism I hopefully will not need to remind you of the track record of imperialist violence and terror all over Africa, in India, and in Latin America. With regard to fascism there were, to my personal knowledge, only three solidly fascist states: Italy, Spain, and Japan. Of these, Italy used terror on the Ethiopians, Spain used terror on the anarchists, and Japan intended to inflict a level of terror, or at least mass violence, on China and America. Indeed, the Kamikaze fighters no doubt used a form of terrorism against the US.

Finally, Nazi terrorism should not need to be excessively dwelt upon, but we should remember that the deaths that occurred during World War II reached as high as 85 million overall of those who died, directly or indirectly, as a result of Nazism; 50 million civilian deaths; 25 million military deaths; 5 million prisoner of war (POW) deaths; 11 million Soviet civilian deaths; 10 million Soviet concentration camp deaths (i.e. Holocaust deaths); and 6 million World War II related Soviet deaths in the postwar period. Not to mention 3 million Chinese military deaths; 8 million Chinese civilian deaths; and 5-10 million World War II related Chinese deaths in the postwar period.

All this, in total, puts the Soviet and Chinese deaths caused by Nazism to be 27-28 million among the Soviets and 16-21 million among the Chinese. All to go with the estimated 6-7 million Ashkenazi Jews, 250 thousand disabled people, 100-200 thousand Freemasons, and 10 thousand homosexuals that died during the Holocaust. To be clear, the Ashkenazim were not the only victims of the Holocaust, they were not even the largest number of those brutally murdered during the Holocaust (that title goes to the Soviets at an estimated 10 million), nor the first to be placed into concentration camps (another title going to the communists, this time predominantly German). In sum, World War II was a global war with global proportions. Thus, no one community has the right to claim they suffered more or worse from Nazi terrorism than any others. The world suffered from Nazi terrorism.

What I hope I have hereby achieved is the successful detachment of terrorism from its current connection to fundamentalism and Islamism. Also to have at least slightly contributed to the weakening or lessening of its use to justify all manner of atrocious acts against Muslim nations, each fighting against what they believe to be – not necessarily American decadence, as is so often believed by most Western narrators – American imperialism, European orientalism, and Zionist annexationism. One of the major problems with creating simplistic, threatening, and villainous daemons like the "terrorist" has perhaps been expressed best by the words of Keen: "an overt and publicly expressed intention to defeat [any] demon enemy – whether RUF rebels in Sierra Leone or the Viet Cong in Vietnam or the Taliban in Afghanistan – has repeatedly created huge opportunities for diverse actors within the counterinsurgency to engage in politically and economically advantageous abuse with minimal international criticism."

Again, it could be said that Death uses national soft power to blind the international community to the truths of what is really going on in the world. All thus bringing us back again to Rwanda, "The Rwandan regime had considerable international sympathy that had been encouraged by collective guilt over the international community's non-response to the 1994 genocide. But this guilt was now feeding renewed suffering – and some began to talk of new genocides *within the DRC*, including mass mortality among the Hutu refugee population. Hundreds of thousands were deprived of humanitarian relief, and in 1996-97 an estimated 232,000 Hutu refugees were killed in the DRC, primarily at the hands of the Rwandan army and its Congolese rebel ally, the Alliance of Democratic Forces for the Liberation of Congo (ADFL)." Moreover, the Hutu/Tutsi genocide continues on, even to this day, in the DRC, and shows little sign of abating. Soft power thus has the ability to vocalise certain voices while muting and silencing others. This is what ultimately makes it so useful to conceptual entities like Death and Hades.

All that being said, there is still an argument to be made, which the prophet Ezekiel would delineate prophetically in one of his earlier scrolls, that Death was in fact, and has been this whole time, a being both subservient to, and in the service of, Allah himself for the purpose of removing systems that he was ready to judge: "Though Noah, Daniel, and Job, were in [a land], as I live, saith the Lord God, they shall deliver their own souls by their righteousness. For thus saith the Lord God; How much more when I send my four sore judgments upon Jerusalem, the sword, and the famine, and the noisome beast, and the pestilence, to cut off from it man and beast?"

Effectively, we can find here the ways of Allah, that he sometimes uses Death and Hades to bring an entity to its ultimate manifestation. True indeed, each of these last four horsemen: War, Famine, Death, and Hades could even turn out to be the mysterious four angels "bound in the great river Euphrates" (9: 14) that had been prepared for that very hour, and day, and month, and year. Therefore, while I personally theorise that the first horseman is most likely the Great Witness from al-Khidr, destined to bring plague and pestilence upon the earth; the four horsemen that follow him or her are far more likely to symbolise the four sore judgments Allah intends to inflict upon the earth nearing the end of his or her testimony.

Herein we can also appreciate how difficulties like death exist in virtually every entity imaginable, to carry them through into their next manifestation. The death of an entity is thereby its transitioning from one state to another in manifestation. Non-existence in itself is actually an absurdity. All things have life as all things have energy. Energy, that is, interactive desire and motion, exists everywhere and in all things, and it can never die. All it does is merely change from one state to another. The same is also true of the human soul. It does not actually die, in the sense of ceasing to be, it merely transitions from one form of existence to another. In this, we understand the Day of the Lord to actually be a time of severe change, when the world shall meet Allah face to face, and shall therefore be changed. Even the apostle Paul said of it "the dead shall be raised incorruptible, and we shall be changed."

But the changing of the world has occurred many times historically: the latest being the rise of modernity. Yet modernism will also have to stand face to face with Death, being, in actuality, nothing more than a European version of Americanism. American neo-colonialism has thus been backed and supported by European idealists who understand that the system itself currently stands by the power and dominance of American imperialism. All nations that are subject to the White House, IMF, World Bank, US Treasury, and USAID (which all make up the current Washington consensus) are all subjects to the GUSE (Great United States Empire) and to US neo-colonialism. By transcending modernism, one effectively transcends the imperial seat of the US and may even rouse their displeasure. True indeed, Europe is not officially subjected to the US as such, but they have still surrendered their power to its empire, as they too follow the modernist agenda.

The intellectual fight back of the twentieth century led up to postmodernism; but modernism was only really triumphed here. Nonetheless modernity reaches its full demise only when a new system, like godbodyism, has become the new establishment, leaving liberalism behind to the darkness. This kind of revolution will set off a true postmodernism. It will also put in place a new standard for living and perceiving. When philosophical movements have reached their height then comes a tipping point at which time anything can set off revolution. The main motivating force behind modernism was humanism. We need a new motivating system in place of humanism's failed mission to improve our lot. While, true indeed, Existentialism seems to be the motivating force behind the current school of post-modernism, it cannot account for the pneumatological realities that exist within the universe. Herein is where the movement of godbodyism becomes seriously interesting.

If we consider one of modernism's greatest strengths it would be its monopoly on intellectual/scientific representation. It seems all intellectual and scientific achievement flows directly from modernists and modernisers. The inferiorising of ancient customs and traditions, the rejecting and neglecting of what is essentially real and true subjectively to other races and people, has brought about the humiliation of tribal knowledge, secrets, and remedies and the glorification of all Western sciences. As concepts like race begin to get triumphed by ethnicity so the concept of modernity is slowly getting triumphed by an anti-modern movement. But anti-modernism should not be a shift back to a past nirvana, it should be a shift into a bright interdependent future. It should recall nature in that all natural beings know their place in nature and operate within that sphere. This more naturalistic future is based on demodernisation into something less intellectually based.

But as any true postmodernism brings on the death pangs of modernism – a system centred on liberalism – such an actuality may seem contemptuous, even blasphemous, to most modern minds. The movement from the rule of law to the rule of Allah means a transition from liberalism to godbodyism must occur. True indeed, far from creating a world of freedom, liberalism has only produced an oppression to surveillance, all in the name of security. Not giving people the freedom to rule themselves is the only way that liberalism can actually ensure that it does not collapse into the pernicious malaise of chaos. This is the psychologic of self-disclosed humanity: not the freedom of humanism but the oppression of dehumanisation. Here liberalism is not the aspiration of subjected humanity but the imposition of modernist effectuation.

Ultimately, what we can conclude here is that Death, having been sent out also to conquer, was not meant to be taken literally, in the physical sense of the idea, but was considered an individual experience we all receive when we come to understand death as an inevitability, a prelude to elevation we all must go through. Here, Death, though preparing for the great battle of the Day of Allah, is also the very messenger of Allah sent to bring humanity to the point of reaching divinity. Thereby, the warfare between Death and Allah, is really just a ruse for the true warfare between the nations and Allah. If there was no fight before, there is definitely about to be one now.

"Fear Not They Which Can Destroy the Body"

At the point when the Lamb opened the fifth seal (6: 9-11) the souls (*psychikos*) of those who were unjustly murdered for the sake of Allah and for their testimony cried out to Allah for justice, for vengeance, and for revenge. It is here that Death and Hades, having already prepared for warfare, and having gathered and assembled their various armies and captives, appear to have been challenging the very sovereignty of the Messiah. Basically, having already conquered and overcome every principality and power of the astral plane, the Messiah was clearly now preparing to conquer and overcome every government and territory of the physical plane – the last perhaps being that of Death himself. It could be, or at least was very likely hoped to have been, that by his conquering of Death the Messiah would thereby have crystallised all his victories; lest having overcome in both the astral and the physical he end up surrendering them all to Death.

Therefore the stage was now fully set for the great battle of Death and Hades; even as the prophet Isaiah exclaimed in his own scroll of governmental prophecies: "And in this mountain shall the Lord of hosts make unto all people a feast of fat things, a feast of wines well refined. And he will destroy in this mountain the face of the covering cast over all people, and the veil that is spread over all nations. He will swallow up death in victory; and the Lord God will wipe away tears from all faces; and the rebuke of his people shall he take away from off all the earth: for the Lord hath spoken it."

The Messiah's final victory over Death would thereby allow for the freeing of the captives belonging to both Death and Hades, and the clothing of them with the clothing of Allah's people. The white robes given to them were to symbolise a sealing of righteousness and give them a place among those who would come later, at the opening of the sixth seal. These suffering and executed martyrs were here clothed in what were essentially white *djellabas* and white abayas, each of them washed in the bleach of the blood of the Lamb. There was believed in this gesture to have been found enough satisfaction to help them overcome the adversity and captivity they were then suffering. These symbols would have all been seen as images of hope to the messianic communities that were enduring persecution from the then Imperial State.

But persecution from imperial powers is nothing new, the scrolls of Daniel and the scrolls of Maccabeus are filled with them. Yet our hope takes on new bounds when we return again to the prophet Ezekiel's astral drama, "Thou shalt fall upon the mountains of Israel, thou, and all thy bands, and the people that is with thee: I will give thee unto the ravenous birds of every sort, and to the beasts of the field to be devoured. Thou shalt fall upon the open field: for I have spoken it, saith the Lord God. And I will send a fire on Magog, and among them that dwell carelessly in the isles: and they shall know that I am the Lord." However, within our modern situation a new level of persecution and torture through psychological methodologies, deserves some significant recognition. The growing reality within colonial systems, and within the current neo-colonial manifestation of the GUSE, is that torture is inescapable so as to maintain political hegemony. But whereas in ancient times they tortured the body and put the body through the extremities of physiological pain, now they torture the mind and create ever newer means of psychological pain.

The political and, indeed, philosophical dimensions of modern torture reveal that the problem is deeper than the use of implements to cause pain; it is found in the ruling ideas of the imperial state. Acculturation methods, with the ruse of integration hopes, are applied to foreign countries with the distinct expectation of isolating and removing any form of political challenge to the imperialist agenda. Disciplining of any defiance to the imperial doctrine is, of course, the essential aim of the neo-colonial state. However, the use of torture under the pretext of what Lou Turner called "enhanced interrogation techniques" for the purpose of coercing compliant behaviour, calls the ethical superiority of the entire imperial edifice into question.

To further explain the realities of the tortured Turner spoke of how, "To break down his resistance, police or military personnel arbitrarily round up ten to a dozen local residents and torture five or six of them to death while the suspected insurgent observes. After several homicidal tortures, the real interrogation begins. According to this method, torture, indeed murder, is used as an agent to condition the response of a detainee and also as a ruse for the dual concealment of the official nonknowing of intelligence and the possible knowing of official nonknowing by insurgents." These extremes to which the state is willing to go to maintain its form of hegemony are problematic as they do more to radicalise individuals than police them. At the same time, torture is a standard procedure within the context of any warfare. Thereby, with this legitimation tactic the use of such enhanced interrogation methods to break *suspected* resistance in fighting their Wars on Terror, Wars on Drugs, Wars on Crime, and various other nondescript wars becomes de-problematised.

Fanon took the argument even further by breaking down the forms of torture used by the imperial power during liberation struggles such as what occurred in Algeria. The first category of torture he spoke of was, what he called "preventive tortures." "We here refer to brutal methods which are directed towards getting prisoners to speak rather than to actual torture. The principle that over and above a certain threshold pain becomes intolerable takes on here singular importance. The aim is to arrive as quickly as possible at that threshold." In these cases, Fanon explained, the interrogator would use methods such as, "Injection of water by the mouth accompanied by an enema of soapy water given at high pressure"; "Introduction of a bottle into the anus"; and "Two forms of torture called 'motionless torture' in which the interrogated are placed in incomprehensible positions requiring movement but should such movement occur they are instantly attacked."

Fanon further articulated how the repercussions of using such methods on some people, who, "Being tortured night and day for nothing seemed to have broken something in these men. One of these sufferers had a particularly painful experience. After some days of useless torturing, the police came to realize that they were dealing with a peaceable man who knew nothing whatever about anybody in an F.L.N. network. In spite of being convinced of this, a police inspector had said: 'Don't let him go like that. Give him a bit more, so that when he gets out he'll keep quiet.'" Clearly, the man was already broken and there was no need for any added humiliation, however, power rarely cares for the needs or pains of those it inflicts with suffering.

Fanon also spoke of a third form of torture, which came about through the imperialist collusion with the medical establishment, "When dealing with a patient who seems to suffer from an unconscious inner conflict which consultations do not manage to exteriorize, the doctor has recourse to chemical methods of exploration. Pentothal, given by intravenous injection, is the most common serum used to liberate the patient of a conflict which seems to be beyond his powers of adaptation." Yet, if with "neurosis pentothal sweeps away the barriers which bar the way to bringing to light an interior conflict, it ought equally in the case of Algerian patriots to serve to break down the political barrier and make confession easier for the prisoner without having recourse to electricity; [even as] medical tradition lays down that suffering should be avoided".

This technique was extremely deceptive, as, though it appeared to be saving the tortured from the physical threat of more severe forms of torture, such as electricity, it still produced psychological traumata within the minds of its victims. Fanon explained that what would happen as a result of using this typology of interrogation was that "the patient [would] not even know whether he has given any information away. [Thus, the] sense of culpability towards the cause he was fighting for and his brothers in arms whose names and addresses he may have given here weighs so heavily as to be dramatic. No assurance can bring peace to these broken consciences." Still, such extreme forms of modern interrogation do bear modest similarities to the forms of torturing used against the early messianic movement during the days of Roman imperialism. These tactics were all applied in the hopes of coercing from the disciple a renunciation of the Messiah and of the kingdom of God.

Then again, if we consider the more up-to-date Black American struggle of our own time: as a result of the hopes generated by the Civil Rights movement and the few wins that had transpired therefrom, many Black people believed that the hegemonic powers were finally starting to concede defeat. However, Huey Newton and the Black Panther Party of the 1960s-80s were not in the least deceived by White supremacy's weakened, yet completely unconquered, position. Singh exclaimed concerning their situation that "even as the legal edifice of segregation was being dismantled by government decree, a much more enduring structure of 'spatial apartheid' had been made visible by its inscription into the urban landscape. In this sense, the vision of the ghetto as an internal colony, or perhaps better, a neocolony, was not simply an analogy. As James Blaut argues, although ghettos clearly lack the ability to press for self-determination as 'politico-geographic units,' [they actually] define the relations of exploitation and oppression that govern relations with dominant power. These relations, moreover, are defined in rigid, socio-spatial terms, because ghettoized/colonized areas are excluded from sharing in social/global surpluses."

Nevertheless, ghetto culture as it stands now is no culture at all; it is in fact capitalism on a hyper and massive scale. Their clothes are more expensive and so are their cars; their jewellery is bigger and their home accessories are flashier. Pretty much everything they buy has to be great or hyped up. It is a hypercapitalism to the extreme. Therefore, for the sake of thearchy we of the godbody culture have for the most part come to see that ghetto capitalist culture is not representative of our reality or of our desire. Effectively, even as Black Panther leader Linda Harrison also said:

> *"We have no culture but a culture born out of our resistance to oppression. No colonial system draws it justification from the fact that the territories [and people] it dominates are culturally nonexistent. You will never make colonialism blush for shame by spreading out little known cultural treasures under its eyes' (quoted from The Wretched of the Earth)."*

So, our counter-culture as a godbody movement must, of necessity, be an anarcho-Islamism even as the current culture of the GUSE has decayed into a Christo-fascist culture. With the devolution of Charismatic Prosperity Theology into a Christo-fascist ideology the dangers ahead are that this Christo-fascism is not only manifesting among the American Republicans but even among the American Democrats. This danger, however, is not from the people as such, but from the leaders, who, for the most part, have adopted the Charismatic view that the inerrancy of the Bible means that only the prosperous are blessed of God, and that any disabled, sick, physically, mentally, or financially othered grouping or person is obviously cursed or abandoned by God. Moreover, with America being the wealthiest, strongest, most powerful nation in its own eyes, God is thereby obviously with them as a people and as a country.

But these Christo-fascist tendencies have existed in America for years. According to Hayes and Kiene, "In the late 1960s, the Black Panther Party gained national attention as an organization of defiant young Black men and women committed to resisting by any means necessary what Malcolm X had called America's White power structure [i.e. White fascist tendencies]. Emerging within the crucible of the Black power movement, these urban revolutionaries symbolized the rejection of Martin Luther King, Jr., and the civil rights establishment's sterile theorizing and ineffectual strategies of nonviolent civil disobedience in the Northern setting. Viewing urban Black communities as colonies occupied by a system of hostile White police, the Panthers fearlessly contested the power of the state to brutalize Black citizens." Indeed, Singh also contributed that, "In developing their [own] brand of 'third worldism,' the Panthers turned to what was by far their most important ideological resource, the writings of Frantz Fanon."

Herein, what we can understand is that Fanon was a major influence on the Panthers in their desire to resist American neo-colonialist annexation. Essentially, "Although he [did employ the] Marxian theory of revolutionary change, Fanon [still] pointed out that it had to be sufficiently refashioned to fit the colonial situation. He contended that anticolonial insurrection emerged in the countryside and filtered into the cities by means of the peasantry or the [underclass] who resided at the urban periphery" (Hayes & Kiene 2005: 160). This aspect of Panther theory, their alliance and siding with the underclass – their considering them to be the revolutionary section of society – was new and powerful. It instilled in the ghetto people a sense of destiny away from the streets. They could see that they were on a mission against a powerful and unbeatable behemoth, a Great United States Empire (GUSE) that cared nothing for them and took few prisoners.

Obviously, for those who have not read Fanon, he is not for the faint of heart. Indeed, like myself, he is and can be a very difficult read for many, particularly those from the hood (ghetto), who for the most part are, if not uneducated, usually undereducated. According, again, to Singh, "Fanon's relevance was by no means immediately evident to the Panthers themselves. David Hilliard, for example, candidly recalls the feelings of self-loathing and futility brought on by his many frustrating attempts to make sense of Fanon's complex prose. Yet Hilliard also tells of his perseverance and increasing excitement as he began to understand new concepts and ways of thinking about the Black experience in America in the discussions of Fanon's writings in the Party's political education classes." Again, through Fanon the Panthers were able to see the relevance of the frequent ghetto uprisings that were transpiring in those days as the spontaneous violence of the colonised fighting against their colonisation.

Moreover, Singh further continued, "The Black Panther Party, though it never developed a comprehensive urban theory or strategy ... was nevertheless the product of [an] emergent understanding of the socio-spatial logic and politics of ghettoization. Once again seizing upon Fanon's work for appropriate concepts, the Panthers emphasized the colonizing, as opposed to the strictly national aspects of ghettoization, and identified Fanon's lumpen proletarian [underclass] as a ghetto archetype and the most 'spontaneously revolutionary' agent of the Black struggle in the overdeveloped world." It would be through this theoretical basis that the Panthers were able to find connections between the liberation struggles going on in Vietnam, Latin America, and parts of Africa, effectively, the colonised world or so-called Third World, and the liberation struggle going on in the urban streets of Oakland, Chicago, New York City, and Boston. Through neo-colonialism, what should have simply been urbanisation, became to Black America ghettoisation.

Based on this understanding and outlook the US police were not seen as protectors or keepers of the peace but as a fascist troop sent to the ghettos of the GUSE to undermine any radical resistance. In effect, through their studying and understanding of Fanon, the Panthers could perceive the coming of "urban revolt [and so] embraced the Black ghetto as the basis of a renewed and very different kind of Black radical vision: the site of a radically dispersed Black nation and the model of the internal colonization of America's Black people. Reappropriating ghettoized spaces from the pathologizing discourse of social science, Black liberation politics instead figured the ghetto as a place of 'irredeemable *spatial* difference' within the nation-state, irrecuperable to unifying temporal narratives of national belonging and citizenship."

Based on this narrative of national citizenship police officers, as a manifestation of the national-state, currently claim their authority is due to their duty and obligation to protect all US communities, further claiming that they will only enter and patrol them in a respectful manner and for their own safety. But they prove they are not obliged to make any Black communities feel safer or they would stop arresting and murdering innocent Black lives for such simple things as playing with toys or sleeping in their beds. They are actually making only one group of people feel safer in this society, White people. But who are they saving White people from?

As any keen observer would be able to put together, the police are sent to our communities to protect White people from the frustration and disillusionment of the underclass. In order to reach the many with the order of the few, terror, intimidation, brutality, and murder are the tactics the police use and have been using. Who suffers? You and I suffer. To them we are the ones that may get out of line; we are the ones that may rage against our exploitation; we are the ones with a revolutionary tendency and nothing to lose by fighting them. In the long run, the police, as pawns in this modern bourgeois society will be the main force used to block any movement within our communities by arresting any members of our communities that show any signs of nonconformity.

Even so, within the current underclass has arisen the super-gangster movement. Having myself been a member of the movement's foundational gang, the Crips, I can say with all honesty, I loved being a Crip. It is for this reason that I believe, not only does Pantherism, but even the super-gang movement, have and has something incredible to offer to godbodyism. While, true indeed, the philosophy, ideology, and lessons of the godbody are without doubt unquestionable. At the same time, the super-gang culture and lifestyle is definitely worth emulating. Here I would like to encourage my godbody brothers and sisters to seek to form an alliance with the super-gangsters, thereby we can both learn from and move with each other as two powerful underclass movements.

True, we, the underclass, currently fill up the jails and prisons of America, whether by bad or good "citizens." Prison as a whole, however, is filled with three kinds of "criminals": those who are inherently incorrigible and anti-social, who commit crimes for nothing but the rush; those that Huey Newton called "illegitimate capitalists," who have conformed to the ideas and ideals of the system but see no legitimate means of survival within it but to break its laws; and finally, political prisoners, who have a major problem with the system and its ideals and take direct actions to change or challenge it, it is this action that landed them in prison.

Illegitimate capitalists and political prisoners can be either apologists or fanatics based on their state of mind. For example, a terrorist in prison may think what they have done was right, they are political prisoners, but their thinking is fanatical. However, there are terrorists that seek to explain their actions and justify them to those outside of their circle, these are apologists for themselves and others like them, either way a terrorist is a political prisoner, even though they should be punished for the evil of what they did.

Furthermore, on the subject of snitching, two very important points must be understood immediately: (i) Snitching only applies to those who use government power, force, and institutions to punish, persecute, or otherwise profit from someone belonging to one of those second two categories of "criminal" mentioned earlier. (ii) A woman using the same government power, force, or institutions against a rapist, paedophile, physical abuser, child abuser, or a man that literally shot her in a car, is hardly a snitch. She is a survivor. If we must employ terminologies like snitch and informer, which I believe we should, we must not dilute their meaning by using them against innocent women that survived traumatic horrors and experiences we could never possibly understand being perpetrated against them by those they trusted.

Effectively, prison is supposed to be for the anti-social, but anti-sociality can come in many forms. The most obvious is violating the law, but one who is anti-social and commits a crime in their anti-sociality, does deserve to be punished for it, even though the penitentiary system can itself be a form of psychological torture in its own right. See, the modern state exists as the only body that holds a legitimate monopoly on violence; and the most prominent symbol of state violence, in our time, is the penitentiary system. Prior to the founding of the penitentiary in the 18th century the symbols of state violence were the whip and the chain.

Prisons, at that time, were merely holding facilities before trial; and punishments were usually state orchestrated corporal punishments such as beatings, amputations, mutilations, placement in the stocks, or being drawn. Having a monopoly on all legitimate violence meant, back then, that these acts of state-sponsored violence were public spectacles that would leave a flesh wound on the body, hence, the name corporal. However, around the 1750s many reformists believed that a more civilised form of punishment would be the carceral form, where people could be put in a quiet location to think about what they had done and the harm they had caused. This, it was believed, would lead to penitence and thereby reform the convicted into an upstanding citizen.

Since those days carceral punishment has become not only legitimised but normalised. Even to the point that society is unable and unwilling to think of non-carceral measures of dealing with deviance. The strongest case for carceral punishment comes from the carceral feminists who say that men who abuse or rape women must be locked away and kept from harming others in the future. This legitimation of carceral punishment fails to see passed the societal gendering of prisons as male or to appreciate the nightmare of female incarceration. True, there is a far greater quantity of males incarcerated. Still, those women that do get locked up face many problematic scenarios as a result of their sentencing.

Even before their sentencing women have to face the sexual abuse of the strip search, in which officers and nurses search every cavity of their bodies: vagina, anus, and mouth, with their fingers. Male officers have even been known to grope vaginas, chests, and buttocks in sexually suggestive ways while on duty; and these are regular occurrences for women in jails and prisons.

On top of that, there are the numerous reports of sexual harassment and vaginal, anal, and oral rape from correction officers. More importantly, they are unable to escape from their abusers being imprisoned by them. I can attest from my own experience on Rikers, correction officers were well known for taking advantage of inmates' vulnerable position to acquire sexual favours from them. This is due to public unawareness and officer vilification of the inmates, hypersexualising and fetishising them.

But we still have not addressed the fear of the carceral feminists. What do we do with all the rapists and paedophiles? This is a loaded question, but it is also a misconception of the situation. These labels used to dehumanise and demonise these people allow us to forget that everybody has a shadow side, and we are all capable of untold atrocities given the right circumstances. By demonising these people as inherently evil and not the victims of circumstances that occurred in their lives to corrupt them, we fail to notice or deal with what creates rapists and paedophiles. Herein, the problem is not the individual (as in them being inherent evil), the problem is in the current system of modernity.

The very popular copaganda circulating throughout society is that prisons are to protect "good people" from the "bad people," usually coded as Black people. This creates the idea that prison is only filled with those who deserve punishment. The police, therefore, like your typical Marvel superhero, save innocent people from these "evil villain" ghetto people. This black and white way of thinking couples the idea of the Black criminal with that of the supervillain and not with that of the misled or misguided human being, capable just as much of good as they have been of negativity. Thereby it also justifies the state's and the law enforcer class' monopoly on violence as ordinary people are potentially too evil to be allowed to use violence at their own discretion.

In all, to envision a world without state-sponsored violence we must first envision a world without the traumatising and distorting realities of carceral punishment. To do this we must now understand, with Angela Davis, that prisons will not be replaced by one all-encompassing solution but with several interconnected solutions. These solutions are: (i) decriminalising all currently illegal drugs and substances. To go with this the allowing of all users that wish to quit easy access to the best programmes and counselling, including Narcotics Anonymous, with which to do so. The example here would be American prohibition. By legalising all forms of alcohol, they put an end to those lucrative criminal enterprises and the mob violence they entailed.

(ii) Decriminalising all forms of consensual sexual performances, including: all forms of public nudity, all forms of consensual sexual public performances, and all forms of consensual sexual media performances. If a woman or a man chooses to provide any form of sexual favours with their own body as a compensation for a given product or service, such is their prerogative. Along with this, teaching, training, and guidance on sexual preferences, performances, and potentials should be provided to all young people as they mature, as well as guidance in sexual safety and contraceptives for all precoital, coital, and postcoital experiences. Finally, the institutions of marriage and divorce should also be abolished in the process, thereby allowing for new forms of relational and intimate interaction to be developed. All this will go a long way in eliminating the need or desire to rape or molest anybody.

(iii) Organising and establishing meeting grounds that are based on livelihood or employment within all neighbourhoods, workplaces, and universities to create social accountability, and to determine service capability. All this will go a long way in eliminating the need or desire to resort to deviant behaviours. (iv) Abolishing all forms of monetary compensation and monetary valuing. Compensation should thereby be through products and services, but the system itself should determine actual compensation through form of employment. All this will go a long way in eliminating the need or desire to steal anything. (v) Establishing a fighting ring as the new form of punitive justice, the rules of which can be decided by the community.

Now, the question: what about rapists and murderers seems somewhat moot. With the abolition of money and decriminalisation of all drugs there will be no reason to kill anybody. Also, with the decriminalisation of all forms of consensual sexual performative there will be no need to rape or molest anybody. With no monetary means of valuing products and persons no individual or group will feel their work is of higher or lower value than others. With punitive justice turned to a more humane form of corporal punishment than tortures, whippings, amputations, and mutilations the psychological trauma of internment and the hyperincarceration complex of the United States can be abolished. Again, prison and state abolition in our time is as unimaginable as slave trade and slave labour abolition were in their time, but it can definitely happen if we are willing to fight for it.

Furthermore, if we consider now the words of Abron, she perceived concerning the formative days of the Black Panther movement, "The 1966 version of the BPP ten-point Party platform included two demands concerning the United States criminal justice system. Point 3 demanded, 'We want freedom for all Black men held in federal, state, county, and city prisons and jails.' In a similar vein, Point 9 demanded, 'We want all black people when brought to trial to be tried in court by a jury of their peer group or people from their black communities, as defined by the Constitution of the United States.' In the early days of the organization, the Party informed community residents of their constitutional rights." These sorts of Panther initiatives allowed the Panthers to gain massive credibility in the

Black communities of America, especially considering that the American government has always harassed and criminalised Black bodies.

Nevertheless, there is still in our time the hope for a new form of social organisation coming about in the global South. Especially in Africa, where modernist dreams have only become the disillusioned nightmare of repressed activism. US neo-colonialism and the American Christo-fascist order have set the pace for the agenda of Black people, whether in the continent or the diaspora. According to Nye, "More than four centuries ago, Niccolo Machiavelli advised princes in Italy that it was more important to be feared than to be loved. But in today's world, it is best to be both. Winning hearts and minds has always been important, but it is even more so in a global information age." Effectively, it is not enough to have military might and weaponry, not enough to have superior financial and technological capacities, not enough to have strategic and tactical advantage, if you are perceived to be unjust or oppressive you will still be hated, period.

To explicate this situation Nye provided the perfect evidential arguments, noting, "For example, in terms of resources the United States was far more powerful than Vietnam, yet we lost the Vietnam War. And America was the world's only superpower in 2001, but we failed to prevent September 11." It is for this cause that he also stated, "The United States may [currently] be more powerful than any other polity since the Roman Empire, but like Rome, America is neither invincible nor invulnerable. Rome did not succumb to the rise of another empire, but to the onslaught of waves of barbarians. Modern high-tech [Islamists] are the new barbarians." What he was saying was that it is important for America to read the signs, the writing on the wall. True, America has historically had numerous preachers, satirists, academics, activists, and politicians predicting their downfall. Maybe they really thought the end was near, maybe they just wanted to advise or humble America. Either way, America's true fall, if it is to ever have one, will be due to its lack of tact and subtlety in appreciating global perceptions of it.

The powerful American behemoth, oddly enough, in many cases, finds itself in conflict with much weaker, and much less technologically or strategically advanced peoples. Like the barbarians in the times of Rome, they seem embarrassingly outmatched and outgunned, yet in a lot of cases (shockingly, more than the American public are aware of) America loses either a decisive victory or an instrumental ally. But, how could any plucky, yet ambitious, country rival the Goliath that is America, especially on the military stage? Here, perhaps, the problem is in the question. Many of America's greatest defeats occur, not because they or their allies lose on the military stage, but because America is not perceived to be a noble player fighting for noble reasons on the global stage.

America is unfortunately perceived to be, as stated in the original question, a Goliath. It is an effectively overpowered monster in the eyes of most people, therefore worthy of getting its head chopped off. Again, the perception of America, to the outside world, is based largely on how America perceives itself, but is subverted in all the areas where it would want the opposite. It is this subversion that distorts most people's views of America's intentions in many ways. What do I mean? Since the 1950s, America has been becoming a global force and participating in the global conversation. Moreover, they have also sought, sometimes covertly, sometimes overtly through force of arms, to overthrow any government that refuses to submit to them. They have also forced any government that *is* willing to submit to do so either monetarily or contractually. To the American people and their government these may all seem to reinforce their idea of "American exceptionalism," but outside of America they are seen as demonstrations of political bullying, deceptive bribery, self-interested greed, media manipulation, and the spreading of immoral consumerism.

This image is more outside of Western spaces than within them. The problem in these situations is not that the ideal of America is not loved: an ideal represented in things like sports; Hollywood; hip hop, and most Black music genres; Amazon and most other online companies; social media and digital media; Smartphones and smart technology; AI and ML; and the various American counter-cultures. This America really resonates with most people all over the world. But juxtapose that with the American government, then it all goes pear-shaped. Many non-Americans would literally rather die than allow the American State to get even a foothold in their country, regardless of the political and economic benefits that could be gained.

From this premise we can see why most non-Americans currently believe that all the martyrs and saints that they see and know are suffering – or may have even lost their own lives, fighting to overthrow this system (that is itself understood by them to be a neo-colonialist monolith) – will one day bring about the eventual *eschaton* of this very system. Many of those victims of the current American Christo-fascist order, are, and have usually been, Islamic in orientation; some of them are *even today* still suffering in torture facilities as a result of the former War on Islam. We must therefore come to understand that our victory in dismantling the various structures of modernity comes about, firstly, through intellectual debate. As all new systems start off in the philosophical realm and then organise into movements so as to bring about social change; even so our own theoretical system of mental and bodily decolonisation will have to continue as such until the time of thearchic activism, when warfare, both intellectual and possibly martial, will be unleashed.

Even so, there is, or at least once was, a tradition within the godbody movement that spoke of a legal and martial harassment that was to come later upon the Black community, and particularly upon the godbody communities. It was believed that this event would be instigated by the United States government eventually leading on to our internment, isolation, torture, and even attempted genocide. Well, such an event may be transpiring before our very eyes right now with the current persecution of Muslims throughout the United States. Yet even despite this tradition we in the godbody presently lack any formal or universally recognised doctrine of death; let alone an understanding of it or of its intricacies.

Not that this book intends to explain or unravel any of its mysteries. Nonetheless, as a contribution, or at least a beginning, so as to lead the way towards the future development of a much more comprehensive adaptation, this book suggests that we borrow and reimagine from the super-gang culture our own, "Divine Army Chant:"

> *"If I should die, feel no shame; my soul will enter,*
> *the astral plane.*
> *So put the peace sign, across my chest;*
> *and tell the parliament, I did my best."*

While this may be a rather simple, and even simplistic, chant, originally created by the Crips due to the ever present reality of death among those in the gang life; it still contains a lot more subtlety than we or they have ever appreciated. Therefore, at least as a beginning to a much more comprehensive and satisfying understanding on our part: of death, life, and the afterlife, it is here being suggested that we adopt this ritual to be expressed at the close of all our ciphers and parliaments. This should also hopefully prepare us for the development of an authentically godbody funerary interpretation, as a God or Goddess enters the astral plane to dwell among the ancestors as themselves now becoming one of the ancestors (regardless of the age when they pass).

The Prophet of Islam shared a similar eschatological vision with his own people. Here, the word we call tribulation in the English language is called *Fitnah* in the Arabic, and it is believed in Islam that there will be six *fitnahs*. The Prophet said, "Enumerate six signs which will occur in close proximity to the Hour – 1) my death; 2) the conquering of Constantinople; 3) death that will take you like the barber of sheep (takes hair from them); 4) an abundant flow of wealth until a man receives 100 dinar yet still remains dissatisfied; 5) a trial that will not leave a single house from the Arabs except that it enters it; 6) then there will be a truce between you and the children of the yellow ones." Each of these signs of the Hour could be called a *fitnah*. Moreover, they, to a degree, also coincide with the various signs of the times in early messianic beliefs.

Yet the Prophet also said, "Between the creation of Adam and the arrival of the Hour, there is no *Fitnah* greater than the Dajjaal." Again, as we stated earlier, the *Dajjal* is the Islamic Anti-Christ, so it was believed in Islam that the *Dajjal* would rise from among the "yellow ones" (symbolic in those days for the Caucasians) and make war with the Muslims. It was further believed that during this warfare he would come to sign a truce with them but would break it halfway in and go right back to war. All this would thus inspire the Messiah (*al-Masih*) to return and defeat the *Dajjal*, basically killing him and all the armies of those willing to go to war for him. What we see therefore is that Islam understood that the Messiah would return, and that there would be a Divine Parousia, but only after the Great Tribulation (or *Fitnah al-Akbar*).

Still, anyone who takes a stand against the iniquities and inequities of the modern system will always find themselves called into question or persecuted as a criminal or extremist for their troubles. This will invoke arrest, torture, or even murder at the hands of a state machine that is said to serve the people. Again, this state machine, being based on a two-party, bureaucratically run, demagogically mandated, chaotically reinforced mechanism; is able to repress and transgress in the name of freedom. Freedom, thus, has become a watered-down excuse and cover for persecution of dissension. Any opinion that runs counter to the hegemony of the GUSE and its modernist agenda is callously targeted for exclusion and tribulation. We know this for sure: US neo-colonialism, in its current form as globalisation, is everywhere prevalent. The GUSE has military bases in virtually every country on the planet. One thing is for certain, imperialism is very much so still alive in our world today.

The Voice that Shakes the Earth

Following the opening of the sixth seal (6: 12-7:17) great and wondrous cataclysms occurred both in the earth and in the heavens. All that could be shaken was shaken, that which was called "the wrath of the Lamb" was unleashed, and all people were held to account for the various sins they had perpetrated. The entirety is reminiscent of where it was written in the epistle to the Hebrews, "See that ye refuse not him that speaketh: for if they escaped not who refused him that spake on earth, much more shall not we escape, if we turn away from him that speaketh from heaven: Whose voice then shook the earth: but now he hath promised, saying, Yet once more I shake not the earth only, but also heaven" (Hebrews 12: 25, 26). It is herein that the great Day of Vengeance prayed for by the martyrs of Allah is finally revealed, and the Lamb will get his revenge for all the blood that had been spilt by the ungodly against his people.

It is also here that the astral vision foreseen by the prophet Ezekiel finally comes to its desperate conclusion: "And, thou son of man, thus saith the Lord God; Speak unto every feathered fowl, and to every beast of the field, Assemble yourselves, and come; gather yourselves on every side to my sacrifice for you, even a great sacrifice upon the mountains of Israel, that ye may eat flesh, and drink blood. Ye shall eat the flesh of the mighty, and drink the blood of the princes of the earth, of rams, of lambs, and of goats, of bullocks, all of them fatlings of Bashan." "And it shall come to pass in that day, that I will give unto Gog a place there of graves in Israel, the valley of the passengers on the east of the sea: and it shall stop the noses of the passengers: and there shall they bury Gog and all his multitude: and they shall call it The valley of Hamon-gog."

For even though these Scriptures ultimately confirmed the following word spoken beforehand by the prophet Zephaniah, "Hold thy peace at the presence of the Lord God: for the day of the Lord is at hand: for the Lord hath prepared a sacrifice, he hath bid his guests. And it shall come to pass in the day of the Lord's sacrifice, that I will punish the princes, and the king's children, and all such as are clothed with strange apparel" (Zephaniah 1: 7, 8); the people of the early messianic movement would most likely have interpreted all this to be both an exaggerated and a distorted representation of the Armageddon War. (For the Armageddon War was believed by many to be a coming struggle in which the Thearchists – which in our time would be referring to the Islamists – went into battle with what, at that time, was presumed to be the Hellenists (that is, the Greeks); but as we can see was really supposed to be the empire of Gog, the last imperial power, representing the Hellenic empire).

So again, who is the real Gog and where is the real Magog? To answer these questions, we must consider again the imperial power in the world today, the power most likely to be a hindrance to the coming of Allah and of his thearchy. As for the man Gog himself, he will actually be the person that drives the world forces into battle with the bringers of the thearchy. The astral and physical warfare that occurs as a result will therefore be eschatological, even to the point that the dead will not be given a proper funeral but will be left out in the streets for the animals and birds to devour. The early messianic movement experienced this kind of Crusade against them, perpetrated by

Nero Caesar when he began his imperial witch hunt of the early messianic communities.

The knowledge of governmental persecution was, again, very apparent to first century messianism, which faced death for their confession of devotion to messianic authority. In those days, the messianic movement was itself condemned as what we would call in our day a terrorist movement. The godbody movement of today has a similar restriction, we therefore will very likely face a similar attack from media onslaught to what they faced. Here tragedies like war, famine, death, and the spectre of Hades (hell), will all represent plagues sent by Allah to judge the world, and particularly the GUSE, for their persecution of us godbodies, particularly those of us that are Muslim. But before Allah can pass his final judgment on the world, he will first send out an astral being, with "the seal of the living God," for the purpose of sealing those he has preserved for glory.

The prophet Ezekiel gave an even clearer picture as to what effectively qualifies someone for such an honour, but this time in a completely different astral vision from the first, stating:

> *"He cried also in mine ears with a loud voice, saying, Cause them that have charge over the city to draw near, even every man with his destroying weapon in his hand. And, behold, six men came from the way of the higher gate, which lieth toward the north, and every man a slaughter weapon in his hand: and one man among them was clothed with linen, with a writer's inkhorn by his side: and they went in, and stood beside the brazen altar. And the glory of the God of Israel was gone up from the cherub, whereupon he was, to the threshold of the house. And he called to the man clothed with linen, which had the writer's inkhorn by his side; And the Lord said unto him, Go through the midst of the city, through the midst of Jerusalem, and set a mark upon the foreheads of the men that sigh and that cry for all the abominations that be done in the midst thereof. And to the others he said in mine*

hearing, Go ye after him through the city, and smite: let not your eye spare, neither have ye pity: slay utterly old and young, both maids, and little children, and women: but come not near any man upon whom is the mark; and begin at my sanctuary" (Ezekiel 9: 1-6).

Obviously, there are many who will disdain this type of language and instantly think, "How do we know the mark on those who mourned and cried for Jerusalem is not, in fact, the mark of the Beast?" For anyone with this sort of question I have given it a greater treatment in chapter 15. For now, however, know that the language is of very little significance. The mark on those who wept and mourned in Jerusalem is not likely to be the mark of the Beast as Allah does not tend to condemn those that are suffering. In fact, the Messiah said that such were blessed, saying, "Blessed are they that mourn: for they shall be comforted" (Matthew 5: 4). Hereby, the mark spoken of here, in the context of the prophet Ezekiel's vision, is in fact very likely to be the seal of the living God, in the context of the apostle John's vision.

This seal was to be a sign and proof of affiliation to the people of Allah, given to those who, like those that mourned at the abominations of Jerusalem, look at the world today and hunger and thirst for a day when it will actually be righteous. Essentially, the seal of Allah was understood to be more than merely an awkward mysticism or some backward traditionalism, but a transcending of both mysticism and traditionalism. Indeed, the stuff that dreams are made of. For even as Queen Makeda of Sheba said in Solomon's Song of Songs, "Set me as a seal upon thine heart, as a seal upon thine arm: for love is strong as death; jealousy is cruel as the grave: the coals thereof are coals of fire, which hath a most vehement flame" (Song of Solomon 8: 6). Yet the Hebrew word used here for love was the word *ahab*, which, though, true indeed, can be defined as love, is not so much the love a person has for their friend or sibling, nor even the love a soldier has for their people. *Ahab* mainly, though not exclusively, denoted love in the libidinal sense, as in romantic love.

On the other hand, the Hebrew word used here for jealousy was the word *qinah*, a word that actually comes from the root word *qana*, and means zeal or passion, not jealousy in the sense of wanting what someone else has, or bitterness over a lover's so-called betrayal. It only got mistranslated as jealousy due to a misinterpretation by certain Greek translators over the years. Still, these issues are only being brought up, not so much as to encourage people towards being more erotic, or to say that women are not allowed to be celibate, or again, to say that we godbody do, or even should, force our female members to give it up more. The issue is being brought up mainly because – though marriage may be generally rejected within the godbody movement, eroticism and romance are not – eroticism, far from being condemned by Allah, was always, in actual fact, the very seal of fidelity to Allah. Indeed, the very first commandment he gave to humanity in the beginning was "Be fruitful, and multiply" (Genesis 1: 28).

Most people have been bought up with a view that eroticism is carnal and unspiritual, that romance is even profane and vulgar, but what the Song reveals, and Genesis confirms, is that romance plays a much more vital role in Allah's plan than has so far been presumed. That is not to say that other interpretations of the seal do not exist. Ephesians 1: 13, 14 says: "In whom ye also trusted, after that ye heard the word of truth, the gospel of your salvation: in whom also after that ye believed, ye were sealed with that holy Spirit of promise, Which is the earnest of our inheritance, until the redemption of the purchased possession, unto the praise of his glory." So, the seal could simply be a reference to the holy Spirit: thereby making what was said later in (14: 4) a lot clearer, especially as it is written there concerning those with the seal of Allah on their foreheads, "These are they which were not defiled with women; for they are virgins. These are they which follow the Lamb whithersoever he goeth. These were redeemed from among men, being the firstfruits unto God and to the Lamb."

The seal of Allah, thus, apparently, being the seal of the Holy Spirit, appears here to have no connection to the seal of passion, let alone of eroticism, spoken of in the Song of Songs; but given a closer inspection the two actually do coincide. The apostle Paul wrote for the messianic communities of Corinth, "Would to God you could bear with me a little in my folly: and indeed bear with me. For I am jealous over you with godly jealousy: for I have espoused you to one husband, that I may present you as a chaste virgin to Christ. But I fear, lest by any means, as the serpent beguiled Eve through his subtilty, so your minds should be corrupted from the simplicity that is in Christ. For if he that cometh preacheth another Jesus, whom we have not preached, or if ye receive another spirit, which ye have not received, or another gospel, which ye have not accepted, ye might well bear with him." When it said in Revelation that those sealed were virgins, it was most likely speaking in this symbolic sense, as in having no other Jesus or Spirit to corrupt them. But in that sense, the holy Spirit alone could hardly be the seal of Allah, as the holiness spoken of there is undefined. What represents the *true* holy Spirit if there are false ones that are able to beguile us?

First of all, I am not suggesting that the true Holy Spirit is erotic as such; however, the seal – which was strong as death – does appear to be such. For there is a distinction between eroticism and lust: the central difference being refinement. Thereby, even a counter-cultural articulation like hypereroticism could be appreciated as holy through the subterranean artistry of transfigured deviation. It also effectively refines *all* forms of erotic act-species, such as the wearing of transparent *djellabas* and abayas, as practices performed to demonstrate holiness. Herein can also be identified the significance of the Hebrew word *qodesh*, as it originally delineated both a classy and a sexy definition for the concept of holiness, even as such would have been understood during the days of the early messianic movement.

Even Frantz Fanon expressed – with regard to his endorsement of the appropriation or re-appropriation of identifiable traditional markers – that such practices be encouraged as forms of anti-colonial resistance, saying, "In the Arab Maghreb, the veil belongs to the clothing traditions of [the women of] the Tunisian, Algerian, Moroccan and Libyan national societies. ... In the case of the Algerian man, on the other hand, regional modifications can be noted: the *fez* in urban centres, turbans and *djellabas* in the countryside" (Fanon 2006: 100). Ultimately, wearing the type of clothing that was traditional to the early messianic movement, particularly the type that we in our day would call hypererotic, distinguishes for us, demonstrably, the holy from the unholy, the clean from the unclean.

Nevertheless, for those who feel that such a definition is far too simplistic for the Most High Allah to recognise, I will proceed to remind you of the covenant that Allah made with Abraham of circumcision, the covenant Allah made with the Baptist of water baptism, and the covenant Allah made with Muhammad of the hijab. The covenants of Allah all have an element of bodily counter-cultural performance. Indeed, within Allah's requirements there is always an enactment of body-politics, a performance of corporeal flesh, that thereby signifies refinement and distinction.

Accordingly, the Holy Spirit of the first century was most likely considered nothing more than a manifestation of erotic class and refinement; and definitely not an inhibitor or disorganiser of words and behaviours. Our self-expression thereby should be a manifestation of our own divinity, as it is based on a classy and sexy spirit, and not a possessed or possessing spirit. In this manifestation it abolishes and destroys all pre-conceived ideas, thoughts, and notions, and impresses itself upon our sexuality. Thus, also actively removing any mental inhibitives and bodily performatives based on the acculturating of ourselves to our surrounding environment. In our day it would be that which demodernises our mind and body through the acceptance of hypererotic and hypermartial honourability.

At the same time, all this has not been an entirely honest account: when (14: 4) spoke of the seal on the forehead of the hundred and forty-four thousand, what it actually said was that Allah's name was written on their foreheads. Basically, it was supposed to be Allah's very signature: and Allah's signature historically has always been some kind of demonstration of power. So, the actual question should now be: what was the significance of the forehead with regards to the seal of Allah? The only apparent answer could be that this is the location of our third eye. The signature of Allah was thus always to be the opening of our third eye, thereby allowing for us the ability to see into the astral plane at will. This truth is hereby apparent in that the Lamb that walked with them had seven eyes. Still, like with all signatures there is always a double signing. The godly sign up with hypererotic classiness (and possibly also with the practice of what I call light exhibitionism, the refusal to wear underwear), and Allah himself signs back with the opening of their third eye.

But herein can also be seen – after that the godly, both male and female, have signed themselves up to this classy and sexy lifestyle, and Allah has signed back by giving them astral vision and other supersensory abilities – that things really start to get heavy as the world now prepares to meet Allah himself at the Day of Judgment. It may therefore be asked at this point: what could those abominations possibly have been that would drive anybody to sign up to adopting a hypererotic seal like light exhibitionism in the first place even if they are classy? In order to answer this question, we must first try to remember that this sixth seal of the book of Allah, as well as the four preceding, also represented both the sixth trumpet and the sixth vial of the wine of the wrath of Allah. Whereby, to gain a better understanding of the sixth seal, particularly in its relation to the sixth vial, we will now consider what happened later on, with the outpouring of the sixth vial.

The apostle John said concerning the pouring out of the sixth vial, which represented the wine of the wrath of Allah, "And the sixth angel poured out his vial upon the great river Euphrates; and the water thereof was dried up, that the way of the kings of the east might be prepared. And I saw three unclean spirits like frogs come out of the mouth of the dragon, and out of the mouth of the beast, and out of the mouth of the false prophet. For they are the spirits of devils, working miracles, which go forth unto the kings of the earth and of the whole world, to gather them to the battle of that great day of God Almighty" (16: 12-14). The imagery painted in this is extremely clear, the warfare that has been looming throughout the course of the epistle is finally ready to transpire.

At this point, Allah prepares the way for the "kings of the east," but who are these mysterious kings of the east? To provide a level of clarity I will now say, the Latin word Orient, in its original definition, meant both rising (as in "of the sun") and the east. How this Scripture would therefore have been read in the Vulgate (Latin Bible), was, "the kings of the Orient." Again, when most of us nowadays think of the Orient we tend to think of China, Japan, Korea, and the Far East. However, this is very unlikely how the early messianic communities – especially considering that it was the Euphrates River that dried up, a river that is nowhere near modern China, Japan, or the Far East – would have interpreted it or would have been meant to interpret it. Remember, the Euphrates is in Babylon in modern-day Iraq, therefore, when the Revelation here said, "the kings of the east," or "the kings of the Orient," the most likely meaning the apostle John intended was the kings of the Near East.

It is also clear at this point that these kings were not intended to be of any royalty, nobility, or aristocracy; the issue at stake was with the wielding of political power. Therefore, we see that it was believed within the early messianic movement that an alliance of Oriental governments, which in our time would most definitely be Islamic governments, will be set and prepared on the one side. At the same time, on the other side, based on what the Scriptures just pointed out, the unclean spirits of the dragon, the Beast, and the false prophet will go out to "the kings of the earth and of the whole world." Herein, we should now be able to see that in this great warfare it will be a case of the Islamic governments, on one side, and the governments under the power of the empire of Gog and Magog, on the other side, when "he gathered them together into a place called in the Hebrew tongue Armageddon" (16: 16).

At this point you should already understand: the governments of the earth (the geo) and of the whole world (the cosmos) being under the power of the Great Empire, were always destined to go to war with the Islamic nations of Allah. Effectively, the West has been fated to go to war with Islam and their rivalry against Islam has been of long standing. Though, historically, there have been great Crusades, several of them; this particular Crusade predicted here was always set to be something different. This Crusade was to be after the time of the Great *Dajjal*. In this case, geographical and geopolitical forces will be driven by the cosmic and cosmological forces of the Dragon, the Beast, and the false prophet, to gather together against the so-called Orientals, to engage in warfare with very Allah in a place in Israel called Tel Megiddon. Tel Megiddon is a geographical area located in the valley of Jezreel where the kings of Israel historically built their palaces. The War of Tel Megiddon, at least in the minds of the children of Israel and Judea, was supposed to be a demonstration to the world of the wrath of Allah: when Allah would judge the nations of the world, those led by Gog and Magog, by the hand of Israel and Judea.

Particularly, if we consider post-exilic theory, the Judeans understood that the armies of the world would all be gathered to do battle against Allah and against his people. They believed, effectively, that, "In that day shall the Lord defend the inhabitants of Jerusalem; and he that is feeble among them at that day shall be as David; and the house of David shall be as God, as the angel of the Lord before them. And it shall come to pass in that day, that I will seek to destroy all the nations that come against Jerusalem. And I will pour upon the house of David, and upon the inhabitants of Jerusalem, the spirit of grace and of supplication: and they shall look upon me whom they have pierced, and they shall mourn for him, as one mournest for his only son, and shall be in bitterness for him, as one that is in bitterness for his firstborn. In that day shall there be a great mourning in Jerusalem, as the mourning of Hadadrimmon in the valley of Megiddon."

So, what is so significant about this valley of Megiddon? In order to fully understand its significance, one must know its biblical history. It was written in the Bible, "And Elisha the prophet called one of the children of the prophets and said unto him, Gird up thy loins, and take this box of oil in thine hand, and go to Ramoth-gilead: And when thou comest thither, look out there Jehu the son of Jehoshaphat the son of Nimishi, and go in, and make him arise up from among his brethren, and carry him to an inner chamber; Then take the box of oil, and pour it on his head, and say, Thus saith the Lord, I have anointed thee king over Israel. Then open the door, and flee, and tarry not." The reason this young prophet the prophet Elisha was sending had to immediately flee after sharing this message was that in a technical sense it could have been used against him to say that he was a conspirator and an instigator of treason, which was then, and still is in some places, a capital offence.

Now when the young prophet found Jehu he was sitting among the captains of the army, he himself being a commander among them, so the young prophet took him into a secret place and did as the prophet Elisha told him to do. When Jehu returned to the captains and told them what the young prophet had said, they immediately bowed down, then they gathered all their troops in preparation for a coup against the house of Ahab. Not too long after storming Samaria, killing the then King Joram of Israel and the then King Ahaziah of Judea, they sent word to Jezebel's servants and eunuchs that if they threw Jezebel down from her place they would be spared their lives. Sure enough, they did exactly what they said, and Queen Jezebel died instantly. Having thus taken over the royal palace, which, as noted, was in the valley of Jezreel, Jehu sent letters to the rest of the house of Ahab: seventy princes that also lived in Samaria, giving them all an opportunity to gather their forces and take back the palace. When they all openly surrendered, Jehu effectively named himself King of Israel and thus founded the Nimishi Dynasty.

One of the first things King Jehu did was then proclaim a celebration for his great victory, even as the event is recounted in the IV Book of Kings, "And Jehu said, Proclaim a solemn assembly for Baal. And they proclaimed it. And Jehu sent through all Israel: and all the worshippers of Baal came, so that there was not a man left that came not. And they came into the house of Baal; and the house of Baal was full from one end to another. And he said unto him that was over the vestry, Bring forth vestments for all the worshippers of Baal. And he brought them forth vestments. And Jehu went, and Jehonadab the son of Rechab, into the house of Baal, and said unto the worshippers of Baal, Search, and look that there be here with you none of the servants of the Lord, but the worshippers of Baal only. And when they went in to offer sacrifices and burnt offerings, Jehu appointed fourscore men without, and said, If any of the men whom I have brought into your hands escape, he that letteth him go, his life shall be for the life of him."

So that day King Jehu massacred all worshippers of Baal that came to the temple of Baal in Jezreel to worship, he also destroyed all the images of Baal and all his statues. For doing this Allah promised Jehu that his dynasty would be established, however, he also told him that for the genocide by which he destroyed them, his dynasty would only last for four generations. Herein, it came to pass that when the fourth generation finally arrived the word of Allah came to the prophet Hosea telling him to marry a promiscuous woman – possibly even a prostitute – by the name of Gomer, "So he went and took Gomer the daughter of Diblaim; which conceived, and bare him a son. And the Lord said unto him, Call his name Jezreel; for yet a little while, and I will avenge the blood of Jezreel upon the house of Jehu, and will cause to cease the kingdom of the house of Israel. And it shall come to pass at that day, that I will break the bow of Israel in the valley of Jezreel" (Hosea 1: 3-5).

To be sure, this historic event has already transpired, way back in 722 BCE with the fall of Samaria, when the Neo-Assyrian Empire officially colonised the Northern Kingdom of Israel. However, that was never intended to be the end of the matter, as the prophet Hosea said later on, "Then shall the children of Judah and the children of Israel be gathered together, and appoint themselves one head, and they shall come up out of the land: for great shall be the day of Jezreel." This was clearly an event that the prophet Ezekiel further confirmed when he said, "And I will set up one shepherd over them, and he shall feed them, even my servant David; he shall feed them, and he shall be their shepherd. And I the Lord will be their God, and my servant David a prince among them; I the Lord have spoken it. And I will make with them a covenant of peace, and will cause the evil beasts to cease out of the land: and they shall dwell safely in the wilderness, and sleep in the woods."

Consequently, just as the prophet Jeremiah prophesied a New Testament, even so the prophet Ezekiel was here prophesying a Testament of peace (or of *Islam*); reassuring those who came after that it would be David who would bring this testament of Islam to us. What can hopefully be discerned therefore is that the War of Tel Megiddon was expected to be different from what most people today have theorised. It is, in fact, most likely to be a war between the anarcho-Islamists and the Christo-fascists, due to the unclean spirits of false prophets, each working signs – which could themselves be technological, scientific, and even military marvels – to inspire them to go out into warfare with the people of Allah and very Allah himself. But what did the Messiah have to say about these events, "Behold, I come as a thief. Blessed is he that watcheth, and keepeth his garments, lest he walk naked, and they see his shame" (16: 15). All of which sounding pretty simple enough, but the wording is actually a gross mistranslation.

In order to give this Scripture a more perfect – or at least a more accurate and true to context – translation, I shall here translate each word of the second sentence, one by one: Blessed (*makarios*: which can translate to beautiful, happy, blessed, great, wonderful, or beatific). Is (*esti*: which can translate to is, are, or be). He (*autos*: which can translate to self, he, she, him, her, us, or they). Watcheth (*gregoreuo*: which can translate to aware, awake, woke, or vigilant). And (*kai*: which can translate to and, but, though, if, that, then, so, or too). Keepeth (*tereo*: which can translate to guard, delimit, prevent, or prohibit). His (*hautou*: which can translate to self, his, her, our, their, or them). Garments (*himation*: which can translate to apparel, fashion, clothes, clothing, or covering). Lest is not in the original texts but was most likely added or edited in to give a level of coherence to their corrupted translation. They (*autos*: which can translate to self, he, she, him, her, us, or they). Walk (*peripateo*: which can translate to live, follow, walk, or go about). Naked (*gymnos*: which can translate to train, exercise, practice, course, or naked). And (*kai*: which can translate to and, but, though, if, that, then, so, or too). They (*autos*: which can translate to self, he, she, him, her, us, or they). See (*blepo*: which can translate to gaze (upon), look (upon), perceive, or regard). His (*hautou*: which can translate to self, his, her, our, their, or them). Shame (*aschemosyne*: which can translate to indecency, immodesty, improperness, impropriety, or inelegance).

Based on these more honest word translations we can hopefully develop far more accurate sentence translations of the words spoken by the Messiah. For example: "Great are the self-aware that keep self-covered, they follow the practices and self-perceive their indecency." Or "Beautiful are they and Woke, who prohibit haute fashion; they live naked, though some gaze at their immodesty." Or "Wonderful is the Self, the vigilant one that guards; the Self, a covering, the Self, alive and naked; though the Self looks upon our inelegance." Or, finally, "Blessed be they, the awakened, that delimit their clothing when they follow this course, for they look so haute, (never) improper."

Though any one of these could make for a more contextually strong translation, suiting more accurately the actual context of early messianic practices, I suppose if I had to choose an even more precise translation for this particular text, one that would also prepare its readers to be sealed with a sexy and classy holiness, I would probably combine a few of them together to produce: "Beautiful are the self-aware that delimit their clothing: they go about naked, though some gaze at their immodesty." Why I say that this makes for a more precise translation is that the apostle John (whose surname was Marcus; see Act 12: 12 and John 19: 26, 27), was clearly, at one time, the author of Revelation, and obviously also, clearly, the most likely author of the gospel of Mark.

Accordingly, however, it is in this gospel that he included a story that may seem out of place if read inappropriately, "And there followed him a certain young man, having a linen cloth cast about his naked body; and the young men laid hold on him: And he left the linen cloth, and fled naked" (Mark 14: 51, 52). What was the purpose of adding this anecdote to his narrative about the Messiah's arrest? The best possible reasons could be, firstly, to reveal the clothing tradition of the early messianic movement: that some of them wore very Afro-chic clothing, such that would wrap-around their naked bodies. Secondly, to reveal the very truth that they were naked underneath such Afro-chic clothing (that is, that they were what I have spoken of as light exhibitionists). Thirdly, as a form of personal testimony, as who else could have possibly known the details of such an obscure story but the very author himself?

Nevertheless, at the same time, we could obviously also say with Littlewood, "A nude man and a nude woman embody [two] rather different images. The man without clothes carries a heightened sexual potential, almost a threat of rape. At the same time [this] nudity partakes of nakedness, 'stripped for action', a prosaic extension of his conventional working role. If the naked man is a self-determining subject, the undressed woman becomes an object, for men. ... [Yet, despite this truth, the] nudity of the female Earth People directly challenges this notion; like the men, they aim at being naked for themselves" (Littlewood 2006: 172) and it is here that my vision of the armed and martially trained Goddess begins to fully take shape.

Here, through the practices of light exhibitionism, sexual train running, and free love, the Black Goddess ultimately attains to a total and absolute independence from men, and even from what I call the Victorian monogamous patriarchal standard. Moreover, anarchist Malatesta made the very interesting point about this free love, "Do you think that enslaved love could really exist? Forced cohabitation exists, as does feigned and forced love, for reasons of interest or of social convenience; probably there will be men and women who will respect the bond of matrimony because of religious or moral convictions; but true love cannot exist, [cannot] be conceived, if it is not perfectly free." Effectively, any choice a Goddess makes to be with a man, or with men in general, should essentially be a decision she makes free from any coercive factors: whether they be those coming from societal pressure to be married and have children; or those coming from the implicit threat of some form of male dogmatic, domestic, economic, or sexual abuse.

In all, what will most likely be the real War of Tel Megiddon? It will most likely be a warfare between the anarcho-Islamists and the Christo-fascists over the land of Israel. The Christo-fascists are at current the Baal worshippers idolising a false god in the form of Jesus Christ. The anarcho-Islamists, on the other hand, coming with the message of the thearchy of Allah, who exists as al-Muhibb (the Libidinal) will manifest their God through the acts of seductionism, militarism, and light exhibitionism. Herein, the war itself is over who will be God in Israel: will it be Jesus Christ or Allah. To the Christo-fascists it will and must be Jesus but to the anarcho-Islamists the only God is Allah and the Messiah was only his messenger. Therein we can see that the Christo-fascists have only been vexing themselves, destroying themselves, subjugating themselves, and handing over control of the earth and of the whole world to the uninhibited powers of Gog and Magog. Accordingly, whereas the dominant empire previously had to deal with the wrath of the Lamb, now they are about to experience at full strength the inviolable wrath of very Allah himself.

Judgment Day as Declared by the Prophets

When the Lamb opened the seventh seal (8: 1-5) silence gripped the heavens for about a half an hour. This prolonged silence was not one of worship or duty but one of intensity. And then it was unleashed: the wrath of Allah longly waited for fell upon the earth to try the hearts of all Allah's enemies. Here they were now standing face to face with their greatest fear and their greatest judge, themselves. The uncleanness and injustice of their ways had been hidden from all creation, and nothing on earth knows a person like they know themselves. As they were now able to see themselves in all their filthiness, all their vanity, all their corruption, all their weakness, and all they had caused to happen within the world; if they could look on and still see the good behind the veil of Death, then, when their destiny to an eternity with likeminded individuals is fully understood, they will actually praise Allah for the final outcome.

However, for those who see failure, misery, shame, and disappointment; that see ruin, sin, and a wasted life and devotion. For them there will be horror, plague, and the unending feeling that when Allah destines them to an eternity of likeminded individuals they are and will effectively be missing out on the fulness of Allah's capacity. Moreover, for such individuals there will also be the understanding that suffering and plague will never come to an end; that they, indeed, are eternal. In this case, even the future they had believed they were striving for had always been a misreading; so that now, surrounded by likeminded, and therefore also jealous and unfulfilled, people, they fully understand the wrath of Allah. When all the voices, and the terrors, and the thunderings, lightnings, and earthquakes have come to pass on earth, and there is nothing left on earth to stand on that cannot be shaken, it is in that moment that we must run to He who cannot be shaken, and running to him we know that he sees us and has always seen us as we truly are.

In the day that the baby bird is about to take to its first flight it calls out to, and can call out to, none other than he who is the Most High Allah. When the war-horse or chariot charges into battle, there is only one who it prays to for victory. When the rain-clouds gather, and the storms brew, there is only one whose command they await. When the rivers rush toward an aggressive coast, or are parched for lack of supply, there is only one who they depend on for strength and support. When the strong winds threaten to rip the tree from its place, or to dash the rocks and mountains with a mighty blast, only one gives them comfort and eases their fears. When the mountain lion is hungry, and becomes famished from the hunt, she stretches out her hand to no lower being. When the mountain goat is pregnant on the hills, and in pain to be delivered, she cries out to no lesser power for the deliverance of her kids. When the crocodile storms through the swamps, and takes his seat in the cloudy marsh, there is only one whom he fears, and only one to whom he does obeisance. When Shaitan is lifted up in victory, and in pride of his mighty haul, there is only one who makes him tremble, and only one who makes him submit.

In the final analysis, when humanity is through with all its fighting, and all its arrogance, and all its vanities, they too will have to stand, alone, before his judgment seat; and they too will have to give an account to none other than Allah, the Beneficent, the Merciful, the Ruler at the Day of Judgment, the Lord of all the Worlds. Yet for those who remain unconvinced, assuming that this is all just a Islamisation of biblical or Christian ideas, just remember that Islam itself was the Prophet Muhammad's attempt to, first of all, remove the various vain superstitions from the culture of his people. Second, to decolonise the minds and bodies of his people from the influence and fear of the various imperial powers surrounding Arabia. Third, and most importantly, to restore to his people a connection to their Abrahamic heritage, which may at that time have been forgotten or lost due to centuries of superstitions, on the one hand, and centuries of Falashic and Imperial Christian influence, on the other.

Essentially, the Islamic movement the Prophet Muhammad led and instigated was always a noble movement that had always been inspired by Allah, again, with the central intent to restore the authentic Abrahamic culture. True indeed, anyone who actually, genuinely does their research will find that the proper Semitic/Falashic name for God given to Abraham in the beginning was actually the name: Allah. Moreover, the proper Hebrew name for God given in the Masoretic Bible (the supposedly authentic Bible) was never properly Elohim. Elohim in the Hebrew language is a plural for God, as in, gods. But even if we now say, alright, maybe a correct translation or transliteration is Elah, again, we find clearly a distortion. The truth is, the proper name of the God of the Hebrew Bible was always, and has always been, Allah. Furthermore, during the days of the New Testament: when the Baptist and the Messiah spoke to the people, the then common language was neither Hebrew nor Greek. The common language in the Israel and Judea of their time was Aramaic, which is another Semitic language. Now Aramaic is also a language still spoken in Palestine to this day by various Palestinian Christians, and what is the name they, in Aramaic, use for God? Again, it is Allah.

Allah is and has always been the name of the Hebrew God from the time of Abraham to the time of the Prophet Muhammad. Muhammad did not make the name up, or develop it by combining this concept with that idea. If anyone made up the name it would have been Abraham, yet even this is questionable. The fact is, Allah is the name of the God of the Hebrew tradition, as noted, from the time of Abraham to the time of Muhammad; a truth that actually gives newer and greater meaning to a Scripture heavily, and intentionally, misinterpreted within Christianity: "And I will pour upon the house of David, and upon the inhabitants of Jerusalem, the spirit of grace and of supplication: and they shall look upon *me* whom they have pierced, and they shall mourn for him, as one mournest for his only son, and shall be in bitterness for him, as one that is in bitterness for his firstborn. In that day shall there be a great mourning in Jerusalem, as the mourning of Hadadrimmon in the valley of Megiddon" (Zechariah 12: 10, 11; emphasis mine).

The one Allah had prophesied that was supposed to be pierced was never meant to be the Messiah, though the apostle John purposely led his followers to believe that. It was not that the apostle John lied, or was even purposefully trying to deceive, but that the original message of the Messiah was always one leading to Allah, in which the God of the Messiah, again, in Aramaic: Allah, was the true and rightful king of his announced thearchy. Even the Prophet had written in these Quranic verses, saying, "The Messiah disdains not to be a servant of Allah, nor do the angels who are sent to Him. And whoever disdains His service and is proud, He will gather them all together to Himself. Then as for those who believe and do good, He will pay them fully their rewards and give them more out of His grace. And as for those who disdain and are proud, He will chastise them with a painful chastisement, and they will find for themselves besides Allah no friend nor helper" (Quran 4: 172, 173).

At this point we can see that the only wall left for the Islamophobic to hide behind is overt self-denial; for anyone, after knowing that they have been emphatically wrong and corrupted, who persists in their own corruption is doomed to experience nothing more than the chaotic existence of perpetual hopelessness. Worse still, "if we sin wilfully after that we have received the knowledge of the truth, there remaineth no more sacrifice for sins, But a certain fearful looking for of judgment and fiery indignation, which shall devour the adversaries. He that despised Moses' law died without mercy under two or three witnesses: Of how much sorer punishment, suppose ye, shall he be thought worthy, who hath trodden under foot the Son of God, and hath counted the blood of the covenant, wherewith he was sanctified, an unholy thing."

The apostle Paul further stated along these lines, "Now this I say, brethren, that flesh and blood cannot inherit the kingdom of God; neither doth corruption inherit incorruption." Thereby revealing that the kingdom of God (or, again, in our own case, Black thearchism), is not for the corporeal, nor is it itself corporeal. Indeed, the Divine Parousia of the Messiah may not even in itself be a corporeal Parousia. It may in fact of necessity be an astral Parousia. A lot of believers, nowadays, love to say how the Messiah will fix all the world's problems at his Second Parousia, when Allah has already given us the means to fix everything that needs fixing right now thanks to the First Parousia. Further, as was also said concerning the Second Parousia: "the Lord himself shall descend from heaven with a shout, with the voice of the archangel, and with the trump of God: and the dead in Christ shall rise first: Then we which are alive and remain shall be caught up together with them in the clouds, to meet the Lord in the air: and so shall we ever be with the Lord" (1Thessalonians 4: 16, 17).

Now the apostle Paul had already said that flesh and blood do not inherit the kingdom of God, also the word he used here for "air" is the word *pneuma* which can also translate to spirit, so this was clearly not considered by him to be a corporeal resurrection. Considering these things a little more thoroughly perhaps the best way to answer this Scriptural question is by going deeper into further Scriptures. The apostle John provided us with an answer to the riddle that has far more depth and weight to it, "After this I looked, and behold, a door was opened in heaven: and the first voice which I heard was as it were of a trumpet talking with me; which said, Come up hither, and I will shew thee things which must be hereafter. And immediately I was in the spirit: and behold, a throne was set in heaven, and one sat on the throne. And he that sat was to look upon like a jasper and a sardine stone: and there was a rainbow round about the throne in sight like unto an emerald. And round about the throne were four and twenty seats: and upon the seats I saw four and twenty elders sitting, clothed in white raiment" (4: 1-5). All this was an experience the apostle John recounted of his own enrapturement, of the hereafter, and of heavenly bliss, yet all entirely *astral* in manifestation, as everything that happened took place while he happened to be "in the spirit," that is in the *pneuma*.

At the same time, this biblical Scripture also presents us with a completely uncommon description of the Ancient of Days and his divine ones from the current White images shown around the world today (seeing that jasper is in fact a reddish brown colour very similar to mahogany and sardius is in fact an orange brown colour in sight very similar to varnished oak). The picture the apostle John seems to have painted here was thereby a picture of Black deities. So now, how do we make sense of this reality? Jose Malcioln becomes most helpful in this instant, especially in his expressing this statement that our ancestors, "The Cushites, [the] fathers of all … black people … [were]

celebrated Cushite kings [and were] usually deified after death, and sometimes metamorphosed to be identified with the stars and constellations". Moreover, as he would further continue, "the Greeks often visited Africa when she abounded in glory, and referred to the Cushites [themselves] as gods."

So what is the godbody outlook of the Divine Parousia? To us it comes though Black people understanding the interconnection between the Black race, divinity, nobility, Africa, and theocentrism. Conversely, according to Boyce Rensenberger, "Evidence of the oldest recognizable monarchy in human history, preceding the rise of the earliest Egyptian Kings by several generations, has been discovered in artifacts from ancient Nubia in Africa." These Nubian people being highly civilised, classy, wise, and beautiful, were also excessively adventurous. Yet, "Once the Nubians traveled to other lands wearing as much gold jewelry as they did, people of paler skin began to visit Cush to trade." Thus giving us an idea of the wonder and impression these ancestors of ours must have had on those people outside of Africa. Indeed, the Parousia of the Gods and Goddesses of our time may not even be able to capture the realities of what our ancestors were really like in those times.

Malcioln further explained the aftereffects of the ancient interactions with these Nubian gods and goddesses, and in particular the Divine Goddesses, saying, "An unusual sight was the Nubian woman in her splendor and beauty. She was beautiful to admire as she approached, irresistible to behold when she passed and gracefully displayed her protruding buttocks. The Nubian woman did not require a crinoline petticoat or hoop-skirt with a wire cage to attract a man of good taste. And when the foreigners discovered that it was not necessary to put a pillow under her to obtain the peristaltic movements so gratifying in harmonious sexual relations, they sought her favors or took her by force."

To understand better the realities of what transpired during this process of Nubian (or ancient Ethiopian) development Malcioln continued, "As a result [of the violent and non-violent sexualisation of the Nubian woman], there are [now] fifty or more tribal groups with separate customs and looks. There are also about fifty languages spoken, and four times as many dialects." Consequently, "The original language group of Ethiopia was Cushitic. It was not until the first millenium B.C.E. that the Semitic people, called Habasat, entered Ethiopia from southern Arabia. ... [Ultimately], the Semitic-Ethiopic languages became Ge'ez, Tigre, Tigrina, Amharic, Argoba, Harari, Gurage, and Gufat." From these beginnings came the Kushite/Nubian people, who were the true fathers and mothers of civilisation, and the first true and living Gods and Goddesses of the planet. Now, any neighbourhood that thereby accepts this reality will also thereby experience, at that moment, the Divine Parousia, and from that moment begin to dwell in the body of God.

It is now, therefore, the declared intention of Black style godbodyism to overthrow all the existing forces of American style liberalism, and thereby to replace the existing rule of law with the literal rule of Allah. To be sure, liberalism will never willing lie down to godbodyism, it will therefore have to be overcome and overthrown. But this overthrowing need not involve terrorism or even coercion. The mature system (if it is really the desire of the people to call it that) is based on socially and theologically ethical people living to manifest their own divinity. This is not the liberalistic "rule of law," amounting to nothing really but the rule of the bourgeoisie; this is the thearchic rule of libido, effectively amounting to the rule of Allah.

Basically, the Day of Allah was to come after the Lamb had judged the nations of the world, led by Gog and Magog, by the hand of his once dispersed, and even now still dispersed, people of Israel in warfare. This Day of Allah, being therefore preceded by the Second Parousia of the Messiah, should not be considered interchangeable with it. At the same time, to the godbody the Divine Parousia is itself in accordance with Black individuals realising in their hearts that they and their ancestors are, and have always been, the true Gods and Goddesses of the planet earth. From that moment on they essentially will dwell in an actually existing millenarianism of poor righteous teachers of Black divinity. Still, the potential of this thearchy coming into the neighbourhoods of the world have already likely caused the rulers and governments of the earth and of the whole world, led by the empire of Gog and Magog, to prepare their own fight back in the form of an Armageddon War.

It is for this cause that Allah, again, said through his prophet Joel that there are, "Multitudes, multitudes in the valley of decision: for the day of the Lord is near in the valley of decision." If, indeed, this valley of decision was always intended to be nothing more than an allusion to the valley of Tel Megiddon, then we see that the decision to be made was, and has always been, the most ultimate decision. Will you allow Allah to overthrow all the false teachings and false deities in your heart, and thus accept the divinity of your own self and kind? If you choose the affirmative then, and only then, will come afterwards an individually experienced tribulation.

Nevertheless, the apostle Paul had this to say on the matter: "we must through much tribulation enter into the kingdom of God" (Acts 14: 22). The individually experienced tribulation they go through will obviously come as a result of state sponsored persecution, a persecution they endure because of the revelation they received of the Messiah in the *pneuma*. However, the Armageddon War comes when those persecuted during this Great Tribulation make the revolutionary decision to fight back against their persecutors, and it is only at that point that the people of Allah will finally be able to liberate themselves in the form of global war.

The Epistle of Revelation in Godbody Eschatology

Though we godbodies all claim cultural Islam, thereby practicing the *culture* of Islam, many of us look to inspiration from the Bible, and particularly from the epistle of Revelation. Indeed, the epistle of Revelation has legendary status for us among the other books of the Bible. Written most likely by the apostle John Marcus (Acts 15: 37) it contains very eschatological imagery. Although a large number of Christians, since the time of Eusebius of Caesarea have connected the Revelation to a an Elder John, Lizokin-Eyzenberg and Shir explained that the evidence for the authorship of the Revelation being by the apostle John is actually stronger than that of the Gospel of John, which was most likely written by a scribe skilled in Greek letters. The unlettered Judean apostle of first century Galilee obviously wrote the Revelation like any child of the ghetto writing in the traditional Judean apocalyptic style; using Greek to the best of his still relatively unlearned abilities. Regardless, the apostolic authorship of Revelation is the direction this book has taken.

In the Revelation John introduced three mythic characters, like any Greek comedy introducing its main villains: First, the Dragon, who is "called the Devil, and Satan, which deceiveth the whole world" (12: 9). This character is introduced as the primary villain, the one who opposes the hero, who is the Messiah. Second, the Beast, who ascended out of the bottomless pit, and goes into perdition. This Beast is called "in the Hebrew tongue ... Abaddon, but in the Greek tongue hath his name Apollyon" (9: 11). Third, Babylon the Great, who is "THE MOTHER OF HARLOTS AND ABOMINATIONS OF THE EARTH" (17: 5). Further, according to the apostle John, the Beast "shall hate the whore, and shall make her desolate and naked, and shall eat her flesh, and burn her with fire" (17: 16). Basically, the house of the villains is already a house divided against itself; this is what allows what would otherwise have been a tragedy to become a comedy.

However, it is not the hope or even the comedy aspect of the Revelation that the godbody adopted within its own eschatology, it is the language of Revelation that is more valuable to us than the visionary elements. Within the 1-10 of the godbody 120 lessons it is asked, "Who is the colored man? The colored man is the Caucasian White man, Yaqub's grafted devil of the planet earth." This answer is open to misinterpretation. Many have taken it to mean that we godbody see White people as evil and wicked because we see them as devils grafted by Yaqub. That is not the case. We see White supremacy as evil and wicked and the White people who follow White supremacy not as an absolute evil, but still as evil, yet only for that reason, as such, and not for being grafted.

Indeed, many White people take serious issue with being called the devil. Such language they claim as racist in its own right. To those in the Black community who buy into this garbage I wish to say: the oppressor never likes being called an oppressor; the exploiter never likes being called an exploiter; the victimiser never likes being called a victimiser; the abuser never likes being called an abuser; the misogynist never likes being called a misogynist; and the transphobic never likes being called a transphobic. The truth is that power rarely sees its oppressive nature as anything unnatural or unjust; it instead sees its power as very natural and justly earned. Hereby, we see the narratives

White supremacy has told itself to maintain power are based on a discourse of White superiority that justifies their right to power, their right to supremacy.

In many ways Cone shared a similar view and encouraged this perception for Black theology, however, he did not consider White people to be devils for their White supremacy. But if we consider where devilishment came from in the first place we get an understanding that what caused the devil to fall at the origin was a superiority complex: the devil felt superior to God and so fell, or the devil felt superior to Adam and so fell. Whatever way you look at it it was a superiority feeling and power imbalance that led the devil to become a devil. Well, the discourse of White superiority and the ideology of White supremacy are the current conclusions of devilishment. In other words, whether Black theology likes it or not, whether we appreciate it or not, White people will be the living devil until proven otherwise.

The godbodies take such a radical approach saying that as long as White supremacy exists in the world White people will be devils, this is because we know what oppression, exploitation, and victimisation look like, and in every case, it comes from a system created by them. The devilishment, however, is not in that the system was created by them, but that it not only heavily favours them, but undermines, oppresses, and victimises all that is other to their standards. This system also makes White people devils by giving them a heavily exalted unconscious opinion of themselves, while subjecting all other races to the threat of their social and systemic privilege being weaponised against them. Moreover, with White privilege having become unconscious through both biases and micro-aggressions being used without thought of hurt, repercussion, or public opinion, the devil, at least to us godbodies, is White people.

To us also, from among the White population comes the Anti-Christ (*al-Dajjal*), but there is also separately a Beast. Many of us view the *Dajjal* as a man, but the Beast as a system: the

Great United States Empire (GUSE). To many of us the *Dajjal* shall lead the Beast to war with the Black race, but the Beast is a system not a person. There are seven heads of the Beast according to Revelation, these are not problematic as such: they possibly represent the political ideals that America stood for and stands for. The Beast being the corruption of those ideals. The apostle John said, "the beast that was, and is not, even he is the eighth, and is of the seven, and goeth into perdition." The Beast was and is not: the was part is the seven heads, the is not part is what the US empire corrupted those heads into. In that sense it never was, as America never really lived up to the ideals it proclaimed it believed in. On an even more Meta level, the Beast that is not is the *Dajjal*, as he is not a head but is of the seven and "goeth into perdition."

But ultimately, to many of us, the GUSE is the Beast and the *Dajjal* rises from within the Beast as its strongest representative. Indeed, he could be called "America personified." In this sense, America is very important to the destiny of the world, as the last great empire it will play the biggest role in global events. Moreover, the Great Tribulation will feature the US persecuting Black people substantially, worse than they have persecuted us since the Civil Rights movement. At least, that was for a long time the belief of those godbodies that believed in the Great Tribulation or *Fitnah al-Akbar*.

Yet, there is another layer to the Beast being Imperial America that should be acknowledged, the belly of the Beast. In this understanding the belly of the Beast is not a country or person but the US prison-industrial complex. Just as the Beast is seen by many godbodies as the system of the GUSE, so the belly of the Beast is seen by these godbodies as the system of the prison-industrial complex. I know this because when I was locked up in prison, I heard many godbodies referring to our prison as the belly of the Beast. Here the eschatological symbolism was removed, and the language was based significantly on the so-called "now of eschatology." Again, being in the belly of any animal means being eaten. The metaphorical idea is that we were consumed and swallowed whole by the Beast (GUSE) and once vomited back onto the streets we would forever have a prison sentence tarnishing our record.

The final villain the apostle John spoke of in Revelation, that we godbody use in our language, is Babylon. In Revelation Babylon was likely either Rome or Jerusalem, however, to us Babylon is the US government and law enforcers. While many would call the police Babylon, following the Rastafarian ideas of Babylon, we would also call the FBI, DEA, SWAT, and USIB Babylon. We would even call the judges, lawyers, politicians, clergy, and professors Babylon. So, while to us the Beast is the system of the GUSE; Babylon, to many of us, is those who maintain the system, oppose street culture, and will oppose Black people as a whole during the time of the Great Tribulation.

As the Beast turns on Babylon so the system will turn on those who maintain it. Or to be more precise, a *dajjal* and his followers will oppose the timidity of the GUSE in its dealing with Black people, especially at the time that the Witness arises. But Babylon will fall, according to the Elijah Muhammad, and will be left without refuge. He said, "America hates the doers of good and seeks to destroy them. This is the cause of the fall of America." Moreover, he continued, "Never before America has there been a nation on the face of the earth where scores of murders take place daily and nightly. In one large metropolitan city of America, the death rate is terrific … children kill children … male is against male and female is against female, destroying each other."

A final terminology that the godbody use that is derived from the Revelation is the mark of the Beast. This mark, used in the Revelation to signify those belonging to the Beast and corrupted by him, indeed, those who worship the Beast and will partake of his judgment, is used by the godbody in a similar way. Those who have been influenced by the Charismatics say the mark of the Beast will be a computer chip, as that is what the Charismatics say. Those who have been influenced by the Jews say the mark of the Beast will be a Scripture or a corruption of the Scriptures (in their case, the Torah), as that is what Deuteronomy 11: 18 implies. Those who have been influenced by the anti-vac crowd say the mark of the Beast will be a vaccine, as such a reality seems very possible in our day. However, those of us who are learned know that the Hebrew name *Neron Qesar* (Nero Caesar) added up to 666, which was defined by the apostle John to be the real mark of the Beast.

Based on this idea there are a small minority of us who say that the mark of the Beast is belief in the White Jesus. This is based on a second opinion about the Beast: that it is the Roman Catholic Church. That is not to say all Catholics are evil or going to hell or anything that morbid, I myself am a practicing Catholic and a cultural Muslim – similar to the Mozarabs of Spain – this is to say that the Roman Empire was never really destroyed after its fall. In the first century, when the apostle John wrote the Revelation, the Roman Empire was still very strong and had no serious signs of ever falling. Yet Rome did fall in 476 CE. At that time all that remained of the Roman Empire was the Roman Catholic Church. But maybe that is it, the Catholic Church remained in Rome and maintained a system of clergy and church government similar to the fallen empire. In that sense, Rome never really did fall, as Catholicism remained. Then, with the return of empire in the form of the Holy Roman Empire, the Popes played a significant role in governing the masses.

However, around the time of the Renaissance something changed: around about that time the Catholics began painting Jesus as a White man. The first instances of this being during the Renaissance, it is for this cause that we consider the White Jesus to be the Beast that was, and is not, and never was. The White

Jesus was created by Catholicism and has corrupted everyone it has encountered. A bold statement but one that is proven by the realities of White supremacy. White supremacy could not have existed without the White Jesus. By painting Christ as a White man, they thereby defined themselves as God-people. There is obviously an irony here in that the godbody, by definition, consider Black people to be divine people; however, we do not define God as they do. To them God is defined by power, and power has always been used to determine White supremacy. To us God is defined by intelligence, hence why always read.

Those of us who call the White Christ the Anti-Christ (*al-Dajjal*) and the Roman Catholic Church the Beast say the battle between the Beast and Babylon – which we still say is America, in this case the Great United States Empire – is more likely a battle between Religion and the State. Hence, the kingdom of the devil (White supremacy) will be divided against itself. Again, all this may be fine and well, but was this really the interpretation the apostle John had in mind when he wrote the Revelation? Indeed, the White Christ and the United States of America did not exist to the apostle John so how could he really, in all honesty, have been writing to seven historical communities in the Roman province of Asia about these realities. Moreover, how do we go about finding the true interpretations that the apostle John had in mind when he wrote the Revelation? Who did the apostle John consider to be the Beast and is this in any ways related to what we godbody teach or have taught?

To find the apostle John's ideas of the Beast and his mark we must first go to (13: 18) where it says, "Here is wisdom. Let him that hath understanding count the number of the beast: for it is the number of a man; and his number is Six hundred threescore and six [666]". This is not the only time wisdom (*sophia*) is mentioned in relation to the Beast. As it said later on, "And here is the mind which hath wisdom. The seven heads are seven mountains, on which the woman sitteth. And there are seven kings: five are fallen, and one is, and the other is not yet come; and when he cometh, he must continue a short space".

As Lizokin-Eyzenberg and Shir (2021) noted, this can be open to a number of interpretations. Their personal interpretation is based on having seen a coin minted in the first century with an image of Emperor Vespasian on one side and an image of the goddess Roma on the other side sitting on seven hills. This evidence is compelling as the first century messianic communities would no doubt have seen this coin and would therefore be more familiar with this than they would have been with a White Christ or with the nation of America. In this sense, the seven mountains are the Seven Hills of Rome, and the seven kings could be interpreted as seven Caesars, seven marking the number of completion to first century Judeans.

However, there were actually twelve Caesars, so the "five are fallen, and one is, and the other is not yet come" quote becomes quite problematic to this interpretation. Also remember, this is for "the mind which hath wisdom," simplistic interpretations like that would therefore stumble the average reader but not the deep thinker. So, if it is not the Seven Hills of Rome and seven Caesars why is there such striking symmetry? The answer to this is found in (12: 1-5) where a woman clothed with the sun, and the moon under her feet, and a crown of twelve stars was with child and in pain at its delivery. Then a red dragon, having seven heads and ten horns stood in front of the woman to devour her child as soon as it was born. This story resembles uncannily the story of the Egyptian goddess Auset. Indeed, the cult of Auset was very popular throughout the first century Roman Empire. Yet it is unlikely he meant for the vision of 12: 1-5 to be interpreted as the story of Auset and her son Horu. Sometimes a little knowledge can be a dangerous thing.

In this case, two far more likely scenarios to have influenced the apostle John were (i) the apostle combining the Auset imagery to his relationship with the Messiah's mother: thereby imagining a dreaded women wearing a twelve point tiara; also having a pregnant body while wearing a topless, fine-spun, golden-orange, African wrapper known as a *Kaftan*; and having her own brazen orange feet standing atop a white circle. (ii) Solomon's Song of Songs where Queen Makeda of Sheba said of herself, "I am black, but comely, O ye daughters of Jerusalem, as the tents of Kedar, as the curtains of Solomon" (Song of Solomon 1: 5), and where, moreover, it was said of her, "Who is she that looketh forth as the morning, fair as the moon, clear as the sun, and terrible as an army with banners?" (Song of Solomon 6: 10). Here, the sun-kissed Queen of Sheba represented the African queen of heaven, carrying many of the symbols used by the apostle John in his Revelation.

So, like with any modern-day rapper that uses a quadruple entendre, the apostle John hid several layers of meaning within the words he used. Not to mention the Author that masterminded the entire visionary sequence. Thereby, the mind which hath *sophia* would have known: the Bible, as a whole, speaks of six mountains that were used by six prophets – five are fallen, and one is, and the other is not yet come. The six mountains that were fallen were Mount Horeb, Mount Zion, Mount Moriah, Mount Carmel, Mount Samaria, and Mount Olivet. The six Kings were Moses, David, Solomon, Elijah, Amos, and Jesus. Based on this picture it is easy to see who the seventh head is, Muhammad, and the mountain is Mount Hirah. Furthermore, within this list there is great chiastic symmetry.

A1. Mount Horeb – Arabian Mountain
    B1. Mount Zion – Davidic Mountain
        C1. Mount Moriah – Religious Mountain
            D. Mount Carmel – Prophetic Mountain
        C2. Mount Samaria – Religious Mountain
    B2. Mount Olivet – Davidic Mountain
A2. Mount Hirah – Arabian Mountain

Herein, the head of the seven that was fatally wounded was not Jesus but Muhammad, as he is the prophet that has been excluded from all Roman Catholic doctrine and ideas.

So again, the question now becomes, was this the apostle John's intention? If you take the author of the Revelation to be the author of the Gospel of John, then something quite interesting becomes apparent. There is a story in John's Gospel that is in no other gospel, which is about a Samaritan woman at a well. In it, "Jesus saith unto her, Go call thy husband, and come hither. The woman answered and said, I have no husband. Jesus said unto her, Thou hast well said, I have no husband: For thou hast had five husbands; and he whom thou now hast is not thy husband: in that saidst thou truly" (John 4: 16-18). We can be sure of two things from this quote, firstly, John was not present when the Messiah had this conversation with the woman, secondly, it is unlikely that the Messiah ever told anybody, whether privately or publicly, what he actually did say to that woman. If that is the case, why did the apostle John say that that was what the Messiah said? To interpret to those with wisdom the mystery of the Beast.

The clue is when the woman said, "Our fathers worshipped in this mountain [Mount Samaria]; and ye say, that in Jerusalem is the place where men ought to worship." Obviously, this interpretation falls apart if the author of the Revelation was not the author of the Gospel of John, so it is up for debate. The more common interpretation of the seven mountains being the Seven Hills of Rome has higher symbolic value: in this case Babylon is Rome and the Beast is the Roman Empire. But if this book is correct then who really is Babylon? Is the Beast really the great prophets of history? And are these ideas not a stretch, even a blasphemous stretch? The answer is found, again, in Revelation, "And the beast that was, and is not, even he is the eighth, and is of the seven, and goeth into perdition." The seven heads are not evil as such; it is the corruption of them by the

Beast that makes them evil. Hence, the apostle John most likely did have in mind the corruption of the Messiah into something that he was not when he wrote about the Beast, thereby making the White Christ a very likely candidate for the Anti-Christ.

The Messiah himself also finalised this point, saying, "When ye therefore shall see the abomination of desolation, spoken of by Daniel the prophet, stand in the holy place, (whoso readeth, let him understand:) Then let them which be in Judea flee into the mountain" (Matthew 24: 15, 16). The apostle Paul, however, gave an even more in depth interpretation, saying, "Let no man deceive you by any means; for that day shall not come, except there come a falling away first, and that man of sin be revealed, the son of perdition; who opposeth and exalteth himself above all that is called God, or that is worshipped; so that he as God sitteth in the temple of God, shewing himself that he is God" (Thessalonians 2: 3, 4). Clearly, when the "son of perdition" takes his seat in the temple of God telling himself that he is God that will be the abomination of desolation spoken of by the prophet Daniel.

Having said all that, let us look more closely at the actual section of the apocalypse of Daniel to see what it said and what the prophet Daniel really believed would be the fate of the Great *Dajjal*: "the ships of Chittim shall come against him: therefore he shall be grieved, and return, and have indignation against the holy covenant: so shall he do; he shall even return, and have intelligence with them that forsake the holy covenant. And arms shall stand on his part, and they shall pollute the sanctuary of strength, and shall take away the daily sacrifice, and [put in its] place the abomination that maketh desolate" (Daniel 11: 30, 31). Clearly, the sanctuary of strength is where the Great *Dajjal* sets up his abomination of desolations, so that now the question becomes: where is this "sanctuary of strength"? Where is this "holy place," or this "temple of God"? To answer these the apostle Paul gave us a clear definition: "Know ye not that ye are the temple of God, and that the Spirit of God dwelleth in you?" (1Corinthians 3: 16). The temple, sanctuary, or holy place of Allah are not in some building in Jerusalem but in the holy people of Allah.

So now, the question is: what kinds of sacrifices will this *Dajjal* seek to put an end to? The sacrifices of praise? The tithes of finances? In theory both, but in truth neither. The *Dajjal* does not end or take away such, he merely directs them toward himself, even as it is written, "Take heed that no man deceive you. For many shall come in my name saying, I am Christ; and shall deceive many." "For if he that cometh preacheth another Jesus, whom we have not preached, or if ye receive another spirit, which ye have not received, or another gospel, which ye have not accepted, ye might well bear with him" (Matthew 24: 4, 5; 2Corinthians 11: 4). So, what is the abomination of desolations? The seating in the heart of the God's people a false Jesus from the historical Jesus.

Returning again to the prophet Daniel, it says, "And the king shall do according to his will; and he shall exalt himself, and magnify himself above every god, and shall speak marvellous things against the God of gods, and shall prosper till the indignation be accomplished: for that that is determined shall be done" (Daniel 11: 36). Let me paraphrase the last part "he shall prosper until the time of the heathen be accomplished." As noted earlier: after Chittim (Hebrew code for Rome) attacks, he will abandon the holy covenant. Sounds like Protestantism to me; that is, the immediate post-Renaissance. From that time, they began to set up an abomination that has left so many nations in the world – the vast majority of the planet even – desolate. The single-eyed mission of this Great *Dajjal* to exalt himself above all that is called God or that is worshipped and to make the people of the world bow down to his image was excessively successful. But he cheated, and Allah knows it.

Still, the question could now be asked: what about America, surely the apostle John did not have in mind a nation as yet unknown to him and his people? This is where it could be said that I personally differ from the godbody in my interpretation. It is clear to anyone who does a deep dive into the epistle of Revelation that the apostle John set up four Manichean dichotomies: God and the Devil, the Lamb and the Beast, the Witness and the false prophet, Jerusalem and Babylon. As New Jerusalem is the redeemed church, even so Babylon is clearly the irredeemable church. This is a church and mosque that is in collusion with imperialism, or in this case the GUSE. Indeed, if this Babylon was to fall, "the kings of the earth, who have committed fornication and lived deliciously with her, shall bewail her," "And the merchants of the earth shall weep and mourn over her" (18: 9, 11).

Still, I have, again, not been entirely honest with you: though most street lifers use the language of Babylon in their discourse, most of us godbodies actually do not. We have, however, been known to use the term Magog as a surrogate for devil when talking about White people. It is rare, and only among a minority, but it is done. Herein, the empire of Babylon, the third villain in the epistle of Revelation, is not as important as the two cameoed villains at the very end, Gog and Magog, as the empire of White people. Effectively, the White Christ is believed by some in the godbody, though admittedly, again, a minority, to be the Anti-Christ (*al-Dajjal*), Christianity (both Catholic and Protestant) to be the Beast, the Western penitentiary system to be the belly of the Beast, images of the White Christ to be the mark of the Beast, and White people as a whole to be Magog or of the empire of Magog.

But how then do we reconcile these ideas with the picture of eschatology painted so far? We say that the Witness from al-Khidr will share the message of the Messiah's Blackness – again, not an ontological Blackness but a physiological Blackness. He or she will also share the message of the White Christ being the Anti-Christ, the message of Islam being a godly covenant, and the message of the Black thearchy being God's kingdom. A little *dajjal* (False Prophet of the Great *Dajjal*) will then hear all these messages and instantly accuse the Witness of racism. But the Witness will be very influential, leading many Black people to the Blackness of the Messiah, thus causing that *dajjal* to lead a grassroots movement against Black people. This will inspire the Witness to fight back in the form of violent uprisings.

When the government gets a whiff of the violence being used against these White persecutors of Black people the state will begin to clamp down on the Witness and on his or her followers. This state-sponsored persecution will become a Great *Fitnah* when Martial Law is put into force as a result of the revolution inspired by the Witness. Then, "the brother shall betray the brother to death, and the father the son; and children shall rise up against their parents, and shall cause them to be put to death. And ye shall be hated of all men for my name's sake" (Mark 13: 12, 13). This will be Magog coming down hard on Black people. The Christians who are good enough will hate Magog for persecuting us Blacks under the rubric of anti-terrorism. Yet the *dajjal* will probably have enough political capital to win for himself the Presidency of the Magog Empire. Finally, the Witness will be caught and arrested for treason. At the behest of the *dajjal* he or she will then be murdered either in his or her cell or taken and brought somewhere no one else knows about to be killed.

PART III
SOTERIOLOGY

In the epistle of Revelation there is presented a brilliant and beautiful story so grand that people have for the most part considered it to be foretelling of a millennium of grace: "And I saw thrones, and they sat upon them, and judgment was given unto them: and I saw *the souls* of them that were beheaded for the witness of Jesus, and for the word of God, and which had not worshipped the beast, neither his image, neither had received his mark upon their foreheads, or in their hands; and they lived and reigned with Christ a thousand years. But the rest of the dead lived not again until the thousand years were finished. This is the first resurrection. Blessed and holy is he that hath part in the first resurrection: on such the second death hath no power, but they shall be priests of God and of Christ, and shall reign with him a thousand years." Also, "For the priesthood being changed, there is made of necessity a change also of the law" (Revelation 20: 4-6; emphasis mine; Hebrews 7: 12).

The unobvious part that has been overlooked by so many people over the past few hundred years is that it is not the physical body that is resurrected in this *First Resurrection* but "the *souls* of them that were beheaded." This misinterpreted symbology of the epistle of Revelation by most modern theologians and preachers of apocalyptic peril, has unfortunately led to many great tragedies and acts of horror. If given its genuine and proper interpretation the relation this Scripture has with the message of the apostle Paul could have easily been seen. Here the apostle Paul, using a language the early messianic movement would have completely understood, revealed how Allah, "Even when we were dead in sins, hath quickened us together with Christ, (by grace ye are saved;) And hath raised us up together, and made us sit together in heavenly places in Christ Jesus" (Ephesians 2: 5, 6). Clearly, it was this resurrecting and rapturing of the soul that was of true importance, because if we fall from this grace shown us by Allah, a grace that has completely saved us, then our souls will not be raised from death into resurrection life.

Basically, the first resurrection was always to be a resurrection of Afrosensuality. Moreover, the word used for soul in the epistle of Revelation was psyche; and in case you forgot *psychikos* was translated in the King James Bible as the word sensual and the Freudian interpretation of psychic activity was itself far more sensual than cognitive; we therefore see that the first resurrection should actually be considered a kind of sensual resurrection. For which cause, and for clarity's sake, I have here called the first resurrection: the resurrection of Afrosensuality, and not of the Black psyche.

Another interpretation that could be very helpful is to understand the translation of the word first in First Resurrection. The word first in its Greek original was the word proto, which, indeed, translates to first but also translates to foremost, chiefest, best, and premier. Looked at in this way the First Resurrection is actually the Premier Resurrection, this is fitting as those that rose were those "that were beheaded for the witness of Jesus, and for the word of God," and as you should expect by now, I believe this was a mistranslation. The word used for beheaded is a word used only once in the New Testament, the word *pelekizo* which is properly translated as executed, as in state sponsored murder, but can also mean to truncate, as in to cut off.

What we can see ultimately is that the First Resurrection is actually the Premier Resurrection, which is a sensual resurrection for those whose souls were cut off due to the witness of Jesus and the word of God. This is what has been lost: the early gnostic doctrine of the truncating, or in their case, imprisonment of soul. That the sensual body was encased in flesh and forced to live out a life of flesh but would one day be set free to dwell in a sexual and martial paradise where they would not be judged by either God or men (and women). The Messiah took this idea even further when he said to the Sadducees sent to test him about marriage, "in the resurrection they neither marry, nor are given in marriage, but are as the angels of God in heaven" (Matthew 22: 30). This parallels completely with the godbody's own prohibition of marriage. Effectively, we godbodies prove to be children of the resurrection, practicing a more messianic lifestyle than even the Christians themselves. At the same time, none of this means that we are modern-day monks, nuns, or hermits. We neither take a vow of celibacy nor are we a part of the Incel/Femcel community. We simply reject the bourgeois forms of marriage, considering ourselves able to have free, and in many cases, polyamorous sexual relationships.

In truth, the earnest expectation of prophecy revealed how all these things were always supposed to take place. For we can read in the scroll of Daniel an episode in which the prophet Daniel prayed to Allah, and was in supplication before Allah, crying to Allah for the forgiveness of the sins of his people, when,

> *"Yea, whiles I was speaking in prayer, even the man Gabriel, whom I had seen in the vision at the beginning, being caused to fly swiftly, touched me about the time of the evening oblation. And he informed me, and talked with me, and said, O Daniel, I am*

now come forth to give thee skill and understanding. At the beginning of thy supplications the commandment came forth, and I am come to shew thee; for thou art greatly beloved: therefore understand the matter, and consider the vision. Seventy weeks are determined upon thy people and upon thy holy city, to finish the transgression, and to make an end of sins, and to make reconciliation for iniquity, and to bring in everlasting righteousness, and to seal up the vision and prophecy, and to anoint the most Holy. Know therefore and understand, that from the going forth of the commandment to restore and to build Jerusalem unto the Messiah the Prince shall be seven weeks, and threescore and two weeks: the street shall be built again, and the wall, even in troublous times. And after threescore and two weeks shall Messiah be cut off, but not for himself: and the people of the prince that shall come shall destroy the city and the sanctuary; and the end thereof shall be with a flood, and unto the end of the war desolations are determined" (Daniel 9: 21-26).

How does one interpret these things? First of all, we know that the call to rebuild Jerusalem took place at the request of Nehemiah (Nehemiah 2: 4-11). Second, history tells us that Nehemiah did not return to Jerusalem until around about 445 BCE. Next, we know that threescore and two weeks (62 seven year periods) would have definitely been around 434 years. Putting aside literal or possibly literal interpretations, we also know that Herod the Great died in 4 BCE, and very likely ordered the murder of those infants sometime between 9-11 BCE. Finally, according to a few historical notes the Messiah Jesus lived for 47-49 years and not the standard 33 years. So now, if we do the math: seventy times seven is 490, 445 BCE minus 434 BCE is 11 BCE, the time of the proclamation to murder all the infants. Add to that now 49 and you get some time between 37 and 39 CE, when it is most likely the Messiah actually died. Seven years after that was the first persecution of the messianic movement after the deacon Stephen's death, 15 years after that James the Messiah's brother was murdered, and 8 years after that Jerusalem was sacked by the Romans and left completely desolate.

Though exact timing in prophecy may be a little problematic, as Allah dealt very rarely in exactitudes, going rather on an event-sequence model (ESM) of time, this timing is pretty accurate. Indeed, the Messiah himself spoke two messages that give us pause to consider this accuracy a little further. First, he said to the Pharisees that requested from him a sign, "Ye hypocrites, ye can discern the face of the sky and of the earth; but how is it that ye do not discern the time?" (Luke 12: 56). This was clearly a reference to Daniel's prophecy, which the Messiah had obviously mastered. Second, as the Messiah entered into Jerusalem upon a young colt, he began to weep, "Saying, If thou hadst known, even thou, at least in this thy day, the things which belong unto thy peace! but now they are hid from thine eyes. For the days shall come upon thee, that thine enemies shall cast a trench about thee, and compass thee round, and keep thee in on every side, And shall lay thee even with the ground, and thy children within thee; and they shall not leave in thee one stone upon another; because thou knewest not the time of thy visitation" (Luke 19: 42-44).

Again, a very skilful interpretation of the words of the archangel Gabriel, where he said to the prophet Daniel, "the people of the prince that shall come shall destroy the city and the sanctuary; and the end thereof shall be with a flood, and unto the end of the war desolations are determined." Anyone who knows a little first century history should know that all this has already transpired, and that the prophecy was already fulfilled, as a result of the First Jewish Revolt (66-71 CE). Here the Judeans fought against the Romans, but the Romans put them to flight, sacked Jerusalem, burned down the city, and burned down the Temple.

So, let us now look deeper at what the archangel Gabriel meant when he said to the prophet Daniel, "Seventy weeks are determined upon thy people and upon thy holy city, to finish the transgression, and to make an end of sins, and to make reconciliation for iniquity, and to bring in everlasting righteousness, and to seal up the vision and prophecy, and to anoint the most Holy." Indeed, this oft-misinterpreted Scripture by so many modern-day Charismatics, theologians, and "prophets" of Christianity has led to many modern-day tragedies in our time. Given a proper interpretation we can, again, see how misinterpretation of Scripture can bring about ruin. Moreover, it is, or perhaps should be, the easiest Scripture to interpret of them all.

The author to the Hebrews probably said it better than anything I could ever say, "Christ being come an high priest of good things to come, by a greater and more perfect tabernacle, not made with hands, that is to say, not of this building; Neither by the blood of goats and calves, but by his own blood he entered in once into the holy place, having obtained eternal redemption for us. For if the blood of bulls and of goats, and the ashes of an heifer sprinkling the unclean, sanctifieth to the purifying of the flesh: How much more shall the blood of Christ, who through the eternal Spirit offered himself without spot to God, purge your conscience from dead works to serve the living God? And for this cause he is the mediator of the new testament, that by means of death, for the redemption of the transgressions that were under the first testament, they which are called might receive the promise of eternal inheritance" (Hebrews 9: 11-15).

Basically, as the old doctrine says, Christ has made an end of sin by becoming sin for us. Thus, the transgression was finished, for he made an end of sins, and brought us both reconciliation from iniquity and everlasting righteousness. Finally, he sealed up the visions and prophecies, at least for that time (we all know that the Prophet Muhammad came after to finalise, confirm, and seal the prophetic office itself). Effectively, the destruction of Jerusalem, prophesied by the Messiah, actually took place in 70 CE as he went on to say to his disciples, "Verily I say unto you, This generation shall not pass away, till all be fulfilled. Heaven and earth shall pass away: but my words shall not pass away" (Luke 21: 32, 33). This is a far cry from the dispensationalist view that the last seven-year period will be taken from that generation into a future generation which will fulfil it at a later date. What we see is that, as that generation has passed away, so all the Messiah prophesied has already come to pass (lest we make the Messiah out to be a liar).

We may herein ask the question now: what then is the significance of the New Testament if that was how we were supposed to attain the promises? To this the prophet Jeremiah provided the best answer, "Behold, the days come, saith the Lord, that I will make a new covenant with the house of Israel, and with the house of Judah: Not according to the covenant that I made with their fathers in the day that I took them by the hand to bring them out of the land of Egypt; which my covenant they brake, although I was an husband unto them, saith the Lord: But this shall be the covenant that I will make with the house of Israel; After those days, saith the Lord, I will put my law in their inward parts, and write it in their hearts; and will be their God, and they shall be my people. And they shall teach no more every man his neighbour, and every man his brother, saying, Know the Lord: for they shall all know me, from the least of them unto the greatest of them, saith the Lord: for I will forgive their iniquity, and I will remember their sin no more" (Jeremiah 31: 31-34).

Victorian Gardens

From here we can see how the words of the Messiah that actually endorsed the concept of marriage can be used quite optimally, "Have ye not read, that he which made them at the beginning made them male and female, And said, For this cause shall a man leave father and mother, and shall cleave to his wife: and they twain shall be one flesh? Wherefore they are no more twain, but one flesh. What therefore God hath joined together, let not man put asunder." This idea, combined with the concept of Afrosensuality, can create a hypersexual standard that challenges the Victorian moral standard. We godbodies currently live by this standard, though from a modernist perspective it may seem somewhat unimportant. Yet to us it still carries a huge weight of responsibility, and as the Messiah here attempted to reveal, it actually played a vital role in the Afrosensual development of the Original people.

Moreover, if we were to consider our current time we could also see how a misconception of Black sexuality has developed based on what transpired since Victorian times, and the spreading of what I have called the Victorian monogamous patriarchal standard. This standard was created as a result of the abolition of slavery throughout the British Empire, receiving its start as what was initially called Apprenticeship (1834-37), a time when the British thought they needed to teach, train, and guide their former slaves into "civilised" and "decent" living and livelihoods.

The project of Apprenticeship inevitably failed, a truth that was not fully appreciated until after the beginnings of the actual Victorian monarchy. Mimi Sheller would also go on to say of those days how, "Female apprentices were punished in large numbers for trying to assert and protect the limited rights they had won as mothers of the slave labor force during the period of so-called amelioration (an attempt to raise the birthrate among slaves following abolition of the slave trade). ... While British abolitionists focused on the cruel treatment of women, [the] women themselves took a major part in protesting the conditions in which they found themselves supposedly free."

From the time Queen Victoria ascended the throne (1837) a new standard for the colonies was beginning to get promoted. First, "Virtuous women [were] required to be pure, chaste and monogamous" (Nzegwu 2011: 254). Second, the propagating of "a phallocentric position that emphasises and legitimises the privileging of men's needs, desires and fantasies" (Nzegwu 2011: 254). Furthermore, as Sheller also stated, "When [the] new order arrived with the abolition of slavery in 1834, European writers like Anthony Trollope argued plainly that civilization would only proceed in the colonized world on the basis of 'a clear gender order with breadwinning husband and father and domesticated wife and mother". Thus was reinforced by the Victorian standard the virtuous monogamous patriarch.

This Victorian monogamous patriarchal standard itself came about due to the popularity of the King James Bible and its use and misinterpretation by various Anglican clergy, particularly concerning where the apostle Paul stated to the evangelist Timothy, "This is a true saying, If a man desire the office of a bishop, he desireth a good work. A bishop then must be blameless, the husband of one wife, vigilant, sober, of good behaviour, given to hospitality, apt to teach ... One that ruleth well his own house, having his children in subjection with all gravity; (For if a man know not how to rule his own house, how shall he take care of the church of God?)" (1Timothy 3: 1-5). Thus, as this philosophy spread further afield, mainly through the popularity of the King James Bible, and its misreading by these Anglican clergies and missionaries, there also arose the Victorian monogamous patriarchal standard of hegemonic masculinity.

Moreover, Sheller also maintained that this "notion of masculinity was [itself] central to the construction of liberal ideologies of citizenship centered on the free white male individual, and this idea of masculinity was rooted in the bourgeois patriarchal family." As the Anglican clergies and missionaries began to narrate, propagate, and impose their general theory and outlook of this Victorian monogamous patriarchal standard on the people of the African continent, what was becoming abundantly clear was the need to "expose the exploitative nature of [their] notion of sexuality [thus] feminist research on battery, rape, incest and child sexual abuse, prostitution and pornography [which all thereby] demonstrated that women within this European and European-derived sexual schema are objects of pleasure rather than subjects who ought to have pleasure" (Nzegwu 2011: 254).

For the purpose of empowering Black women to become, not only subjects appreciating their own sexual value and right to enjoy pleasurable (read orgasmic) sexual experiences, but empowered sexual objects with autonomy and will; even Nzegwu went on to talk about how, "Sexuality discourse in the *kpanguima* curriculum lays out the culturally approved boundaries of behaviour, the culturation of the natural body for sexual expression and the conditions under which sexual encounters can be pursued ... Because sexual pleasure is [actually considered] a social good, sexual desire is not subject to punitive laws unless one engages in practices that are deemed culturally unacceptable [Furthermore, these types of Black] communities emphasise the right of women to enjoy sex. Students learn about the critical stages – pre-coital, coital and post-coital – as well as a range of techniques for the different phases."

In presenting her case for early Black forms of marital arrangement Nzegwu further introduced the concept of nuptial advisers, "The institution of [these] nuptial advisers ... emerged to facilitate pleasurable experiences, and to instruct young women and couples in the art of lovemaking. These advisors are found in different regions of Africa, and include the Sande *sowei* (Boone 1986) and the *laobé* in Senegal; the *nwang abe* of the Ubang of Nigeria (Uchendu 2003); the *magnonmaka* of Mali (Diallo 2005); the *ssenga* of Buganda (Tamale 2005); the *shwen-kazi* among the Banyankore in Uganda; the *tete* among the Shona of Zimbabwe; the *alangizi* of the Yao of Malawi and the *chewa* of Zambia; the *nacimbusa* of the Bemba of Zambia (Richards 1956); the *mayosenge* in parts of Zambia and the *olaka* of the Makhuwa of Mozambique" (Nzegwu 2011: 261).

It is with these nuptial advisers within these various African settings that we find the words of Pyotr Kropotkin ringing ever truer: "The first thing which strikes us as soon as we begin studying [indigenous] folk is the complexity of the organization of marriage relations under which they are living." Indeed, based on Fredrick Engels' estimation we also find that, "[John] McLennan knew only three forms of marriage – polygamy, polyandry and monogamy. But once attention had been directed to this point, more and more proofs were discovered of the fact that among undeveloped peoples forms of marriage existed in which a group of men possessed a group of women in common; and Lubbock (in his *The Origin of Civilization*, 1870) acknowledged this group marriage ("communal marriage") to be a historical fact."

Herein can be understood how Allah, in his infinite glory and power, could not have remained alone in the universe; not with the potential for so much great beauty and wonder. The Bible says of the creation, "And the Lord God said, It is not good that the man should be alone" (Genesis 2: 18). Well, nor is it good for Allah to be alone, hence, the creation. We must also remember that Moses, the most likely author of the book of Genesis, was a grandmaster (*Sebi*) in the ancient Egyptian Order of Amen, hence why the ancient Hebrew theogony shows such great similarities to the ancient Egyptian theogonies; in which from one god Tum came all the other Heliopolitan gods. These gods, through Khepru (evolutionary motion), in turn created the heaven and the earth at the origin. The Hebrews themselves would also have learned from these ancient Egyptian traditions while living in ancient Egypt for four hundred and thirty years. (This Hebrew experience in ancient Egypt, being of similitude to the African experience in the West, where they lost their freedom, their religion, their culture, their language, and their traditions; also demonstrates an unconscious link with the past as in both cases it was Black people being enslaved).

The biblical Scriptures also reiterate that Allah, who in the beginning created the universe, also made humanity to be in his own image, saying, "And God said, Let us make man in our image, after our likeness and let them have dominion over the fish of the sea, and over the fowl of the air, and over the cattle, and over all the earth, and over every creeping thing that creepeth upon the earth. So God [Elohim] created man [Adam] in his own image, in the image of God created he him; male and female created he them." (Genesis 1:26, 27). Thus Elohim, or to be more accurate Allahi, in making us human beings in his image and after his likeness, created both male and female: Or two different sexual compositions, even as Neteru are a Collective of two different sexual compositions in the ancient Egyptian traditions; and we can be sure of one thing, they all practiced a kind of free love lifestyle among each other.

Consequently, the free love lifestyles and hypersexual experiences of the ancient Egyptian people, both male and female, allowed for a much greater level of sexual independence among the women of ancient Egypt. Nzegwu even furthered this point when she wrote concerning the ancient songs of the Chester Beatty Papyri I, "The songs are [very] passionately charged declarations of love and intense sexual desire. They speak in smouldering erotic tones about the male whose 'heart is afire with desire for {his beloved's} embrace' (Obenga 2004: 598); or the female lover whose 'heart flutters hastily / When I think of my love of you / ... / It lets me not put on a dress' (Chester Beatty Papyri I)." These kinds of dramatic and erotic act-species essentially played a part in giving ancient Egypt a reputation and self-identification as a highly sexual, one might even say hypersexual, people. However, such a hypersexuality did not remain, and has not remained, only in ancient Egypt. As Nzegwu also noted, "The pan-ethnic Sande and Bundu *kpanguima*, and all other similar sexuality schools, taught young women about the force of [their ability to give and gain] pleasure".

In this, Nzegwu virtually gave herself a mission: to enlighten Black people, and Black women in particular, as to their authentic Afrosensual heritage, so as to give to modernised Black women a pride in these kinds of Afrosensual schools. Also to remove from us the shame developed from indoctrination into the Western outlook, especially when related to our sexual behaviours and desires: "Because the [Black] theorisation of sexuality takes place in the context of producing a good society and healthy social living, Sande instructors work on firmly moulding girls into self-assured women. They induct them into community-wide fellowships of women and transform them into Sande *nyaha* or mature adult women, complete with an adult personal aesthetics and a female-identified consciousness."

Again, if we return now to Engels, he noticed how sexual fellowships like "group marriage, when observed more closely, does not appear quite so horrible as is fancied by the philistine in his brothel-tainted imagination." For even, "[Lewis] Morgan, in agreement with the majority of his professional colleagues, arrived at [an indigenous] stage at which promiscuous intercourse prevailed within a tribe, so that every woman belonged equally to every man and every man to every woman." In all this, "Mutual toleration among the adult males, freedom from jealousy, was, however, the first condition for the formation of those large and enduring groups in the sole midst of which the transition from animal to man could take place." "If anything is certain, it is that jealousy is an emotion of comparatively late development."

Concerning these sorts of ancient familial and societal customs Engels had this to say, "We are indebted to the English missionary Lorimer Fison for the most substantial enrichment of our knowledge of group marriage … He found the lowest stage of development among the Australian Negroes of Mount Gambier in South Australia. The whole tribe is here divided into two large classes – Kroki and Kumite. Sexual intercourse within each of these classes is strictly proscribed; on the other hand, every man of one class is the born husband of every woman of the other class, and she is his born wife."

To further explain how the system worked in practice, Engels continued on, "In all forms of the group family it is uncertain who the father of a child is, but it is certain who the mother is. Although she calls *all* the children of the aggregate family her children and is charged with the duties of a mother towards them, she, nevertheless, knows her natural children from the others. It is thus clear that, wherever group marriage exists, descent is traceable only on the *maternal* side, and thus the *female line* alone is recognised." And as Kropotkin so generously reminded us, "The natives of Australia do not stand on a higher level of development than their South African brothers."

In further explaining this system more in depth he consulted the words of, "Lumholtz, a missionary who sojourned in North Queensland: –

> *The feeling of friendship is known among them; it is strong. Weak people are usually supported; sick people are very well attended to; they never are abandoned or killed ... The parents love their children, play with them, and pet them. Infanticide meets with common approval. Old people are very well treated, never put to death. No religion, no idols, only a fear of death. Polygamous marriage. Quarrels arising within the tribe are settled by means of duels fought with wooden swords and shields. No slaves; no culture of any kind; no pottery; no dress, save an apron sometimes worn by women.'"*

With regard to Lumholtz's views concerning Aboriginal polygamy, it is probable that what he meant was more likely a kind of polyamorous group sexuality custom, and not necessarily a system of many marriages. Engels furthers this by relating, through his own studies, "Group marriage, which in the case of Australia is still class marriage, the state of marriage of a whole class of men, often scattered over the whole breadth of the continent, with an equally widely distributed class of women ... the law according to which an Australian Negro, even when a stranger thousands of miles away from his home, among people whose language he does not understand, nevertheless, quite often, in roaming from camp to camp, from tribe to tribe, finds women who guilelessly, without resistance, give themselves to him; and according to which he who has several wives cedes one of them to his guest for the night. Where the European can see only immorality and lawlessness, strict law actually reigns".

Grinker et al. would explain deeper the current Black predisposition towards polygyny in certain African customs today. Most likely having derived from former group marriage (or group sexuality) customs, polyandry "in which a woman has more than one husband ... is [currently] uncommon in Africa, having been outlawed in Nigeria and elsewhere during colonization," which in turn caused the growth of polygyny throughout Africa to expand without the counterbalance of polyandry. The West effectively prohibited the more traditional forms of Afrosensuality, forcing upon Black people European forms of sensuality. After condemning the sacred forms of sexual practice as that between the uncivilised and the wicked, making our ideal form of sexual partnership the same as that of the slave-master/colonizer. Polygamy, by that time, had long been going extinct in Europe, while among the Blacks of Asia, Africa, Latin America, and Australia group sexuality, still existed deep into colonisation.

Whether the practices of polyamorous and group sexuality were really customs acquired from the Original divines or not one thing is for certain: as the early humanities were made in the image of a God-Collective so they originally followed their customs no matter what they were. Whereas it was the narration of those who taught the Victorian monogamous patriarchal standard that the divine beings were and are all heavily robed, asexual, males (or male-dominated), the onus is in fact on them to prove that; especially as, all single-gendered species – that is, species in which male or female only have the sexual properties of one gender – copulate with the opposite sex to reproduce. The ancient Egyptians (ancient Kemetics) did not share their enthusiasm for divine male-dominated asexuality accepting that the divine not only had sex and offspring, but that their system heavily favoured females too. Based on this understanding it becomes imperative that we consider the early customs of early humanity to determine the cultural evolutions or devolutions in the world of what would today be called human sexuality.

Here Engels provided us with what could be called an acceptable explication of Eurocentric sexual devolution: "the transition [from group sexuality] to monogamy ... implied the violation of a primeval religious injunction (that is, in fact, the violation of the ancient traditional right of ... other men to the same woman), a violation which had to be atoned for, or the toleration of which had to be purchased, by surrendering the woman for a limited period of time." Effectively, even though the Victorian monogamous patriarchal "notion of sexuality has made tremendous gains in various parts of the world, this does not mean its view of the erotic is correct ... or that it is the only appropriate way of thinking about the erotic" (Nzegwu 2011: 254).

The True Bodily Resurrection

Engels accepted the idea of a correlation between humanity and nature throughout his studies of the natural sciences, making clear to the readership of his time; "The most simple type found in the whole of organic nature is the cell; and it certainly is the basis of the higher organisms. On the other hand, among the lowest organisms there are many which are far below the cell – the protamoeba, a simple albuminous particle without any differentiation whatever, and a whole series of other monera and all bladder seaweeds (Siphoneae). All of these are linked with the higher organisms only by the fact that their essential component is albumen". Moreover, Engels also effectively informed us that "an albuminous body absorbs other appropriate substances from its environment and assimilates them, while other, older parts of the body disintegrate and are excreted. Other, non-living, bodies also change, disintegrate or enter into combinations in the natural course of events; but in doing this they cease to be what they were. A weather-worn rock is no longer a rock; metal which oxidizes turns into rust. But what with non-living bodies is the cause of destruction, with albumen is *the fundamental condition of existence*."

But whereas albumin is an organism that is the key component for most white organisms and therefore repels light; melanin is an organism that is the key component for most black organisms that, like all black substances, absorbs light.

Therefore, the darker a body the more colour it can see and even consume, the more sound it can hear, and the deeper sensation it can feel. Light is no more than electromagnetic energy waves, but a body is also no more than positive and negative energy waves in balance. All races possess melanin and albumin, but whereas Black people contain a higher percentage of melanin White people contain a higher percentage of albumin.

What I have attempted to show throughout my body of works is that the physical attributes of Allah can be found in electromagnetism; however, by godbody definition, his embodiment can also be found in all melinated people, particularly the Asiatic Black man. These ideas should not be too difficult for the Muslims to accept seeing as how it is written in the Quran: "Allah is the light of the heavens and the earth" (Quran 24: 35) or for the Christians to accept as it is written in the Bible: "This then is the message which we have heard of him, and declare unto you, that God is light, and in him is no darkness at all" (1John 1: 5). If Allah is light and light is a form of electromagnetism then Allah is really electromagnetism; and as any knowledgeable scientist is able to confirm a black body of whatever kind must always attract and absorb light, thereby showing that the embodiment of Allah is and will always be in black bodies.

In actual fact, the idea that we are all born equal is respectable politically but is biologically flawed. All races are in fact different. Not to say that one race is better than the others, just that we all contain a veritable distinction. We Black people *are* more emotional, sensual, and spiritual because there is more melanin in the pineal gland of our brain absorbing the lightwaves of the sun. At night these light rays convert the tryptophan aminos into melatonin, which produces dream and vision states. During the day it converts them into serotonin, which makes us more emotional, sensual, spiritual, and more susceptible to mental so-called abnormalities. (The fact is that the standard of mental normality is White people, whose pineal gland calcifies by age thirteen).

To give further explanation to this phenomenon Engels said, "If therefore tree-frogs and leaf-eating insects are green, desert animals sandy-yellow, and animals of the polar regions mainly snow-white in colour, they have certainly not adopted these colours on purpose or in conformity with any ideas; on the contrary, the colours can only be explained on the basis of physical forces and chemical agents. And yet it cannot be denied that these animals, because of those colours, are purposively adapted to the environment in which they live, in that they have become far less visible to their enemies. In just the same way the organs with which certain plants seize and devour insects alighting on them are adapted to this action, and even purposively adapted."

A further consideration of these biological distinctions within the evolution of social relations has been, and still is, the subject of great debate. Still, the revolutionary potential of biological and ecological relations should at this time be beyond doubt. As Sheller also made note, "It offers another version of embodied freedom – [one] embodied not only in human subjectivities," thereby revealing to us Black people the various forms of "liberation flora and fauna," to build off of Geri Augusto's key concept, that demarcate, present, represent, and reproduce certain meanings and dynamics in a given society. Sheller further explicated how these "relations of power, resistance, and oppositional culture building [get] inscribed into living landscapes of farming, dwelling, and cultivation. Claims to power (both elite and subaltern) are marked out by landscape features such as plazas, roads, pathways, vantage points, and significant trees, all of which proclaim use rights over, ownership of, or the sacrality of particular places."

Such ideas are and have been reinforced by the colonisation of nature theory. If you believe and accept the monism of the universe then it becomes clear that humanity's territorial acquisition and exploitation of nature, natural resources, natural environments, and natural bodies (human and non-human) is both colonial and oppressive in essence. Sheller, speaking here specifically about plants, also continued, stating, "Finding new plants and their uses was not only a primary concern in exploration of the New World; it also underwrote an entirely new attitude toward the natural world, in which it was demystified, classified, and secularized (Sheller 2003: 43). An acquisitive and utilitarian attitude toward natural entities prevailed in the eighteenth century in a cornucopia of botanical plenipotency" (Sheller 2012: 196).

With regard to the revolutionary potential of these "liberation flora" Sheller went on to say, "In these hidden regions, powerful *obia* … could be cultivated in traditional balm yards, and knowledge of plants with unique medicinal and magical properties could be maintained and passed on through the generations. Black studies has begun to explore a wide range of geographies of these plant-based knowledge systems, in which the enslaved are now understood as skilled botanical practitioners whose knowledge of plants was crucial in shaping landscapes and agricultural systems throughout the Americas." The same could also be said for the African continent as various "liberation flora and fauna" people a variety of landscapes with such terminus concepts as: the bush, the jungle, the desert, the mountains, the caves, the mines, the rivers, the seas, the forest, the field, the grasslands, the woodlands, the highlands, and the lowlands.

Sheller, however, was also able to notice the threat to such spaces and locations from oppressive forces: "Not only [are] subaltern 'superimposed' landscapes culturally rich and materially productive, but they also [have] effects back on the landscapes of power. A thousand hands working in small ways to shape the land to their own needs, a thousand feet trudging up into the remote hills, could easily outweigh the overweening gestures of the planter's prospect, the impotent laws of the colonial administrators, or the imperious gaze of the traveler." Herein she was also further able to disclose that, "Nature is not only socially constructed; it is … always fraught with competing practices of using, ordering, and imaging: natures are plural and contested [and] especially in colonial contexts."

Such environmental and arboreal significance was especially pronounced in the Afro-Caribbean context through which Sheller was able to discover their reverence for trees, "From the sacred Kindah tree of the Accompong Maroons in Jamaica (Besson 1997: 214) to the famous *mapou* tree of Bwa Kayiman in Haiti and the great silk cotton trees venerated as places of the spirits in Trinidad, particular trees have special symbolic meanings and social functions within African Caribbean and Indo-Caribbean cultures." Indeed, "the trees, seemingly bereft of symbolic or spiritual significance for Europeans, were in fact full of multiple meanings to various communities of indigenous, African, and East Indian origin and were drawn into a complex web of religious practices and material interactions, including Vodou in Haiti, Obeah in Jamaica, Candomblé in Brazil, and Santeria in Cuba."

Also, as we move on to considering what could be called "liberation fauna" and their potential for mutual aid Kropotkin further delineated that, "In the great struggle for life – for the greatest possible fullness and intensity of life with the least waste of energy – natural selection continually seeks out the ways precisely for avoiding competition as much as possible. The ants combine in nests and nations; they pile up their stores, they rear their cattle – and thus avoid competition; and natural selection picks out of the ants' family the species which know best how to avoid competition, with its unavoidably deleterious consequences. Most of our birds slowly move southwards as the winter comes, or gather in numberless societies and undertake long journeys – and thus avoid competition. Many rodents fall asleep when the time comes that competition should set in; while other rodents store food for the winter, and gather in large villages for obtaining the necessary protection when at work. The reindeer, when the lichens are dry in the interior of the continent, migrate towards the sea. Buffaloes cross an immense continent in order to find plenty of food. And the beavers, when they grow numerous on a river, divide into two parties, and go, the old ones down the river, and the young ones up the river – and avoid competition. And when animals can neither fall asleep, nor migrate, nor lay in stores, nor themselves grow their food like the ants, they do what the titmouse does, and what Wallace (*Darwinism*, ch.v) has so charmingly described: they resort to new kinds of food – and thus, again, avoid competition."

For the best example of what Kropotkin meant his description of the ants is perfectly fitting:

> *"If we take an ants' nest, we ... see that every description of work – rearing of progeny, foraging, building, rearing of aphides, and so on – is performed according to the principles of voluntary mutual aid": "In that immense division of the animal kingdom which embodies more than one thousand species, and is so numerous that the Brazilians pretend that Brazil belongs to the ants, not to men, competition amidst the members of the same nest, or the colony of nests, does not exist" at all, even to the point where "If an ant which has its crop full has been selfish enough to refuse feeding a comrade, it will be treated as an enemy, or even worse. If the refusal has been made while its kinsfolk were fighting with some other species, they will fall back upon the greedy individual with greater vehemence than even upon the enemies themselves. And if an ant has not refused to feed another ant belonging to an enemy species, it will be treated by the kinsfolk of*

the latter as a friend. All this is confirmed by most accurate observation and decisive experiments."

"And yet the ants, in their thousands, are not much destroyed by the birds, not even by the ant-eaters, and they are dreaded by most stronger insects. When [François] Forel emptied a bagful of ants in a meadow, he saw that 'the crickets ran away, abandoning their holes to be sacked by the ants; the grasshoppers and the crickets fled in all directions; the spiders and the beetles abandoned their prey in order not to become prey themselves;' even the nests of the wasps were taken by the ants, after a battle during which many ants perished for the safety of the commonwealth. Even the swiftest insects cannot escape, and Forel often saw butterflies, gnats, flies, and so on, surprised and killed by the ants. Their force is in mutual support and mutual confidence."

Basically, mutual support and avoidance of competition are here shown to be prerequisites for the continuance of species or breeds within the animal world. Herein, it is a hope of mine that we godbodies could ourselves develop such bonds of mutual support: unity, solidarity, and brotherhood/sisterhood that we also become an unstoppable force. True, it is social combining and associating that allowed time within communities like those of the ants to be spent productively, and it is their avoidance of competition and jealousy that keeps them from social breakdown. With social disorder thus curbed by the non-existence of competition or jealousy, the ants can find and maintain a high level of balance and equality within their surrounding habitat regardless of their location. In fact, the same could be said of most other animals too, as Kropotkin continued:

"life in societies enables the feeblest insects, the feeblest birds, and the feeblest mammals to resist, or to protect themselves from, the

most terrible birds and beasts of prey; it permits longevity; it enables the species to rear its progeny with the least waste of energy and to maintain its numbers albeit a very slow birth-rate; it enables the gregarious animals to migrate in search of new abodes. Therefore, while fully admitting that force, swiftness, protective colours, cunningness, and endurance to hunger and cold, which are mentioned by Darwin and Wallace, are so many qualities making the individual, or the species, the fittest under certain circumstances, we maintain that under any circumstances sociability is the greatest advantage in the struggle for life. Those species which willingly or unwillingly abandon it are doomed to decay; while those animals which know best how to combine, have the greatest chances of survival and of further evolution."

This adaptation and sociability within the animal world coincides with what is written in the Bible of these events, "And out of the ground the Lord God formed every beast of the field, and every fowl of the air; and brought them unto Adam to see what he would call them: and whatsoever Adam called every living creature, that was the name thereof. And Adam gave names to all cattle, and to the fowl of the air, and to every beast of the field; but for Adam there was not found an help meet for him" (Genesis 2: 19, 20). At which point another appropriate lesson comes to us from Kropotkin concerning mammalia: "the first thing which strikes us is the overwhelming numerical predominance of social species over those few carnivores which do not associate. The plateaus, the alpine tracts, and the Steppes of the Old and New World are stocked with herds of deer, antelopes, gazelles, fallow deer, buffaloes, wild goats and sheep, all of which are sociable animals. When the Europeans came to settle in America, they found it so densely peopled with buffaloes, that pioneers had to stop their advance when a column of migrating buffaloes came to cross the route they followed; the march passed of the dense column lasting sometimes for two and three days."

Again, we must appreciate the communal lives these animals live under and have lived under for millennia. When and if they were bought before Adam by God they would have already perfected and found their place in nature; and understood what it was they were able and supposed to do. And as Kropotkin stated, "Life in societies is again the rule with the large family of horses, which includes the wild horses and donkeys of Asia, the zebras, the mustangs, the *cimarrones* of the Pampas, and the half-wild horses of Mongolia and Siberia. They all live in numerous associations made up of many studs, each of which consists of a number of mares under the leadership of a male. These numberless inhabitants of the Old and the New World, badly organized on the whole for resisting both their numerous enemies and the adverse conditions of climate, would soon have disappeared from the surface of the earth were it not for their sociable spirit."

Even so, as he continued, "Many striking illustrations of social life could be taken from the life of the reindeer, and especially of that large division of ruminants which might include the roebucks, the fallow deer, the antelopes, the gazelles, the ibex, and, in fact, the whole of the three numerous families of the Antelopides, the Caprides, and the Ovides. Their watchfulness over the safety of their herds against attacks of carnivores; the anxiety displayed by all individuals in a herd of chamois as long as all of them have not cleared a difficult passage over rocky cliffs; the adoption of orphans; the despair of the gazelle whose mate, or even comrade of the same sex, has been killed; the plays of the youngsters, and many other features, could be mentioned."

To further explain the sociability of these "liberation fauna," Kropotkin went on to say, "Let me only remark that with the beavers, the musk-rats, and some other rodents, we already find the feature which will also be distinctive of human communities – that is work in common." In fact, "Almost all free grass-eating animals and many rodents in Asia and America being in very much the same conditions, we can safely say that their numbers are *not* kept down by competition; that at no time of the year can they struggle for food, and that if they never reach anything approaching to over-population, the cause is in the climate, not in competition."

Kropotkin also noted how the same is true of the birds, which according to the above quoted also passed before Adam. "Hunting and feeding in common is so much the habit in the feathered world that more quotations hardly would be needful: it must be considered as an established fact. As to the force derived from such associations, it is self-evident." "In fact, it would be much easier to describe the species which live isolated than to simply name those species which join the autumnal societies of young birds – not for hunting or nesting purposes, but simply to enjoy life in society and to spend their time in plays and sports, after having given a few hours every day to find their daily food." But for an obvious proof of the sociability that exists in these bird societies, "we have that immense display of mutual aid among [them] – their migrations – which I dare not even enter upon in this place. Sufficient to say that birds which have lived for months in small bands scattered over a wide territory secure for each separate individual the advantages of better food or shelter which are to be found in another district – they always wait for each other, and gather in flocks, before they move north or south, in accordance with the season."

But of all these varieties of "sociable bird, the parrot, stands, as known, at the very top of the whole feathered world for the development of its intelligence." Indeed, "There can be no doubt that it is the practice of life in society which enables the parrots to attain that very high level of almost human intelligence and almost human feelings which we know in them.

Their high intelligence has induced the best naturalists to describe some species, namely the grey parrot, as the 'birdman.' As to their mutual attachment it is known that when a parrot has been killed by a hunter, the others fly over the corpse of their comrade with shrieks of complaints and 'themselves fall the victims of their friendship,' as [John] Audubon said ... Very few birds of prey or mammals dare attack any but the smaller species of parrots, and Brehm is absolutely right in saying of the parrots, as he also says of the cranes and the sociable monkeys, that they hardly have any enemies besides men; and he adds: 'It is most probable that the larger parrots succumb chiefly to old age rather than die from the claws of any enemies.' Only man, owing to his still more superior intelligence and weapons, also derived from association, succeeds in partially destroying them."

Obviously, "No one will deny that there is, within each species, a certain amount of real competition for food – at least, at certain periods. But the question is, whether competition is carried on to the extent admitted by Darwin, or even by Wallace; and whether this competition has played, in the evolution of the animal kingdom, the part assigned to it." To do this he showed how it could quite easily be seen that "if the evolution of the animal world were based exclusively, or even chiefly, upon the survival of the fittest during periods of calamities; if natural selection were limited in its action to periods of exceptional drought, or sudden changes of temperature, or inundations, retrogression would be the rule in the animal world. Those who survive a famine, or a severe epidemic of cholera, or small-pox, or diphtheria, such as we see them in [aboriginal] countries, are neither the strongest, nor the healthiest, nor the most intelligent. No progress could be based on those survival – the less so as all survivors usually come out of the ordeal with an impaired health ... and subsequently shows a quite abnormal mortality. All that natural selection can do in times of calamities is to spare the individuals endowed with the greatest endurance for privations of all kinds."

On the whole, for Engels, the entire story was summed up as such: "the first to develop, as it is permissible to assume from the whole analogy of the palaeontological record, were innumerable species of non-cellular and cellular Protista ... of which some were gradually differentiated into the first plants and others into the first animals. And from the first animals were developed, essentially by further differentiation, the numerous classes, orders, families, genera, and species of animals; and finally vertebrates, the form in which the nervous system attains its fullest development; and among these again finally that vertebrate in which nature attains consciousness of itself – [humanity]." Yet the classification of humanity is not fully defined until we consider their social element in mutual aid and the avoiding of competition.

Ancient Egyptian Theogonies

The Original people actually started life as the Homo erectus, the most advanced species of the Homo genus at the time. Engels further takes us on an even deeper journey into the most evidential reasons for their development into the Homo sapiens sapiens and the proper Homo sapiens they became. By Engels' nineteenth century understanding of anthropology, the science itself still being in its infancy; he conceived that what would otherwise be the earliest breeds of hominidae inhabited certain tropical or semi-barren regions of Asia (which we have now come to find was in actual fact East Africa in the Great Lakes region and along the Nile Valley). "Fruits, nuts and roots served him as food; the formation of articulate speech was the main achievement of this period."

Indeed, "the development of labour necessarily helped to bring the members of society closer together by increasing cases of mutual support and joint activity, and by making clear the advantage of this joint activity to each individual. In short, men in the making arrived at the point where they had something to say to each other." But again, "Just as the gradual development of speech is inevitably accompanied by a corresponding refinement of the organ of hearing, so the development of the brain as a whole is accompanied by a refinement of all the senses." Thus our mental development was and is tied in to our sensory and, indeed, our sensual development.

All this would obviously correspond to the biblical account of Adam, created in the image of the angels and given dominion over the world; for here Adam, which is ancient Hebraic for Original man, that is, the Original humanity; was the Homo erectus Black man able to arise from among his hominid forebears to take his seat as ruler upon the earth and over its environments. In the account of Genesis Allah said to Adam, "Be fruitful, and multiply, and replenish the earth, and subdue it: and have dominion over the fish of the sea, and over the fowl of the air, and over every living thing that moveth upon the earth. And God said, Behold, I have given you every herb bearing seed, which is upon the face of all the earth, and every tree, in the which is the fruit of a tree yielding seed; to you it shall be for meat."

However, the mental and sensual accomplishments of Adam were from a social, that is, group perspective. Moreover, to provide Engels' fuller explanation, "Group marriage, the form in which whole groups of men and whole groups of women belong to one another ... [left] but little scope for jealousy", and most likely "arose at a time when ... intercourse between parents and children *had already been* proscribed by custom when the classes arose," which Kropotkin also confirmed, stating, "Societies, bands, or tribes – not families – were ... the primitive form of organization of mankind and its earliest ancestors." Or as he later continued, "The first human societies simply were a further development of those societies which constitute the very essence of life of the higher animals."

So the basic reality of the Black people as we developed from a non-sapiens to a sapiens people was that need and desire for social development – and in particular as sexual beings. Here the words read earlier from Genesis prove particularly fitting: "And the Lord God said, It is not good that the man should be alone; I will make him an help meet for him." And this help which he made would be to him a queen among princesses, the beautiful

Black woman: the receiver, the bearer, the womb for the cream of the planet, the mother of civilisation, and Goddess that gives birth to worlds.

At the same time, and at the risk of making a somewhat broad generalisation, all Black woman have deep within their spirit a drive toward unashamed hypersexual behaviours that makes them all divine. Interestingly enough, when each younger generation of Black woman inherit this spirit they usually find, against all the odds, and even against the wishes of the older generations, newer and more explicit, sometimes even shocking, ways of manifesting it. It is for this cause that we need a "relocation to [a more] African ontological scheme and an examination of its foundational beliefs [so as to] highlight the sexual component, as well as [paint] a different picture of sexual desire and passion. Deemed a personal and social good [in Africa], sexual fulfilment is highly valued by families and communities because it produces well-adjusted individuals" (Nzegwu 2011: 259). Indeed, hypersexual deviance is also – contrary to older generation's own current testimony and reality – exactly what those they did in their own youth, though obviously through different ways and under different circumstances; making it all the more necessary to understand the roots.

In this scenario, Nzegwu pointed out how, "Egyptologists Théophie Obenga and [Cheikh Anta] Diop established generic kinship affinities between ancient Egyptian cosmogony, language, concepts and thought and other continental African languages and cosmogonies … Their work mapped out an older African conceptual universe that not only provided a better interpretation of cultural phenomena in diverse regions of Africa, but also, when supplemented with archival records in Greek, Ge'ez and Arabic, a robust, intellectual universe of discourse many millennia old." It is hereby that we understand that there is a need within the Black community to return to the ancient Egyptian sources so as to find, define, and know ourselves.

The first place Nzegwu took her readers to was to the graphic illustrations of Kemetic sensual songs, "Although *The Pyramid Texts* (sometimes referred to as the *Book of Going Forth by Day* or *Book of the Dead*) can be read as philosophical treatises on divine love, divine adoration and eternal love, the images of sexual intercourse in burial chambers speaks eloquently and audibly through the secular love songs of the Chester Beatty Papyri." Essentially, "The sheer openness of the songs, the unabashed willingness to expose the depths of desire, and the frankness between lovers yield a conception of passionate desire that aims for sexual pleasure and satisfaction. The 'brother' and 'sister' terms of endearment reference not an incestuous relationship [contrary to popular Egyptological thought], but a relationship of equality and belongingness that approximates that of siblings" (Nzegwu 2011: 256, 257). Consequently, these ancient Egyptian women were able to form a kind of spermicide from a gum they crafted from acacia tree sap, which they then applied within their vaginas as an ingenious form of birth-control for their sexual liberation. Indeed, pre-marital sexual relations was encouraged for both male and female. It was only when a marriage agreement had been entered into that infidelity was looked down on and was potentially dangerous.

Hopefully, now we can perceive that when our White counterparts – blinded by the Victoria monogamous patriarchal standard, and to the truth of our own hypersexual forthrightness – tell our Black women that their beautiful manifestations of hypersexuality are nothing more than an immoral and immodest expression of ignorance and subordination; or that they are an embarrassment to women everywhere and are only being used, bullied, and exploited by us brothers; that they are thereby demonising us and isolating them from us. Therefore, at present the actual reality of most of our Black sisters is a far cry from their sensual nature. Having lost themselves and a knowledge of themselves and of their origins in the world, they have become like the proverbial Eve, seduced by a desire to be what she already was by nature, a Goddess, she became a fool and fell from the beauty and grace given to her and her husband by Allah, who formed them in his image.

That said, we learn that the tragedy of Adam and Eve, which itself carried great similarities to the Kemetic apocalypse of Horu and Hethor and also bore similarities to that of Geb and Nut. The apocalypse, which tells us how the two lovers, who made love continually and everywhere, were separated when Ra Atum, unwilling to allow one as irresistible as Nut to remain in the hands of one so vain as Geb, sent his son Shu to divide them. Then, sometime after he ascended again to Pet, the realm of the heavens; he began a ritualistic process of being swallowed by Nut every night and being birthed by her every morning; basically meant to be symbolic of the daily rise of a man at these his most libidinally suggestible times. Finally, when Geb could take no more, he rebelled against his father's unjust punishment and seized the crown from his head, causing Shu to retreat into Pet. Unable to wear the stolen crown Geb then placed on his head the wig of Ra Atum and so was able to wear the crown and rule over the earth.

This story, mainly spoken to encourage the people towards Ra Atum, that is, all-knowledge of self-creation, shows Geb's own internal weakness at the time was his lack of self-knowledge, which caused him to be separated by his father Shu from his beloved Nut. The correlation between the two stories is considerable: Geb, which means land, ground, earth, and solidity corresponds substantially to Adam, whose Hebrew root is *Admah*, meaning, land, ground, and soil; while at the same time Nut, which means sky, Nature, and lucidity corresponds to Eve, whose Hebrew root is *Khavah*, meaning life, Nature, and motion. Hence, Adam and Eve's falling coincides with Geb and Nut's separation, in which knowledge of self was the key issue. The terrible tragedy of these original people (Black people); was due to the false moralistic traditions that damaged the innocence of their former cultures, where it is said of them that "they were both naked, the man and his wife, and were not ashamed"(Genesis 2: 25).

But godhood, which was personified through knowledge of self or Ra Atum, allowed Nut to see the beauty of her own nakedness and sexuality and Ra Atum to experience the pleasures of his morning and nightly suggestibility, which Geb only experiences again when he gains the wig of Ra Atum and becomes *Peraa*. So, every morning, no matter how bad the night before was, the goddess Nut births god, while every night, no matter how bad the day has been, the goddess Nut swallows god.

But within this Kemetic story of early humanity there is also a marked difference from that of their Hebrew descendants: when Nut and Geb were together they had a liberal sexual relationship, which produced four (and in some stories five) children: Ausar and Setekh, Auset and Nebthet and sometimes Horu. Of the four Auset was given to Ausar and Nebthet was given to Setekh. Being children of the soil and sky, Ausar and Auset, Setekh and Nebthet were all Black. The throne of Kemet passed from father to son in those times so Ausar received the throne from his father Geb. Ausar, the fourth *Peraa* of Kemet, taught the men to irrigate lands, cultivate fields, domesticate animals, worship deities, obey laws, and practice sanitary rituals; while Auset taught the women to work magic, understand mysticism, appreciate holism, learn sciences, become beautiful, practice healings, and consume the right herbs.

Again, considering the fantasy element of this situation does an injustice to the intellect of the people of Kemet, known for their knowledge of mathematics, science, and architecture. So from a more symbolic perspective this apocalypse of Ausar and

Auset takes us back into the story of the early hominidae, and in particular the Homo erectus. The Homo erectus created laws and rituals which were mastered in ancient Kush. They also mastered the art of cultivation and domestication. They then migrated out of Kush to other parts of the world: to Arabia, Kemet, Sumer, Melanesia, and China spreading civilisation as they travelled. This bears remarkable similarity to the apocalypse of Ausar where he travels the earth spreading civilisation wherever he goes.

However, these Original people had no anticipation of the dissimulation to come about from that old snake in the grass. "Now the serpent was more subtle than any beast of the field which the Lord God had made" (Genesis 3: 1). This serpent, taking every advantage, would go on to bring about Adam's complete demise even as Setekh brought about the demise of his brother Ausar in the ancient Kemetic version: first throwing him into a box built only for him, then, after he was finally found by Auset, chopping up his body and scattering it around the world. Even so, the Black man, like Ausar: whether in the box built just for him, scattered from hood to hood, or taking over Dwat to become *Peraa* and god of the Dwat; is still in a state of near shock and pain over his brother's betrayal; while his Black woman today stands like an Auset without her Ausar: lost, alone, and driven to near madness. But as mentioned in the apocalypse of Geb and Nut: it was the demonising of our Kemetic exhibitionism and seductionism by moralistic opinions, effectively, White lies, that turned the ancient traditions of our ancestors into something evil, sinister, ignorant, and animal thus leaving our poor Black families dehumanised and semidetached from their true nature and natural self-identities.

In fact, the poisoned fruit in the garden was more likely a fruit of trick knowledge, which corrupted their minds leading them to follow unreal and unnatural ideas. The Black man and Black woman both ate of this fruit and found themselves lost and naked in a world in which they were no longer free to be naked. And as those who we looked to to restore our freedom and give us a knowledge of ourselves were usually those who had no knowledge of us as Black people our Black women were now left with a false consciousness: loving sex and their own sexuality while feeling and believing they are wrong or immoral for it. Or wanting to be loved and seen as sexy while fearing being seen as vain or base, or as a user, manipulator, or the disreputable "harlot," for these desires.

Nevertheless she still has hope. Even as Auset in the Asarian apocalypse was eventually able to restore Ausar to life again through her feminine charms, sensuous spells, and seductive faithfulness; so the Black woman as an Auset contains within herself and a love for herself the power to restore her Ausar to life and sanity. Not to become like Setekh or those snakes that were with him, but to become the god of his own domain through regaining a true knowledge of himself and dispelling the trick knowledge that corrupted him. It is through our Auset, that we see self as strong, confident, and psychologically stable, so that through their manifestation of beneficence and mercy to us, we too may become manifestations of beneficence and mercy to them, till we both return to that paradise we fell from in the beginning, or till we turn this hell on earth into an even better paradise.

For which cause, it is best and necessary for the Black woman to look at Allah not as a Judge, nor as a Ruler, nor even as a form of Justice; but as a Lover; one who, though not being a pervert, can be seduced and one who loves to seduce her with the pleasures, beauties, and benefits he showers on her. This is not the God called Reason; this is the God called al-Muhibb (the Libidinal One). This is a God who, if our women were to view him as a loving husband, it would allow them to find a deeper and closer insight into the deeps of his essence, carrying with it beautiful images of his own seductionism.

Obviously, we brothers should also learn to appreciate the godhood within our sisters: that they, through his Essence, are Goddesses; even as we, through his Essence, have become Gods. They are not bitches or hoes, but temples of the living God and should be reverenced as temples of God no matter how promiscuous they are. We should, therefore, view any service or benefice we do to them or for them as an act inspired by the one God to she in whom he has chosen to dwell. Her black body and her black skin are the house of very God, thus she, to us, should be a sacred shrine of honour; a living monument to God, and therefore a Goddess on the earth. And if she is a Goddess then we should protect her, stand up for her, and respect her. The same with our women, they should view us as the Lord God himself, and whatever good they do to us or for us as being done to God and for God. We should therefore be considered and treated as divine by her. Not as fools, idiots, slobs, embarrassments, wastes of space, or walking dildos, but as God in the flesh, one in whom the essence of her Benefactor and Messiah dwells. And if we all have Christ within us, then what she does for him is being done for Christ and what he does for her is again done for a transfigured Goddess.

"Don't Do That…"

All this is through the divine nature of that libidinal love through which we can see that though the serpent seduced the Black woman out of Eden, Allah is able to seduce her back into Eden, for he said, "behold, *I will allure her*, and bring her into the wilderness, and speak comfortably unto her. And I will give her her vineyards from thence, and the valley of Achor [loosely translated: valley of tribulation] for a door of hope: and she shall sing there, as in the days of her youth" (Hosea 2: 14, 15; emphasis mine). Now the word used here for allure is the Hebrew *pathah*, which means to open, to entice or to seduce; so, we can now see clearly a new soteriology for the Black community based on seductionism. We can also find how through our seductionism, which includes light exhibitionism (the permanent non-wearing of underwear), we godbodies are able to build up a thearchy, assuming the full expression of the Godhead.

All these sorts of lessons, though buried and denied, still exist within, and have existed all along within, our transgenerational, transhistorical, and translocational soul. It is for this cause that we of the Black diaspora have struggled for so long with our sexuality in the midst of this Western "culture shock." Again, if we take, for example, the so-called Earth People of Trinidad. According to Littlewood, "For a country long familiar with the religious charisma of the Spiritual Baptists … and also with the newer Rastafari movement introduced from Jamaica in the 1970s, the Earth People remain an enigma. Their appearance in the villages or in the capital Port-of-Spain causes public outrage, for they go about naked. Local opinion favours the view that these taciturn young men, carrying staves and cutlasses, and with the long matted dreadlocks of the Rastas, are probably crazy" (Littlewood 2006: 1). True, any radical movement with any hints of the sexual, like the Earth People obviously have, will be rejected by the mainstream for a time so as to preserve the status quo, but what happens when what is being said and done by them makes perfect sense, just like with the Tantric schools?

Littlewood said concerning the historical precedent for apocalyptic and millennial movements such as the Earth People, that they do tend to have a tendency toward "a radical revision of marriage, and social equality for women; together with … free love and the ultimate salvation of all people." Within this group he placed the Earth People, however, he also identified some forms of relation between them and their Rastafarian predecessors: "The Rasta term for the deity, 'Jah', has an established radical pedigree, and 'Babylon' represents for Rastas and the Earth People the established state, as it has for the countless groups which have returned to the Book of Daniel for their inspiration." Here, whether in their name for God or their name for this world system, the influence of the Rastas on the Earth People cannot be denied; though, at the same time, that in no ways means they belong to or identify within the Rasta collective.

In order to distinguish themselves from the Rasta movement the Earth People, whether in public or in their own community, have for the most part developed for themselves an injunction towards nudity, as Littlewood continued, "The most scandalous characteristic of the Earth People is certainly their refusal to wear clothes. … Although the community are sometimes referred to as the Naked People, we may argue that they are 'nude' rather than 'naked', for they defiantly engage in an activity motivated by a recognition that they are contravening a fundamental value. 'To be naked is to be oneself', says John Berger, 'to be nude is to be seen naked by others'. The Western notion of 'nudity' entails a way of seeing which is conventionalised and idealised; a deliberate shedding of clothes on behalf of other meanings of the act, whether sexual display or antinomian."

Just as the Earth People's rejection of clothing is in direct response to what they call "the Europeans' obsession with garbing the 'naked children' of the colonies" (Littlewood 2006: 168); Black thearchism also recognises the beauty in uncovering and self-exposition, however, with us it is through the practice of light exhibitionism and not through total nudity. That obviously means we will have to keep our private areas excessively clean, in public and in private, and use various lotions, colognes, and perfumes on these areas after every time we shower, but it will be our practice of light exhibitionism that will, firstly, create in our sexual partners the desire to transfigure us (maybe even to overload); and, secondly, set us free from the Victorian monogamous patriarchal standard of sexuality.

Naturally, the idea of prohibiting underwear appears at first glance as very restrictive, but on closer examination it is actually quite liberating, even disinhibiting. It is to a certain degree exhibiting the Black body, and the private areas of the Black body, in a way that is yet and still classy. Within the White community they call this act "going commando," for whatever reason, but it has no social or revolutionary connotations behind it. It is done just for its erotic value. The Black community has pretty much followed the White thus far with regard to this subject; they wore underwear when Whites told them to wear them and they considered it erotic so long as White people considered it erotic. As far as the counter-culture of not wearing it: such is practiced by a minority of Whites, let alone Blacks, though not consistently and mainly among women.

Conversely, while erotic agency will play a central role in bringing down the systems of inferiority; even as "intimate inter-bodily relations are the fundamental basis for human dignity[,] and thus for freedom in its widest sense" (Sheller 2012: 22); even so, light exhibitionism will be a method of unifying and inspiring the Black community towards manifesting that agency. Hence, within the struggle against White supremacy the Black woman will play a dominant and imperative role in both frustrating and complicating the White man's socio-sexual, heteronormative imagination.

In this, the Black woman will thereby become for him a Goddess of sexual ecstasy and counter-discursive erotica, thus reclaiming from him the offensive by using her attractive, indeed, seductive, charms as a means of prostrating the devil to her divine nature. That said, a devil of this calibre will unlikely prostrate himself easily, he will try to dominate, try to degrade, try to insult and belittle. But any negative reactions to the emotions she will be stirring in him will just be his normative and his instinctive drives working against each other: his striving for domination and control going against his libidinal drive. But the fact that his striving is not as prominent in the other races is no proof of the White *man's* destiny (teleology) to rule, it is more proof of his collective neuroses.

At this instance we can see that light exhibitionism is a form of militant self-exposition – a meta-discursive militancy no doubt, but a militancy, nonetheless. Again, as we are not infants, we have no need to wear diapers. This is said in spite of the doctrine of hygiene that has been spoon-fed to large quantities of us as a people, but I repeat, it is far more hygienic to thoroughly clean your private areas, before and after you bathe or shower. Indeed, the golden rule of light exhibitionism is: Whenever you take a shit take a shower. Add to that the added responsibility for Black women to start using tampons over panty-liners and it becomes even more complicated. Obviously, the Black woman may object, saying, tampon makers use unhealthy substances in their products. To this I will say that if Black women were to write to the tampon manufacturers and brands, not via email but through either TikTok or direct mail, and complain about this discrepancy demanding that they make a more natural tampon they would eventually correct it.

For this cause, it cannot be overemphasised how imperative it is that any Black man or Black woman who participates in light exhibitionism – those under the age of 18 should be restricted – should clean thoroughly both private areas of their body so as to keep their aesthetic value. Exhibitionism will also mean they will have to drop activities like the sagging their jeans. Leave sagging of jeans to the kids, we, being grown, should act grown. In fact, practicing light exhibitionism even forces us to be more sanitary than those who wear underwear, so as to avoid public humiliation or personal uncleanness. We will basically reach a point where we despise filth so much that we soap our anus at least three times, sixty times each before rinsing, after every time we defecate and thus show ourselves more hygienic than our opponents.

In the process of decolonising our minds and bodies we in the godbody must acknowledge that in the tradition of the transfiguration of the deviant, "If the Whites were those who clothed themselves to an extraordinary degree, some, by simple opposition, [may take] the line that the original 'natural' state had been, or should have been, one of naked harmony with their land. ... Nudity [thereby] [passes] backwards and forwards between marginal prophetic groups, the collective millennial moment and such temporary individual roles and situations. [Even] Shirley Ardener argues that the sexual display of the Eastern Nigerian 'women's war' against the British colonialists in 1929 deployed, against a new threat, the established response of local women when faced with a collective insult to their sex" (Littlewood 2006: 169). The Victorian monogamous patriarchal standard that was propagated within the colonies established a system of social organisation by which the man became the superordinate and the woman became the subordinate. This standard gave to White people the idea that they were superior due to their Christian values and rules of propriety, thereby denigrating any form of Black cultural expression.

Though it could be relatively easy to call the cultural expression of public nudity, or even light exhibitionism, primitive or backward, maybe even primal; such occurrences have transpired even among White women – even among White feminist women – as Littlewood further assured us when he said "many Ecofeminists style themselves 'witches', following that antiquarian history which argues that medieval agrarian cults revering a female deity were persecuted by Christian priests; women, the ritual celebrants, were [still] identified as … traditional healers in early modern Europe [and] are affirmed as women whom the growth of professional medicine pushed, along with their natural remedies, to the margins of 'superstition': the wise woman became transformed first into a witch and then into a demented old woman. Contemporary feminist witches now go *skyclad* (naked), have *moon huts* for menstruation and subscribe to *Earth Religion News*."

Still, in order to help us attain to this heightened state of sexual liberality the romance between King Solomon of Israel and Queen Makeda of Sheba in the Song of Songs presents us with a most beautiful means of attaining to a sensual resurrection. It is undeniable throughout the pages of this Scriptural masterpiece the amount of sexual innuendos exchanged between Solomon and Makeda; and as it is still holy Scripture, the hypereroticism and seductionism of today's Black woman is justified. Again, within this tale Solomon, in the holy Spirit, said to Makeda:

"DON'T DO THAT..."

> "How beautiful are thy feet with shoes, O prince's daughter! the joints of thy thighs are like jewels, the work of the hands of a cunning workman. Thy naval is like a round goblet, which wanteth not liquor: thy belly is like an heap of wheat set about with lilies. Thy two breasts are like two young roes that are twin. Thy neck is as a tower of ivory; thine eyes like the fishpools of Heshbon, by the gate of Bath-rabbim: thy nose is as the tower of Lebanon which looketh toward Damascus. Thine head upon thee is like Carmel, and the hair of thine head like purple; the king is held in the galleries. How fair and how pleasant art thou, O love, for delights!
>
> "This thy stature is like to a palm tree, and thy breasts to clusters of grapes. I said, I will go up to the palm tree, I will take hold of the boughs thereof: now also thy breasts shall be as clusters of the vine, and the smell of thy nose like apples;" "Thy lips, O my spouse, drop as the honeycomb: honey and milk are under thy tongue; and the smell of thy garments is like the smell of Lebanon. A garden inclosed is my sister, my spouse; a spring shut up, a fountain sealed" (Song 7: 1-8; 4: 11, 12).

To which Makeda responds:

> "I am black, but comely, O ye daughters of Jerusalem, as the tents of Kedar, as the curtains of Solomon. Look not upon me because I am black," "I sleep, but my heart waketh: it is the voice of my beloved that knocketh, saying, Open to me, my sister, my love, my dove, my undefiled: for my head is filled with dew, and my locks with the drops of the night. I have put off my coat; how shall I put it on? I have washed my feet; how shall I defile them? My beloved put in his hand by the hole of the door, and my bowels were moved for him. I rose up to open to my beloved: and my hands dropped with myrrh, and my fingers with sweet smelling myrrh, upon the

handles of the lock." "*Awake, O north wind; and come, thou south; blow upon my garden, that the spices thereof may flow out. Let my beloved come into his garden, and eat his pleasant fruits.*" Solomon, "*I am come into my garden my sister, my spouse: I have gathered my myrrh with my spices: I have drunk my wine with my milk: eat, O friends; drink, yea, drink abundantly*" (Song 1: 5, 6; 5: 1-5; 4: 16).

The same could also be said of Christ and his Church, which the apostle John saw, "coming down from God out of heaven, prepared as a bride adorned for her husband." Again, the word used here – and throughout the New Testament – for bride is the word *nymphe*, which might as well have been the word 'nympho,' as, though her body is said to be of the colour of jasper, which is mahogany, she is adorned in clothing of "pure gold, as it were transparent glass" (Revelation 21: 11, 21); all coinciding completely with the psalms, where it says, "Kings' daughters were among thy honourable women: upon thy right hand did stand the queen in gold of Ophir" (Psalms 45: 9). Remembering also that the Hebrew word for holy is also their word for harlot we can see the relation this Scripture has with the Messiah's own exclamation, "Verily I say unto you, That the publicans and the harlots go into the kingdom of God before you. For John came unto you in the way of righteousness, and ye believed him not: but the publicans and the harlots believed him". Basically, fully consensual female sex workers, "porn stars," and "freaks" have just as much right to practice seductionism as their male counterparts. Through knowledge of self these women can even become the *nymphe* of Christ.

Again, like within the kaula school of Tantra, through becoming one with either an Ausar or an Auset an initiate would be a part of a kind of polyamorous group sexuality. (And for the record, growing up in Brooklyn I also experienced this kind of polyamorous group sexuality in the street life: we called it running a sexual train, and both men and women would do it. This practice was very well respected back then as everything that happened was all in the family. What happened to the days of "It ain't no fun if my homie can't have none"? White people began calling it gang rape and our Black women began to feel ashamed of their actions and blamed the men. The truth is, it is neither sin nor shame to have multiple sex partners, as the ancients did it all the time. The godbodies used to do this time-honoured practice all the time too, but now they want to marry according to the government so as to avoid persecution. We should actually be more concerned about our ancestors' opinions than a little persecution from White people, but I digress.)

As a movement we godbodies should focus on considering the sacredness of the body that our ancestors used to respect, which modern minds have now vulgarised and made embarrassing by their moralistic corruptions, and not in accordance with the Black soul. The body (even the astral body of angelic beings) was always held as a holy temple, a thing of beauty, not to be gawked at or lusted over, but to be enjoyed and appreciated along with all the beauties of Allah's creation. The sacredness of the body is what causes we Black brothers and our Black sisters to be in awe of its naked presence as to us its beauty is something to be awed. Tyldesley also said on the subject, that the "overtly sexual images [of ancient Egypt] contributed to a general misinterpretation – fuelled by the apparently damning evidence of incest, polygamy, transparent dresses, sensual poetry and erotic papyri, and the complete absence of any wedding ceremony – of the Egyptians as a louche, even lewd, people. Yet there is no evidence to suggest that the Egyptians led [overly] promiscuous lives" (Tyldesley 2011: 45). Herein, Black sensuality and sexuality can be traced back to these early origins, and also an early group sexuality.

When Kings Die

Considering again the Asarian apocalypse we come to the place of his sensual resurrection; where Auset, after gathering together the scattered pieces of Ausar's body and mummifying them with spices and oils and strips of fine spun linen; is able to reanimate him by unifying his *khat* with his *ba* and *ka*. Then she gets impregnated by him and conceives a male child, who was to rule all nations with a rod of iron.

The ancestors anticipating this reality for the Black man and Black woman designed a psychological system suited to the Black soul and the attaining of its sensual resurrection. Here the being is divided into three, or more, technically four, parts: The *khat*, which is the lower self, representing the flesh or physiological body. The *ka*, which is the higher self, representing the soul or astral body. The *ba* or lower mind, representing what Freud called the id or instinctual mind; which physiologically resides in the brain. The *akh* or higher mind, representing those ethical and cultural mores we acquire in life; which physiologically resides in the heart or what the Kemetic people called the *ab*. According to the Heliopolitan view the unifying of the three (or four) attributes allowed one to attain to divinity. (As the heart was the only thing preserved in the *khat* during the process of mummification it was only the *khat*, the *ba* and the *ka* that needed reunion after death.)

Auset, by now subsumed in the diabolical drama, represented the Black woman. It is she who reunifies the body and soul of Ausar and allows him to reanimate, thus orchestrating Ausar's empowerment and resurrection. By the powers she gives him through her magic he then goes on to overcome the Dwat and become god and Pharaoh of the Dwat, taking his seat upon the square of morality. By this square he would also judge all those who came before him: any who were found perfect would enter his paradise, any who were not would suffer the tortures of chaos, or, from the time of the New Kingdom, Ammit – a monstrous combination of crocodile, lion/leopard and hippopotamus – would swallow their heart: the seat of the *akh* or the moral conscience. (Contrary to the view of most Egyptologists that the intelligent Egyptians – the Kemetic people – were ignorant of brain matter thought, this book states that they not only knew that thoughts took place in the brain, but that they also understood, even back then, that the heart produces more electricity than the brain and thereby was more sensitive, and sensual, than even the thought producing brain; making it the most likely seat of the conscience.)

This square of morality, to those in the godbody, is articulated in the Build Allah Square, a fighting ring in which we fight it out one-on-one with anybody we have a personal problem with, or six-on-one with anyone who breaks a godbody rule. By so doing we godbodies and street lifers use our square to show and prove our devotion and morality, but not to any person in particular but to our God – who, while being Intelligence, also represents Love, which to us is the highest form of understanding. This square being that fighting ring in which we fight it out with our brother so as to learn and train in mixed martial arts (MMA) having been guided by a God or Goddess that is proficient. Then after fighting them, whether we won or lost, showing them love and brotherly forgiveness, even to the point of forgetting anything we may have had against them. Thereby we also kept it real with each other, instead of hypocritically holding a grudge against somebody and yet smiling in their face. It was our repentance, penance, and trial court all at the same time.

Kropotkin also confirmed that the ancients used to practice these kinds of traditions by stating of the nineteenth century tribal people, "feuds are not uncommon – not in consequence of 'overstocking of the area,' or 'keen competition,' and like inventions of a mercantile century, but chiefly in consequence of superstition." In fact, according to all research early Homo sapiens people were a blood-vengeance people, keeping to the tradition of "eye for eye" justice long before Moses' celebrated exposition of it. Kropotkin said, "All savages are under the impression that blood shed must be revenged by blood. If any one has been killed, the murderer must die; if any one has been wounded, the aggressor's blood must be shed. ... Now, when both the offender and the offended belong to the same tribe, the tribe and the offended person settle the affair. But when the offender belongs to another tribe, and that tribe, for one reason or another, refuses a compensation, then the offended tribe decides to take the revenge itself."

At the same time, Ausar, being the Kemetic god of vegetation was murdered by his brother Setekh, who was the Kemetic god of desert; hence blood-vengeance was required of him. This is where Horu became all important to this Kemetic tradition. The people of Kemet, being very educated and intelligent, learned history and anthropology from ancient Kush, in which was discovered in our time the fossils of the earliest homo sapiens sapiens man. From this information we can piece together a general overview based on the Kemetic tale of Horu and Setekh even if the traditional story is obviously lost.

In considering the development of the Homo erectus, Engels put their physiological change from Homo erectus to Homo sapiens sapiens (otherwise known as Cro-Magnon man) down to their slow change in diet. In sketching out his theory in his

Transition from Ape to Man, Engels said, "A meat diet contained in an almost ready state the most essential ingredients required by the organism for its metabolism. By shortening the time required for digestion, it also shortened the other vegetative bodily processes that correspond to those of plant life". Thus, according to Engels, as the early hominidae began to change their diet they began to change their own metabolism also, which as we know has actually been proven.

However, Engels went further within his theory to show how, "Just as becoming accustomed to a vegetable diet side by side with meat converted wild cats and dogs into the servants of man, so also adaptation to a meat diet, side by side with a vegetable diet, greatly contributed towards giving bodily strength and independence to man in the making." This would have also contributed to the hormonal shifting of the proto-Homo sapiens, allowing for the upping of various hormones that they otherwise had in limited supply: such as, progesterone, testosterone, endorphins and enkephalins. These hormonal changes would come to have a direct effect on the endocrine systems of both genders around about this time allowing for humanity's sensual reshaping also.

The hypothalamus part of the brain, which interacts with the endocrine system and the pituitary complex; is where all our spontaneous, dietary, sexual, emotional, thermal, violent, and growth activity is co-ordinated. It is also that part of the brain that produces and modulates the hormones best suited to the development of these activities. So here Engels demonstrated how, "the body benefited from the law of correlation of growth, as Darwin called it. This law states that the specialised forms of separate parts of an organic being are always bound up with certain forms of other parts that apparently have no connection with them." But these hormonal adjustments were merely a part of our premature development into the Homo sapiens people we are today.

Around the time the ancient Homo erectus died out or were replaced by the Homo sapiens sapiens the whole situation must have appeared like a killing off. For this cause vengeance was sought for by Neter, by Nature, or by some other supernatural force. Even so, the environmental adjustments occurring in the world about this time triggered an ecological consequence that would shake everything: the last ice age. Kropotkin sheds a little more light on this situation, saying, "Now it must be borne in mind that the glacial age did not come to an end at once over the whole surface of the earth. It still continues in Greenland. Therefore, at a time when the littoral regions of the Indian Ocean, the Mediterranean, or the Gulf of Mexico already enjoyed a warmer climate, and became the seats of higher civilizations … territories in middle Europe, Siberia, and Northern America … remained in early post-glacial conditions".

Herein we see how the hope that Ausar – whose name in the language of Kemet was the masculine of blackness, and who represented the agricultural form of the Homo erectus – would have found an afterlife in which his agricultural lifestyle and mentality would be, not only the norm but also the mandatory and customary practice, was presented and propagated in ancient Kush as a result of his demise. This afterlife of simplicity and peaceful coexistence being no longer available to these still developing hominidae, was, in their view, the realm of the divine Black, a now unreachable past that can no longer be attained but by moral uprightness. But according to the tradition, to gain for us, and himself, this eternity he first had to conquer that great serpent of darkness and chaos: Apop, and thus take control of the Dwat taking his seat upon the square. And sure enough Ausar would eventually charm Apop and take over the entire Dwat, coinciding with his title as god of the Dwat.

The agricultural ideal that Ausar represented, the nostalgia he brought to the minds of his descendants and successors, caused him to have that high place within the social and intellectual soul of the ancient world. Again, the tragedy of his demise at the hands of his fellow hominidae made it all the more tragic. This obviously played a big part in why, as Kropotkin said, "All savages [were] under the impression that blood shed must be revenged by blood. If any one has been killed, the murderer must die; if any one has been wounded, the aggressor's blood must be shed. There is no exception to the rule, not even for animals; so the hunter's blood is shed on his return to the village when he has shed the blood of an animal."

The square of morality, upon which Ausar would sit in his judgment hall, thus also became a representative of that by which one has to prove one's heart pure and free from all vanities and unnecessary attachments to this life and world. The violent testing practiced by us godbodies coincides with this scalar testing of the Kemetic; by which the heart was weighed with that of a feather, the feather of Maat, to see if they were worthy of *Sekh-t* (or paradise).

To the Kemetic when someone died they would stand before the ancestors, who were all personified in Ausar, who judged them according to the inaccurately named *42 Negative Confessions* to see if they were worthy of initiation into *Sekh-t*. The soul of the righteous dead would thus be judged as right and exact (equal to Maat) having completed this process. It was also very closely related to the idea of freedom from sin; that is, a sinless life. This also meant the mature practice of seductionism and militarism by the individual, so as to keep them from any social or moral imbalance. All these also produced a hormonal rebalancing within their bodies all leading them back to sensual fulness.

But such a fulness, in our time, requires more than a refining and purifying of our militarism and seductionism; it also requires a purifying of our interactionism. Yet, how does one go about refining their interactionism? What even is interactionism? For the sake of our purposes we will define interactionism as a form of micro-sociology that studies and analyses the interactions and act-species that develop between physical and astral bodies and the forces around them. Again, if one wishes to refine such interactions the keys to this are: (i) developing over time greater empathy for one's environment; (ii) enduring and persevering within such interactions as, in spite of counterintuitive behaviour, or even resistant behaviour, from said environment, the environment, forces, and circumstances themselves are all alive and seeking to test said perseverance; (iii) expending hard work, effort, and time so as to achieve mastery.

Where development by hyperintelligence, hypermartiality, and hypersexuality occur all spatial elements come into play allowing the body to be at one with its environment in ways that are most perfect for our ability and appearance. Effectively, as our hormones, like progesterone, testosterone, endorphins, enkephalins, oestrogen, and androgen, get distributed through our own bodies; even so, through improving our social life, martial life, and sexual life we can develop a more balanced life; which is not too dissimilar to what occurred with our Asarian ancestors.

At the same time, according to Engels, "The reaction on labour and speech of the development of the brain and its attendant senses, of the increasing clarity of consciousness ... gave both labour and speech an ever-renewed impulse to further development. This development did not reach its conclusion when man finally became distinct from the ape, but on the whole made further powerful progress[;] its degree and direction ... has been strongly urged forward, on the one hand, and guided along more definite directions, on the other, by a new element which came into play with the appearance of fully-fledged man, namely, *society*."

Blood Vengeance By Default

The environmental conditions of ancient East Africa allowed for the intellectual capacities of the Homo sapiens to develop further than those of the Homo erectus through the realising, quite early on, that their survival would be far more achievable through having large groups working in unison than having a few people working alone. This development in human reasoning allowed for the creation of large groups and societies in early human history. Thus, as Kropotkin continued, "Common hunting, common fishing, and common culture of the orchards or the plantations of fruit trees was the rule with the old gentes. ... In short, communal culture is so habitual with many Aryan, Ural-Altayan, Mongolian, Negro, Red Indian, Malayan, and Melanesian stems that we must consider it as a universal – though not as the only possible – form of [aboriginal] agriculture."

This helps us substantially to understand the development of the Homo sapiens people. From these practices came new traditions, which would be formed and passed down via the communal societies of the time from generation to generation. Engels said, "The work of each generation itself became different, more perfect and more diversified. Agriculture was added to hunting and cattle raising; then came spinning, weaving, metalworking, pottery and navigation. Along with trade and industry, art and science finally appeared. Tribes developed into nations and states. Law and politics arose, and with them that fantastic reflection of human things … religion." And though it may be obvious to most that religion, or something comparable to religion, was in existence from the earliest human communities, Engels' general theory of the evolution that occurred in the development of the human societies during the Pleistocene epoch becomes clear.

As to the development of human families, Kropotkin stated, "far from being [an indigenous] form of organization, the family is a very late product of human evolution. As far as we can go back in the palæo-ethnology of mankind, we find men living [mainly] in societies – tribes similar to those of the highest mammals; and an extremely slow and long evolution was required to bring these societies to the gentile, or clan organization, which, in its turn, had to undergo another, also very long evolution, before the first germs of family, polygamous or monogamous, could appear." And sure enough, even "when the bonds of common descent had been loosened by migrations on a grand scale, … the development of the separated family within the clan itself had destroyed the old unity of the clan, a new form of union, territorial in its principle – the village community – was called into existence by the social genius of man."

All corresponding to the Asarian apocalypse in that the now pregnant Auset was forced into wandering in the desert during the time that her brother Setekh was ruler over the earth. This may also have been a symbolic representation of the historical events of the Kingdom in ancient Kush known as Ta Seti. The fall of Ta Seti, which itself corresponded with the general ending of the ice age, would prove to have a lot to do with the mass migrations occurring from South to North in those days. As the ancient people began to migrate up the Nile Valley area, and beyond the Mediterranean northward, westward and eastward, they carried with them their agricultural methods.

Again, during this time the system of most of these Black and Kushite tribes were matrilineal and semi-matriarchal. Women were then hailed as goddesses (all deities were predominantly female, the priesthood was also exclusively female and sensual; and the cultural lessons and secrets were held by women in common). If a patriarchal system existed at all during these times it is most likely (based on the Kemetic tradition) to have been in Ta Seti (which means the land of Set (Setekh)). And to be a little clearer, the matriarchal systems were usually tribal and scattered; they practiced gypsy and Bedouin style migration and had no hugely centralised authority system, as discussed earlier by Kropotkin. These, though somewhat beautiful and free, were no match for any patriarchal system of war-ready fighters, hunters, and chieftains, all energised and ready to conquer. And though the matriarchal systems had warriors and warlords within their structure they were still no match for any patriarchal tribe. It seemed the only way for the female to gain or maintain any form of substance was for her to have a male authority with her.

Here we see the significance of the male-child Horu; he was to rule the two kingdoms with two-fold strength, and to take back the throne of his father Ausar. According to the Asarian apocalypse Setekh, knowing Auset was pregnant with Ausar's son, went out searching for her to destroy whatever child she gave birth to. At this time, Auset then took upon herself the wings of a great eagle that she might fly to the Nile River and hide by the bulrushes. It is there that she was met by Djehwti, the god of wisdom and law, who prophesied that Horu would grow to avenge his father's murder and to overthrow the kingdom of Setekh that was then still in operation. And it would be his coming that was the hope of all the Kushite tribes of the time.

Blood vengeance would soon be sought for by Horu against Setekh in revenge for the murder of his father, so that Horu confronted Setekh having reached full maturity; at which time a tribunal also ensued. This tribunal being won by Horu gave Horu an open right to the throne of his father, a fulfilling of his own destiny as prophesied by Djehwti, and a form of vengeance for the murder of his father. But this was not good enough for some of the gods, particularly Ra, king of the gods and definition of godhood, who said Horu was too young and premature; he could hardly handle the responsibilities of governing the rebellious and corrupted ways of nature, let alone those of humanity; which caused the heavenly court to then be divided.

Horu was thus forced to fight Setekh in a contest in which Setekh and Horu both became hippopotami. At this point, Auset was then able to harpoon Setekh and thus draw him close to the pangs of death; where he would have inevitably entered the Dwat to meet his brother and victim Ausar face to face, facing trial and judgment under his authority. Realising what awaited him should he die Setekh cried out to his sister Auset for mercy, who, taking pity on her brother, healed his wound, and he was made whole. This caused Horu to get vexed and cut off his mother's head for helping his father's enemy. For this insult to his sister and to get revenge for his own humiliation Setekh then beat up Horu and plucked out his eyes leaving Horu blinded.

Now, as eyes in ancient Kemet carried a very distinctive quality about them – they symbolised righteousness, truth, and justice – the symbolism of this act is undeniable. The right eye in the Kemetic language was the *maa* and the left eye the *maa-t* and they both bore significant meaning to the Kemetic people of the order underlying the physical order of the universe; and Horu, being the god of kings, bore a mathematical symbolism in his eyes – primarily in the language of the *Metu Neteru* (hieroglyphics), as a fractional sequence.

The symbolisms contained in these Kemetic apocalypses – being of the similitude to the symbolisms contained in the Hebrew apocalypses, and where the symbolic language of the

Revelation came from – was to tell the story of how the ancient Kushites (and by extension the Kemetics) came to be one people. Here the Horu son, in cutting off the head of his Auset mother proved to be unjust and unrighteous (that is, unworthy of his eyes). The evident conflicts between the Black woman and her Black son are understandably also quite problematic. Inasmuch as the single-mother Auset is chastised for aiding her brother and widow-maker Setekh; the action was not of truth as Auset was Horu's first teacher and his most faithful supporter. The eye in itself symbolised balance, truth, and order: the eyes of Horu symbolised the divine order of mathematical integrity. If the divine order was to be unjust then no one would be able to see the truth from falsehood, like Setekh plucking out Horu's eyes.

In the story at this point Horu is left wandering, lost, blind, and alone. Seeing him virtually powerless the goddess Hethor (Het-Hor, Kemetic for house of Horu, that is, the divine woman) takes pity on the lost and lonely Horu and calls for the god Djehwti to make for him two new eyes, which he makes using her breast-milk. This is part of the reason why Hethor's hieroglyph usually has cow horns covering a sun-disk or the image of a light skinned woman with a crown of cow horns covering a sun-disk. Even so, the man without the nurturing of his woman is lost, blind, and lonely. It is she who gives him eyes to see himself as she sees him, as majestic.

However, when Horu had regained his sight and right mind from Djehwti he later returned to the court of the gods, making some of the gods vexed, in particular Ra. To add insult to injury, Babi, the baboon god of sexual potency, then called Ra an old wind-bag whose temples were deserted; causing Ra to lock himself away vowing never to return again, thus turning the universal orders back into darkness and chaos. It is then that Hethor entered into his secret chamber, wearing her usual fine spun linen, and performed a strip-tease sun-dance for him in which she fully exposed her vagina to him. The sun-dance ritual she performed broke his spirit and made him forget his wrath.

Now some within the feminist community may overlook the beauty contained in the concept of a woman saving the world with no more than her vagina and instead focus on the sexualisation or the toxicity of the male pornographic gaze or some other pretentiousness to undervalue this tradition. At the same time, Nzegwu was not shy to mention the actually empowering lesson that could be gained if looked at genuinely. Within Black traditions, "The capacity and functionality of the vagina [made] it both a desirable and dreaded organ. Its moist (or dry), warm chamber allures and arouses men and drives them to seek copulation. Its muscular walls rhythmically grip and pull the penis into its recesses and impel the male to an emotional peak. … As owners of this passage, women dictate the terms of entrance. They can make entrance a pleasurable experience through muscular rhythmic contractions or they can frustrate that experience by lack of cooperation."

Herein, we also see how the ritual of the sun-dance and of the strip-tease would come to be re-enacted by future generations of Black women in their regional exhibitionist traditions; which all sprang from this Kushite and Kemetic source. Those areas that needed rain would have the rain-dance, while those areas that needed the sun would have the sun-dance. And as mentioned earlier, the unashamed brazenness of these strip-tease practices, and of the light exhibitionism involved – all themselves being manifestations of their unapologetic, seductionistic, hypererotic performativity – were performed at special tribal events accompanied by music and exotic dances. The so-called lewdness and hypersexuality of the dances of most Black, Latin, and Asiatic women today also mark an unconscious link with this event.

Moreover, in her research on the different sexual-school communities of Africa, Nzegwu could not help but mention how "it is necessary to establish what happens when women are positively affirmed; how our understanding of sexuality differs when the vagina is perceived as an important organ. At the very least, cultural songs and dances are [now] rich with sexual allusions to the power and strength of this organ. Cultural dances and contemporary dance moves, such as *makossa*, *mapouka*, *ndombolo*, *soukous* and *ventilator* speak of this power in fluid, circular gyrations of the hips and quick forward and backward thrusts of the pelvis. These dances can be energetically or slowly enacted, delivering the … sexually charged moves that suggest the penis will be devoured." Or in plain English, within Black pro-sex traditions the female has always had far more autonomy than in the Victorian monogamous patriarchal tradition, regardless of the screams of the anti-sex feminists to the contrary.

As can also be seen from the story: it was literally the act of exhibitionism (which is usually considered the act of exposing the private areas of the body in public for the sake of sexual self-gratification: basically the getting off on practicing a form of nudity in front of someone else) that effectively brought back the sunshine. Essentially, by our own identification with the so-called worthless, low life, and vulgar, we develop such a consciousness of self that we feel no shame over the past, nor any serious shame in public deviation. In this relation, "Cooper's tongue-in-cheek, yet serious, call for 'bottoms-up history' (Cooper 1993: x) reminds us of the 'pubic' that is the root of the word 'public' and the 'sexualised representation of the potent female bottom in contemporary Jamaican dancehall culture' … these nether regions that are not spoken of in polite/political society" (Sheller 2012: 42).

Acknowledging thereby, there is an orgasmic rush that can be gained from hypersexual practices, a rush that definitely reaches large numbers of we Black people. Nevertheless, this rush is slowly becoming more and more lost to those Black people that are accepting the Victorian monogamous patriarchal standard of morality and are thereby counting piety as something unsexed and unsexual. Notwithstanding, as can be detected from their apocalypses the people of Kemet obviously gave great significance to free love and hypersexuality. Indeed, when Tum himself arose from the primordial chaos and created light and darkness: the light he called Ra and the darkness Apop. The first thing Tum did was choose the light over the darkness thus becoming Ra Atum. The second thing Tum did as Ra Atum was create Hethor as his lover and daughter and technically his hand.

It is from here that Ra Atum began the process of creation producing first the male sexual deposit (Shu) then the female sexual deposit (Tefnut) to be fertilised. At this point, Tyldesley articulated the White misconception of this sexuality, showing how "thousands of years later, scenes of Atum impregnating himself caused many Victorian Egyptologists to blink, while images of the unashamedly ithyphallic gods Geb, Min and occasionally Amen led to such absurdities as strategically placed museum labels designed to conceal the gods' true nature from the eyes of delicate lady visitors." In this regard, the types of hypersexual practices Hethor embarked on would have definitely been considered anathema.

But it all coincides with the Kemetic love for scientific exploration. As the Kemetic people viewed Ra as godhood, knowledge, and as the sun – even as the godbody view the Black man as Allah, knowledge, and as the sun – their studies of the self-reproducing species of amoebic, plant, and marine life, as well as their knowledge of pollination and its role in the procreation process allowed their creation stories and apocalypses to be more scientifically correct than most were. The Kemetic were thereby able to develop a high regard for the creative and transfigurative powers of sex and sexuality. They understood that sex also plays a huge role in self-creation and in the process of self-knowledge.

But Auset, by now tired of her son constantly getting rejected, and of the stubbornness of the gods, particularly that of Ra, chose to go to her husband Ausar for help. But when even the messages sent by Ausar seemed to meet the stubborn moanings of the gods, Ausar gathered together the hoards of hell and of the entire Dwat. He also prepared that ancient serpent Apop, who represented the darkness of ignorance, madness, anarchy, and chaos; and who even Ra was powerless against, and reminded Ra that he dwelt among innumerable daemons, who feared neither god nor goddess, and that if they were to destroy any of the deities their heart would be bought before his square to be judged even as all hearts were. So that through the militarism of Ausar in the Dwat and the seductionism of Hethor in Pet, Ra came to the conclusion that Horu was the rightful heir to Ausar, as Ausar's testimony took precedent over Setekh's kinship position. Horu was thus given authority over all the kings of the earth, that is, over Kush; and chose for Hethor to be his main wife and beloved, as she was the goddess who supported and believed in him from the beginning.

Where to Find the Real Ark of Noah

From the etymology of this literary masterpiece the Hebrews took three concepts that would effectively be unified within the Christian traditions: that of *Ashar*, which the Hebrews defined as happiness, righteousness, and honesty; that of *Ra*, which the Hebrews redefined in their concept of the Evil One; and that of *Satan*, which was based on what Setekh represented to the forces of righteousness in the story. Etymologically the word *satan* does go a little deeper though: in Hebrew the word *sậtan* means to attack or accuse and comes from the root *shotet*, meaning to flog or scourge. But *shotet* also bares some similarities to the word *setekh*, which means negativity, but mainly in the sense of violence, harshness, calamity, aridity, and barrenness. Basically, the Hebrews saw Ra as a socio-cultural evil and Satan as a kind of natural and supernatural evil. To be sure, neither Ra nor Satan carried any favourable position in the Hebraic jargon or mindset; both were treated with contempt and ambivalence even as they were in the Asarian apocalypse.

Nevertheless, any Black boy who is raised as a Horu develops an interconnection to the ancient Pharaohs of Kush and Kemet and will see self as a divine manifestation. Moreover, as the Messiah himself represented Horu in his own time and the living Pharaohs represented Horu in their own time; even so, Ausar represented Allah in the Asarian apocalypse, being the personification of agape and of the dead ancestors of the Black family. Where the Messiah reigns in the heart the person must, like the Messiah, fight against all manifestations of injustice and unrighteousness. By struggling for freedom, justice and equality the Messiah proved himself to be a true Horu, but by dying on a cross he proved himself to be a true Ausar.

The elevation of the Black person from Horu to Ausar (or Hethor to Auset) must be a process by which the dictatorship of the Messiah (Horu) exorcises all vanities from self to open self up to a place where it will be ready to suffer and suffer long. But while they are still a Horu the individual should be taught to value the right and exact, the pure and clean. Purity should in fact be so important to them that they can see it in all things, as said by the apostle Paul, "Unto the pure all things are pure: but unto them that are defiled and unbelieving is nothing pure; but even their mind and conscience is defiled" (Titus 1:15). Pure and clean living is thus for the interior, exterior and anterior of the purified soul.

The Black Horu son and Hethor daughter should be taught this pure and clean lifestyle along with sexuality so as to understand their sexuality from a young age for the purpose of heightening their sensuality and understanding of their erotogenous zones. That is not to say that they should be allowed to do adult things, like start having sex or stop wearing underwear: they should merely be taught about sex to know their bodies more and how to control their baser, more instinctual sensations better. Learning control over their sexual energies from a young age would give them a closer connection to the deity by the time they reach adulthood so that they would be able to become true Ausars and Ausets before death.

That said, it is my hope that the sexual revolution I am calling for with these hypererotic ideas may broaden into a sensual resurrection. How I see this is with Black eroticism being introduced into our movement, together with the use of perfumes, colognes, and lotions to keep our private areas smelling clean, and martial training in armed and unarmed combat at the godbody meetings that we hold weekly, so that our women can protect themselves from violence or rape; we would effectively be creating a situation where we as a people will be able to resurrect our own souls. We godbodies should be the centre of this Black eroticism movement but it will spill over into the Black community as a whole, especially if our women are granted the right to dress how they choose to with no limitations but perhaps the underwear thing.

At the same time, both the concepts of eroticism and pornography are exhibitionistic articulations of libidinal energy; but there are still two fundamental differences between them that must be acknowledged: first, erotica has class, and, second, erotica has narrative substance. Indeed, one of the most expertly explained definitions of eroticism comes to us from the eminent philosopher Socrates in Plato's *Symposium*. Though I may disagree with Socrates' categorising Eros as a daemon I cannot fault his systematic delineation.

Consequently, Socrates saw erotic agency as the instigator of five progressive desires: (i) Love for a singular beautiful body: the love object himself or herself succumbing to standards of both the familiar and the sublime. (ii) Love for all beautiful bodies: the lover learns at this stage that scores of people possess as much, if not more, beauty than the original locus and so desire to see as many as possible. (iii) Love for *psychikos* beauty, that is, love for sensual beauty as *psychikos* was originally translated as sensual: at this stage they realise that a beautiful body is not enough as even a physically unattractive person who is sensually beautiful is more beautiful than the person who is beautiful in body only. (iv) Love for *ergetikos, nomikos*, and *epitdeumikos* beauty or the action, regulation, and practice of beauty: at this higher stage they come to narrow in on which sensual activity or practice always applies to beauty and so desire to see only that. (v) The highest stage, love for *epistemikos* beauty or the science of beauty: at this stage they reach the point of seeking that Absolute Beauty which surpasses all these. Conversely, all these stages, according to Socrates, are inspired by erotica.

Nevertheless, these five stages in *Black* erotica could be articulated as: (i) Black beauty, (ii) polyamory, (iii) Afrosensuality, (iv) light exhibitionism, and (v) seductionism. At the first level would be Black beauty. Basically, the perfume, cosmetics, hair, clothing, and body sculpting industries make billions of dollars convincing ordinary women that they can make themselves and others see them as beautiful. Putting aside all the politics of whether there are actually any "ordinary women," or whether they should have to devote themselves to looking beautiful at all, or even care so much about beauty, let us try to remember that Socrates claimed he learned these stages of beauty from Diotima of Mantineia, who he called a *wise woman* with many kinds of knowledge. The fact is, if the products and methods of the beauty industries were ineffective at raising women's beauty, or at least their confidence in their beauty, they would not be generating the multibillions of dollars they currently do. Effectively, perfumes, cosmetics, hairstyling, good clothing, and an incredible body can make a woman beautiful. Black beauty is when these industries are designed specifically for Black women. Those Black women who use them will ultimately inspire first level erotic feelings.

At the second level is polyamory or plural love. If a Black woman, regardless of her physical beauty, even if she despised the beauty industries and vowed never to care about any of them, she can still inspire erotic desire. She even gives herself an edge over all those beautiful and beautified women, by letting it be known that she is not intimidated if a man has sex with other women. Again, putting aside the politics of male societal dominance, and the ethics of cheating, if a woman genuinely lacks jealousy and has confidence in her own abilities and relationship she will be perceived as sexy. Far sexier even than a woman with just a pretty or beautiful face. With that one move she would have not only reached a place where she can inspire second level erotic feelings, but she would have made herself a regular in his life, not simply a one-night stand.

At the third level is Black sensuality or Afrosensuality. Sensuality itself is when someone uses their sexual energy to drive or inspire others to think of sex with them. Thus, they inspire third level erotic feelings. Afrosensuality is when they consistently, devastatingly, and Africanly use sexuality in their words or behaviours. Again, a Black woman can be subtly or overtly sensual: from talking openly about her body or sexual skills to touching his body or her own. However, when a woman is able to use techniques like anchoring, triggering, amplifying, flirting, or word emphasising in an overtly sexual way, whether she is polyamorous or not, whether she is society's standard of beauty or not, she will leap miles ahead of the women who are any one of the two without doing so. Indeed, the libidinal techniques she uses on the first day she meets him will stay in his mind months after they develop a relationship, even if she is a jealous woman.

The fourth level, however, is the money level: light exhibitionism. Any woman, even if she is absolutely ugly by her own standards and the worlds; even if she is not polyamorous but in fact insecure about her chances if there is another woman; even if she never has had or will have any sexiness at all and has no idea how to get it; she can still leap lightyears above whole groups of women who have great beauty, and practice expertly both polyamory and Afrosensuality, and she can do it with just one practice.

There is a story about a fox and a hedgehog. The fox is crafty, cunning, quick, and dangerous, much stronger and more sophisticated than the lowly hedgehog. The hedgehog is dowdy, ugly, and much slower and clumsier than the fox. Usually the hero of most European folk tales, the fox wins every time. However, when the fox, with his multiplicity of moves and tactics, jumps in front of the hedgehog to catch him, the hedgehog just performs one simple move and the fox is defeated every time. Curling up into a ball, with spikes pointing in every direction, the fox stands no chance and has to admit defeat. Even so, that same ugly, jealous, insecure, and unsexy woman can leap lightyears ahead of a group of very beautiful women, who practice, expertly, both polyamory and sensuality with just one activity.

Let us say the man she desires is a rich, handsome, player with a group of beautiful, polyamorous, expert seducers on call, and an even larger group of beautiful and gorgeous women throwing themselves at him regularly. Well, love is love, the heart wants what the heart wants, and her heart wants him to love her and only her. What chance does she really have, remember, she is ugly by her own standards and the worlds. The truth is, all she needs to do to accomplish her goal is buy a ton of dresses, both simple and complex, that reveal when a woman is not wearing any underwear, then she needs to wear one of them, while practicing light exhibitionism, in front of him.

The first time he sees her he will notice her, and as a player he will pursue. That one action would have effectively not only put her in a league with all the beautiful and sexy women he sees on a regular basis, it would have put her ahead of all of them. Whether they have sex that night or not he will want to see her again. If the next time he sees her she is wearing another, different, dress that also reveals that she is not wearing underwear then she will automatically leap to the top of the list of women he desires. Effectively, she would have inspired fourth level erotic feelings in him. If the next time he sees her she is again wearing a different dress that also reveals that she is not wearing any underwear she will from that time become his only standard of beauty (remember, she even used to see her own self as ugly). Not only so, but he will see her as an extremely beautiful woman, more beautiful than all the other women in his life, who will also feel boring and unimpressive to him (again, remember, these are all expert seducers).

If the fourth time he sees her she is again wearing a different dress that, in its own way, also reveals that she is not wearing any underwear, he will fall madly in love with her. Whether he confesses his love or not is of no concern, the act of light exhibitionism and the consistency of the repetition would have anchored in him the idea that this woman always wears beautiful dresses (the dresses themselves may be cheap and ugly, the point is that he will see them as beautiful) and never wears underwear. She would have effectively taught him to fall madly in love with her with the power of anchoring and fanatical consistency.

At this point, he will be ready to tell her he is giving up all other women for her and with all honesty do it, as very few other women really go without underwear with such consistency. Still, she will have to regulate this practice and make it very permanent, otherwise the inconsistency at whatever stage of this process will cause the outcome to vary. Human beings crave consistency and fear loss. By her not wearing underwear the first day the first manifestation of this fear will be that this is a onetime thing never or rarely to be done again. By her not wearing underwear the second time he sees her the fear will now be manifest in the idea that she sees this as an occasional thing but generally she will be just like every other woman. By her not wearing underwear the third time he sees her the fear will be that she will get bored or give up and just wear underwear the next time he sees her. By the fourth time she would have effectively anchored in his mind that she herself equals no underwear, and all the pleasures that entails. Now his fear of loss will be of losing her. That is the power of true light exhibitionism, and why I encourage it as a godbody practice, so long as the Goddess keeps her lower regions clean and smelling good, she will have this power.

At the final level is seductionism. At this level the Black person (but continuing on with our analogy of a Black woman) applies all four methods of inspiring hypereroticism. She makes herself beautiful regularly; she is polyamorous and not intimidated by her man having sex with other women; she is hypersexual in both words and behaviours; and she is a light exhibitionist. This woman will ultimately inspire fifth level erotic feelings from any and all men. No woman has to be all four, but the Black woman who is all four has mastered the science of beauty. She is a seductionist. Such a woman is obviously like hen's teeth, if not imaginary, but she will be the desire, love, and obsession of all the men she interacts with, especially on a regular basis. The level of erotic desire this woman will inspire within the men she interacts with will be the greatest amount they could possibly experience in that moment, and as that will be where she gets her pleasure from she will be like an eroto-masochist.

Again, no woman is being forced to do any of these things, or to climb any of these levels. In fact, the example I have been using throughout of a woman may have been a little deceptive. It has purely been based on the understanding that there are a lot more complexities to women than simply those that desire power or wealth, many actually desire to inspire erotic feelings in other people, men or women or both. For those women that have this desire I have used this example. However, any seductionist, whether the seductionist be male or female, is an eroto-masochist. If you desire to be such, whether you are a man or a woman, then you must climb the ladder.

As to the ancient tale of early humanity, we received that via ancient Kemet and it provides the best portrayal of the events of how humanity evolved into the Homo sapiens people we are today. Here Horu, representing the Shemsu Hor tribes and Setekh, representing the tribes of Ta Seti, face off for ultimate supremacy over the world, that is, over ancient Kush. In both cases these early societies were most probably polyamorous: that is, they most likely practiced a kind of free love and group sexuality; so that ideas like competition and jealousy would have been alien to these tribal communities within their territorial jurisdictions. Whereas to the modern mindset and to modern moral standards their systems may seem shocking, in the traditional nations such practices were quite valued, and have only been losing their value as modernism has replaced the ancient and more traditional ideas of the past.

So now, based on the understanding that in the resurrection we shall once again be like the divine, al-Muhibb, and seeing that early humanity were themselves made in the image of al-Muhibb; early humanity presents the clue as to how we shall live in the resurrection. Again, in considering the story of human development, it begins in the form of the proto-human: Homo erectus, who first learned "the utilisation of fish (under which heading, we also include crabs, shellfish and other aquatic animals) for food and ... the employment of fire. These two are complementary, since fish food becomes fully available only by the use of fire," as Engels informed us. "But all that was not yet labour in the proper sense of the word. Labour begins with the making of tools. And what are the most ancient tools that we find ... and of the rawest of contemporary savages? They are hunting and fishing implements, the former at the same time serving as weapons. But hunting and fishing presuppose the transition from an exclusively vegetable diet to the concomitant use of meat, and this is another important step in the process of transition from ape to man."

Indeed, Engels revealed to us that, "This new food, however, made men independent of climate and locality. By following the rivers and coasts they were able, even in their savage state, to spread over the greater part of the earth's surface. ... The newly occupied territories as well as the unceasingly active urge for discovery ... made available new foodstuffs ... and game, which was occasionally added to the diet after the invention of the first weapons – the club and the spear." These early people, Homo erecti, also tracked the stars, studied the celestial cycles, and developed traditions based on the electrical currents flowing through the earth. The extent of their calculations is such that even to this day we are unable to accomplish what was accomplished in the ancient times, and this is before Ta Seti. In fact, even ancient Egypt would not have been able to master the arts, sciences, technologies, and calculations they mastered without the teachings, guidelines, and maps worked out by these early civilisations.

It is undeniable that a change in diet and in scientific discoveries affected these Homo erecti allowing civilisation to begin. And these fathers and mothers of civilisation definitely had advanced technologies in their time that bastardises our own modern technologies. "But [as] animals exert a lasting effect on their environment unintentionally and, as far as the animals themselves are concerned, accidentally", whether by fluke or by chance, the tribes of the Homo erectus, by their change of diet and by adopting new scientific practices may have not only superseded their hominid forbears but may also have bought on the ice ages that followed in the Pleistocene epoch. It would be during these glacial periods that the greatest developments in humanity would occur in our transition from the Australopithecus africanus into proper Homo sapiens people.

All this presents us with a definitive relation here to the story in Genesis of Noah and the flood: a flood reported of in all ancient traditions but those of Kemet, reflecting the reality of what happened after the last glacial age on the earth. For the results of the last glacial age, when the ice sheets melted, was mass rain and mass flooding, the forty days and forty nights being symbolic of a more lengthy time period of rains and rising sea-levels. By this time the Ta Setian tribes would have already died off and the Shemsu Hor tribes would have been developing into the matriarchal tribes of pre-Dynastic Kemet. Again, the ark that Noah built is in actual fact more likely to have been symbolic of wooded forestland than a wooded boat or ship. This wooded planting expedition in which he hid all the wildlife of the ancient world, still works even now. For even today wildlife is and can be preserved for future generations from ice ages or other natural disasters by conserving them in forests, woodlands, and savannahs. We also see in these stories an opposite view of a state-of-nature to that of Thomas Hobbes. Rather than the random chaos of all against all we have the sociable relatedness of early human and animal societies.

And so, in that the genuine resurrection of the father is in his son; Noah, representing himself a Horu figure, is given a command of the similitude to that given to Adam that proves very fitting at this time, for "God blessed Noah and his sons, and said unto them, Be fruitful and multiply, and replenish the earth. And the fear of you and the dread of you shall be upon every beast of the earth, and upon every fowl of the air, upon all that moveth upon the earth, and upon all the fishes of the sea; into your hand are they delivered. Every moving thing that liveth shall be meat for you; even as the green herb have I given you all things. But flesh with the life thereof, which is the blood thereof, shall ye not eat. And surely your blood or your lives will I require; at the hand of every beast will I require it, and at the hand of man; at the hand of every man's brother will I require the life of man. Whoso sheddeth man's blood, by man shall his blood be shed: for in the image of God made he man." (Genesis 9:1-6).

Conclusion

As the godbody, we seek to bring into existence neither a utopian nor an idealistic system but an already existing system, our motive is therefore not the ultimate overthrow of the bourgeoisie entirely, it is merely the defending of our already existing culture, traditions and theodical perspectives as they stand. We also refuse to allow modern standards and opinions to corrupt or contaminate our current system of doing things; regardless of how much persecution we will receive for it. Moreover, we also seek independence from the current system, while at the same time recognising our interconnection to it.

The independence we seek works on the obvious and means in a somewhat bourgeois sense, to not need or be dependent on state power or any other entity for our existence, basically to exist in our own right and on our own terms. By interconnection we understand in a more doctrinal, monistic, and naturalistic sense our coexistence alongside and in relation to the current system; not to overthrow it but to be of benefit to it, even as it, of necessity, will be of benefit to us. We are presently of benefit to very few. But we seek to allow that grace which has been shown us by Self to be shown to those outside of ourselves. Thus, our independence as a Nation of Gods and Earths serves as a means of allowing us to not simply gain autonomy but also as a means of benefiting those we are now given the privilege of helping, basically, interdependency.

CONCLUSION

The obvious question of those within the status quo at this point would be: so "what's the catch?" The catch is that with full independence we stand a chance of being a rival nation or system that opposes the current one, and even, in time, overthrowing the current one; but this risk is the reality of any new system. Though well-meaning they all have the very same potential. The reality of an actual overthrow is, however, far more complicated. For this cause the modern state and modern society need not fear too strongly this thearchic entity I bring into being as it is merely an informative training to an already existing organisation not a political movement to destroy civilisation.

Epilogue

With this book I have tried to reveal that early messianism started out as a street movement in the urban slums of the Galilean territories and evolved to become an anti-imperial movement throughout the early Roman Empire that adopted Afrosensual culture and Platonian ideas. I have also tried to show that modern godbodyism started out as a street movement in the ghetto slums of New York City's five boroughs and is now evolving into an anti-colonial movement throughout the Great United States Empire, adopting Neo-Soul culture and thearchic ideas. Moreover, I have sought to show that as the main categories Cone set out for Black liberation theology were: epistemology, theophany, theo-linguistics, anthropology, Christology, ecclesiology, historiology, and eschatology; even so, the main categories for Black godbody theology are: Adamology, Christology, ecclesiology, historiology, cosmology, eschatology, and soteriology.

Furthermore, I have tried to demonstrate the closeness of the godbody tradition to that of the anarchist tradition; and though I am also willing to say with Bey (2020), "I care little ... about bringing people into the institutional fold of anarchism" (Bey 2020: 51), I do care about the anarchic themes that demonstrate themselves through godbody interpretations and illustrations. We godbodies, as believers in and practitioners of righteousness, and as refusing to be corrupted by pressures from the United

States government to submit to their authority; already have striking similarities with anarchism that we definitely need to appreciate.

Even so, due to the current illegalism of some of our members, and our own aggressive hatred of the police and penal system, most of us are already anti-state seeing the state as a means of oppression against the people that corrupts nations. Herein, we godbodies seek the overthrow of the state and to replace it with ghetto parliaments and ciphers. This is the second area where the godbodies agree with anarchism: we have a syndicalist structure. Our parliaments operate similar to labour syndicates and would be very effective as labour syndicates if put into practice as such. A third area where the godbodies are similar to anarchism is with the use of social revolutionism, predominantly called illegalism. Though most anarchists are ideologically social revolutionaries we godbodies have thus far had no ideological training. But our righteousness is an even higher righteousness than that of the state, whose laws we do not recognise, therefore there is some serious significance to our illegalism. Finally, our prohibition of marriage according to the government means that we also advocate for free love, and some even go so far as practicing plural love. It is in these ways that we have much in common with anarchism, therefore, it is my hope, that through introducing these truths to us godbody I may help us to achieve the goal of becoming a world class Black ideology.

With this goal in mind, I foresee four new revolutions, that are already beginning to transpire in the world. As the mid-modern age brought four revolutions that would define modernity, so late modernity has begun the process of experiencing four new revolutions. In mid-modernity these revolutions were: the bourgeois revolution, which instigated the industrial revolution, which further instigated the capitalist revolution, which finally instigated the liberal revolution. In late modernity these revolutions are: The entrepreneur revolution, which has instigated the digital revolution, which is further instigating a syndicalist revolution, which will all make up the godbody revolution I am here instigating.

The entrepreneur revolution is the rising of professionals and small business teams to become the dominant class. The digital revolution is the rising of digital enterprises to fund these entrepreneurs and their ventures. The syndicalist revolution is the rising of small business syndicates and parliaments to plan, organise, and co-ordinate labour and consumption. Finally, the godbody revolution is the democratisation of divinity and the internal obligation to empathically improve the world. Herein, the godbody movement effectively expands to become a godbody revolution as more and more people awaken to these truths. For this cause, I would like to suggest before closing that you re-read this book multiple times to gain the most from its outlook and lessons. In this way you will progress to become not only a Black freedom fighter in the age ahead but a Black divine.

APPENDAGE CHRISTOLOGY

APPENDAGE

The history of the early messianic movement marks a turning point in world history and the beginning of a rival institution to all politico-religious superstructures then and today present in the world. The messianic communion founded by the apostles Peter and James in Jerusalem began as merely a branch of the Judean liberation movement started by the Baptist at Qumran.

This Jerusalem branch practiced the same rituals and traditions but they were a more urban form and tailored towards urbanised individuals outside of the desert oasis of Qumran. Moreover, whereas the Baptist mainly preached the coming of a messianic redeemer and revolutionary deliverer to overthrow Roman imperialism; the Messiah came preaching to those who followed him, "The kingdom of God cometh not with observation: Neither shall they say, Lo here: or, lo there: for behold, the kingdom of God is within you." What the apostles Peter and James did was continue on this vision the Messiah began before his disappearance up the mountain.

Now, for the record, the Bible says concerning the Messiah, "And he came and dwelt in a city called Nazareth: that it might be fulfilled which was spoken by the prophets, He shall be called a Nazarene" (Matthew 2: 23); or to give a more in-depth quotation: "Now therefore beware, I pray thee, and drink not wine nor strong drink, and eat not any unclean thing: For lo, thou shalt conceive, and bear a son; and no rasor shall come on his head: for the child shall be a Nazarite unto God from the womb: and he shall begin to deliver Israel out of the hand of the Philistine"(Judges 13: 4, 5). Again, in the first century the name Nazarene did not imply being from in a certain city by the Galilee called Nazareth. It meant belonging to the sect of the Nazarenes (who were also called Nazarites, and grew their hair long like most modern-day dreadlocks). In that sense, saying he was from Nazareth was to first century Israel what saying someone is from Bobo Hill is to modern-day Jamaica, it implied that he was a Dread.

So if therefore the Messiah was a dreadlock that meant that he did not cut his hair. Seeing that he was also said to have been "clothed with a garment down to the foot", and having "feet like unto fine brass" (Revelation 1: 13, 15) the description of the historical Messiah falls much closer to the Afrocentric spiritualist – even down to his wearing a *djellaba* that went down to his feet – than to the European hippy they keep shoving down our throats. Indeed, the historical Mary, James, Jude, Thomas, Matthew, and even the Baptist himself were all believed to have been Nazarenes, i.e., dreadlocked, in their day too.

Though it is true that the canonical books absent a lot of the details about the Messiah prior to his joining the Qumran movement, which at the time was led by the Baptist – though they do mention that following that experience he was rejected as a leader by the Nazarene community – there is good authority from Egyptian and Ethiopian sources that say that the Messiah and his family lived among the Judeans of Alexandria for many years, possibly returning to Jerusalem only for high feast days and immediately returning back to Alexandria. If this is true then an explanation of how he was so learned at such a young age could be that he had been studying various books from the Library of Alexandria since his youth. Moreover, the vast amount of ancient books contained in the Library of Alexandria could clearly explain where the Messiah developed his own theories of monism, on the one hand, and corporeal resurrection, on the other. Both being two concepts and ideas he would have been able to master through reading and studying the ancient Egyptian book of *Asr Uhem Ankh* (the Asarian Resurrection).

Conversely, it is currently explicated by many modern-day historians, based purely on the evidence of the canonical books, that the historical Messiah only knew Aramaic and that his father was nothing more than a lowly carpenter. However, various other subterranean sources claim that Joseph was not a carpenter at all but in fact a stonemason. Putting aside all the modern connotations of that word, historically speaking, masonry was not only a well-paying profession, it also allowed one to be well travelled and well learned. Furthermore, if his family really did move to Egypt, as the tradition claims he did (Matthew 2: 13-15), then no matter which city of Egypt they went to (most had large Judean populations in those days), they would have at least had to have learned Coptic, let alone Greek, to survive.

At the same time, if we consider his actual ministry – as the Messiah mainly spread his message, ideas, and Injil among uneducated and unlearned Aramaic farmers, artisans, workers, and villagers in Galilee, Samaria, and Judea, the Messiah most likely spoke the language of the common people of the Israel of the time, which language was Aramaic. But so as to provide a more subaltern level of depth: as the language the Messiah used in spreading his Injil, message, and lessons was most definitely Aramaic (a truth which no modern scholar would dare challenge or deny) then the only name the Messiah would have used for God – as in kingdom of – would have been none other than the Semitic name for God which was Allah. Basically, Allah is the name the Arabic, Aramaic, and even the ancient Hebraic people would have used for their God. Effectively, making the God of the Messiah none other than Allah.

At any rate, before he formally started his ministry the Messiah would have still most likely returned to Alexandria in his twenties to study various empathic and psychotherapeutic treatments as well as various monist and spiritualist philosophies, so as to develop his ideas and methods into a system. Again, I know that the idea that most of the healings the Messiah performed were through empathic and psychotherapeutic treatments instead of miraculous powers may seem somewhat repugnant to most Christians; especially considering the other great miracles he was able to do, which I in no ways deny. However, though it is fair to say the Messiah was definitely a *karim* (Arabic for Noble One and Miraculous One), due to the poor sanitation, general illiteracy, and basic lack of education of most first century villages at the time (which is where he supposedly performed most of his healings), it is again far more likely that many of the early claims concerning his healings were greatly exaggerated.

Nevertheless, the Messiah definitely saw therapy (literally meaning healing in Greek) as the basis for his own messianic movement; and this movement, at the time, consisted mainly of traditions already existing within the community at Qumran:

- Baptism was simply a full-body washing followed by the daily ritual of washing to symbolise both death and resurrection, and spiritual cleansing and purifying, for the renewal of the soul. Thus to them the physical cleansing was a seal and sign to mark their spiritual cleansing.

- Rejection of wealth was the renunciation of the world and the temptation of riches for a place in Allah's kingdom. Upon entering the brotherhood they were told to distribute their possessions within the brotherhood as they were to have all things common. And nothing was bought or sold among them. Distribution was made according to need at the time of asking. Thus they had all their daily needs satisfied.

- Public confession was an outward display of rejection of the world and its values, and its morals, and its standards; and a recognition of Allah and his Messiah as the only authorities worth respecting; all ideas very confusing and insulting to Rome.

 For this cause public confessions were considered martyrdom, as the subaltern followers of Christ faced daily persecution and hostility; not to mention the Roman worship of the Emperor as the living expression of the deity on earth. The messianic devotion to Christ over Caesar and the kingdom of Heaven over the empire of Rome destroyed all Roman religious preconditionings. The threats of the kingdom of heaven and kingship of Christ were not only challenging but explosive.

 To confess publicly one's devotion to Jesus as Christ and self as a sinner was as brave an act as it was ridiculous. The Roman world could accept neither idea as conducive to intelligence or sanity; and definitely could not accept them as religious or acts of piety.

- Devotional pursuits and exiles were usually expressed in times of solitude, personal suffering, and patient obedience; which also produced within the mind and heart a longing and searching for Allah. In these instances the loneliness of the situation was transfigured into a world where nothing but the divine exists to the pursuing or exiled individual as it forced them into closer union with Allah.

Even so, times of solitude, personal suffering, and tests of fruitless obedience can and usually do produce within the mind and heart of the pursuer a desire and need for Allah. Furthermore, it is not the attaining that counts but the performative of pursuing; not necessarily to gain from pursuit but to basically pursue Allah for the sake of pursuing Allah – to pursue him because he is real, and can be found inside every one of us. And even though the ultimate purpose behind these periods of isolation and pursuit was to find Allah and self; the self, when found, was to be made subordinate to Allah by the end of the pursuit.

Without finding the self and loving what you have found, the finding of Allah would ultimately have proven pointless and most dangerous. This in no ways negates the unity of Allah or submission of Shaitan to Allah; all the gospels show *jinni* trembling before the Messiah, and following in complete subordination the directives he gave them. This does, however, show the ignorance of modern people, who believe they can find Allah without finding self first.

Ultimately, to the early messianic movement, for someone to come to Allah without first having knowledge of self as sinner was basically coming to Allah as a hypocrite and not as the sinner you are. But this self-knowledge never meant to the early messianic movement weakness, guilt, or unworthiness, nor did it mean selfishness, self-concern, or outright self-interest; it meant self-realisation, being true to self and honest to self. It was the coming to the ultimate self-discovery: that though sinners we can still attain the divine, being the people of the one true Allah. And by presenting this truth Allah reveals that knowledge of self is in actual fact knowledge of himself, as by walking in his love we manifest divinity.

But the Messiah also made very clear to his disciples, "thou shalt not be as the hypocrites are" "But seek ye first the kingdom of God, and his righteousness" (Matthew 6: 5, 33); so that to these already existing Qumran traditions the messianic movement added acts of penance and agape feasts:

- Acts of penance were to make or show oneself worthy of Allah's kingdom, and were performed in remorse for having broken, after initial baptism, any one of Allah's laws as prescribed in the Torah. As the breaking of any of these was considered worthy of excommunication from the messianic brotherhoods in the world here and in the world hereafter; the act and proof of repentance was of necessity performed openly by the penitent.

    The first act of repentance would be the confession of guilt before the assembly, at which time the entire assembly and the assembly leader, the bishop, would decide based on the gravity and reason of the sin what manner of punishment they required. This usually consisted of prayers, fastings, abstinences, or beatings until the sin was atoned for; after which point they would be accepted again back into the eternal kingdom of Allah for having suffered their penalty.

- Agape feasts were the truly blessed coming together of the brotherhood celebrated on the Lord's Day every week to give thanks to Allah for the death and resurrection of the Messiah. It was also a declaration of their undying devotion to, and union with, the Messiah both in the world here and in the world hereafter as one body, to the eternal glory of Allah Most High; and an expression of allegiance to Jesus' dictatorial Messiahship and Lordship until righteous enough to submit to Allah's own authority. Thus severing all ties to this world and social order in anticipation for a newer and better world and social order.

But still, perhaps the most important and yet complicated teachings within the early messianic schools were their doctrines of the incarnation, crucifixion, and resurrection of the Messiah. These three fundamental doctrines and teachings of the messianic movement were the most difficult to understand and explain. Such that even the most studious masters of the late classical times had immense difficulty reporting and explaining them in their own day. Still, the main stone of contention was a God who suffers and dies a criminal's death. It is for this reason that Arius challenged the international bishopric after the Council of Nicaea.

See, the Council of Nicaea was a gathering of all the bishops within the Roman Empire organised by Emperor Constantine himself. At this gathering he wanted to put an end to the then violent and non-violent divisions and conflicts between the early messianic communities throughout his empire. Of these warring communities the two most notable were two very dominant African communities: those of Carthage (in modern-day Libya) and those of Alexandria (in modern-day Egypt). This conflict began over a century earlier, a little after the ever popular Irenaeus began his attack on heresy. Both communities henceforth would thereby name the other heretical for whatever reason.

In the early 200s, immediately following Irenaeus' attack, Clemenus of Alexandria and Terullianus of Carthage were the two most popular anti-heretical theologians. Of them, it was Terullianus who came up with, or better yet stole from Heliopolis, the trinity concept of a long-suffering God. Thus Ausar, Horu, and Auset were transformed into the trinity of Father, Son, and Holy Mother respectively; based on a literal reading from the gospel of Matthew, "Go ye therefore, and teach all nations, baptizing them in the name of the Father, and of the Son, and of the Holy Ghost" (Matthew 28: 19). Clemenus, on the other hand, employed the concept of *gnosis* – a term somewhat tainted by Irenaeus as foreshadowing heresy – in a positive way so as to connote science. This was for the highly educated Greeks and Romans of their time so as to paint messianism in a positive light to them and steer them away from the somewhat silly and disreputable ideas and traditions of the movement.

While Clemenus was not himself an African his successor to the Alexandrian seat, Oregenes, was. Oregenes, another anti-heretical theologian, like his mentor Clemenus, followed in his footsteps and presented the idea of *gnosis* in a positive light, hoping thereby to dispel ignorance, which he felt was the real cause of heresy. Oregenes is also credited with having come up with the term *Theotokos* (God-bearer or mother of God), which he himself obviously stole from Heliopolis, where Auset was said to be the divine mother of Horu (the God of kings). At the same time, Cyprianus, the successor to Terullianus to the Carthagian seat, established and reasserted the idea that baptism in the name of the Holy Trinity was the central means of avoiding heresy; and that those not baptised as such, being thereby apostate, had no right or power to impart guidance, connection, or power to anybody. This conflict between these three great African Fathers would, however, eventually be resolved through the doctrine of the greatest of all the African Fathers: Augustine of Hippo (in modern-day Libya).

By the time the Emperor Constantine brought all the bishops of his empire together in order to himself reconcile their differences at the Council of Nicaea, according to the tradition, the order of the day was to clear certain issues up once and for all. These issues were mainly focused on: the question of whether the messianic movement considered the divinity of Jesus Christ to be substantial or accidental; whether the conception of Jesus was by the Holy Spirit or by the word of God; also which books of the Bible should be considered a part of the messianic canon and which messianic heroes should be canonised.

At the actual council, however, the central argument was over the question of the Messiah's divinity. This dispute was, finally, resolved when Emperor Constantine suggested that instead of arguing over whether the Messiah had the substance or presence of divinity they could reframe the proposition by saying that he had the con-substance of divinity. This idea of con-substantiation, it was hoped, could thereby put an end to their heated debate. So, at that, all the bishops of this otherwise ghetto movement, both intimidated and flattered by the presence of the Emperor in their private and personal discussion, chose to heed his suggestion. A suggestion which would ultimately lead to such mathematical absurdities as Jesus being both 100 percent God and 100 percent man(?). And so, at the Council of Nicaea Carthage effectively won the day over the Alexandrians, hence why Arius, the then Bishop of Alexandria, refused to agree to any of it; and was therefore absented from history, excommunicated from the now Catholic Church, and considered henceforth a heretic.

Godbodyism itself is also a non-trinitarian movement, we teach that Jesus Christ was 100 percent man and was only the son of Allah by the grace and adoption of Allah. The Christian may retort, "But what about the virgin birth?" The Muslims have an answer for that, "The likeness of Jesus with Allah is truly as the likeness of Adam. He created him from dust, then said to him, Be, and he was" (Quran 3: 59). They may then turn around and say, "But, 'In the beginning was the Word, and the Word was with God, and the Word was God. ... And the Word was made flesh, and dwelt among us, (and we beheld his glory, the glory as of the only begotten of the Father,) full of grace and truth'." The thing is: in the beginning was the Logic, and the Logic was with Allah, and the Logic was divine, and the Logic was an attribute of divinity; but the moment the Logic was made flesh it ceased to be divine and became flesh.

The apostle John said somewhere else, "Beloved, believe not every spirit, but try the spirits whether they are of God: because many false prophets are gone out into the world. Hereby know ye the Spirit of God: Every spirit that confesseth that Jesus Christ is come in the flesh is of God: And every spirit that confesseth not that Jesus Christ is come in the flesh is not of God: and this is that spirit of antichrist, whereof you have heard that it should come; and even now already is it in the world." Something very important for us to note is that the word translated as flesh is a very loaded word. It translates as flesh, skin, body, and humanity; but it also translates as the word carnality. Therefore, every spirit that confesses that Jesus Christ was not fully human, i.e., fully carnal, is an Anti-Christ spirit. Again, as soon as the Word was made carnal it lost its divinity. You cannot be 100 percent carnal and 100 percent divine at the same time. Not only is that bad mathematics, but it is also bad ethics. Saying, the Messiah was 50 percent divine and 50 percent carnal is itself bad theology: it turns the Messiah into a demigod; though such still negates the idea of trinity. Truly, the Messiah was 100 percent man, the son of man, and his divinity, like ours, was by the grace of Allah.

Effectively, to the godbody: God is one, Jesus is one among many, and we are all capable of entering the God-Collective through accepting our own divinity and learning the science of everything in life, including the Universal Laws of Existence. Still, godbodyism also includes a fight; yet it is not a national fight nor a spiritual fight. Godbodyism accepts the idea that Black nationalism is a dead end as it only takes from the neo-colonial and imitates it, it also understands that Black spiritualism is a dead end as it only takes from the neo-colonial and reverses it. The end sought for by godbodyism is therefore a world of love, peace, and happiness enveloped in the vicissitudes of Black empowerment.

APPENDAGE

Attention African American Theologians!!!
What if Everything you Thought you Knew About God Was Wrong?

Demystifying God: Redefining Black Theology in the Age of iGod [Remastered] is the second instalment in Shahidi Islam's Shahidi Collection series. With the world manipulating Black history we need to find a way to get to our truth.

Demystifying God

Bibliography

The Five Percenter Vol 22.2; 2016: 3

Abraham, N (1994); "Notes on the Phantom a Complement to Freud's Metapsychology." In N. T. Rand (Ed), *The Shell and the Kernel*; University of Chicago Press.

Abraham, N (1994); "The Phantom of Hamlet or The Sixth Act preceded by The Intermission of 'Truth'." In N. T. Rand (Ed), *The Shell and the Kernel*; University of Chicago Press.

Abraham, N & Torok, M (1994); "Mourning or Melancholia: Introjection Versus Incorporation." In N. T. Rand (Ed), *The Shell and the Kernel*; University of Chicago Press.

Abron, J. M (2005); "'Serving the People': The Survival Programs of The Black Panther Party." In C. E. Jones (Ed), *The Black Panther Party [Reconsidered]*; Black Classic Press.

Adogame, A (2011); "Introduction." In A. Adogame (Ed), *Who is Afraid of the Holy Ghost: Pentecostalism and Globalization in Africa and Beyond*; Africa World Press.

Afrika, L (2013); Dr Llaila Afrika We Are Different; http://m.youtube.com/watch?v=r6aaP6Ynoj4, accessed in May 2014.

Albert, M (2004); *Parecon: Life After Capitalism*; Verso

Alexander, M (2011); *The New Jim Crow: Mass Incarceration in the Age of Colorblindness*; The New Press.

Aptheker, H (1996); "Maroons Within the Present Limits of the United States." In R. Price (Ed), *Maroon Societies: Rebel Slave Communities in the Americas*; The John Hopkins University Press.
Asante, M. K (2003); "The Afrocentric Idea." In A. Mazama (Ed), *The Afrocentric Paradigm*; Africa World Press, Inc.
Asante, M. K (2013); "Afrocentricity Imagination and Action." In V. Lal (Ed), *Afrocentricity Imagination and Action*; Multiversity & Citizens International.
Ashby, M (2003); *Sacred Sexuality: Ancient Egyptian Tantric Yoga The Neterian Guide to Love, Sexuality, Marriage, Relationships and the Secrets of Sexual Energy Cultivation, Sublimation, and Spiritual Enlightenment*; Sema Institute of Yoga.
Avineri, S (1968); *The Social & Political Thoughts of Karl Marx*; Cambridge University Press.
Balibar, E, Wallerstein, I (1991); *Race, Nation, Class: Ambiguous Identities*; Verso.
Baudrillard, J (2012); *Simulacra and Simulation*; The University Press.
Bauman, Z (2016); *Liquid Modernity*; Polity Press.
Bauman, Z (2003); *Identity Conversations with Benedetto Vecchi*; Polity Press.
Ben-Jochannan, Y (2002); *The Need for a Black Bible*; Black Classic Press.
Bey, M (2020); *Anarcho-Blackness: Notes Toward a Black Anarchism*; AK Press.
Blackburn, R (1988); *The Overthrow of Colonial Slavery 1776-1848*; Verso Books.
Brandchaft, B, Doctors, S, and Sorter, D (2010); *Toward an Emancipatory Psychoanalysis: Brandchaft's Intersubjective Vision*; Routledge.
Brown, F, Driver, S and Briggs, C (2014); *The Brown-Driver-Briggs Hebrew and English Lexicon*; Hendrickson Publishers.
Buber, M (2008); *I and Thou*; Simon & Schuster.

Callinicos, A (2003); *An Anti-Capitalist Manifesto*; Blackwells Publishing Ltd.

Chittick, W (1989); *The Sufi Path of Knowledge*; State University of New York Press.

Chiu, C-Y, Leung, A. K-Y. & Hong, Y-Y (2011); "Cultural Processes: An Overview." In A. K-Y. Leung, C-Y Chiu & Y-Y Hong (Eds), *Cultural Processes A Social Psychological Perspective*; Cambridge University Press.

Churton, T (2015); *Gnostic Mysteries of Sex: Sophia the Wild One and Erotic Christianity*; Inner Traditions.

Collins, J (2006); *Good to Great and the Social Sectors: A Monograph to Accompany Good to Great*; Random House Business.

Collins, J (2020); *Good to Great*; [ONLINE] Available at: https://www.audible.co.uk/webplayer?asin=147359202X&contentDeliveryType=SinglePartBook&ref_=a_minerva_cloudplayer_147359202X&overrideLph=false&initialCPLaunch=true. [Accessed 07/12/2023].

Collins, J & Porras, J. I (2005); *Built to Last: Successful Habits of Visionary Companies*; Random House Business Books.

Cone, J. H (2012); "Theology's great sin: silence in the face of white supremacy." In *The Cambridge Companion to Black Theology*, eds. Dwight N. Hopkins and Edward P. Antonio; Cambridge University Press.

Cone, J. H (2018); *Black Theology and Black Power: Fiftieth Anniversary Edition*; Orbis Books.

Cone, J. H (2020); *A Black Theology of Liberation: 50th Anniversary Edition*; Orbis Books.

Davis, A (2003); *Are Prisons Obsolete?*; Seven Stories Press.

Davis, D (1984); *Slavery and Human Progress*; Oxford University Press.

Degnbol-Martinussen, J, Engberg-Pedersen, P (2005) *Aid: Understanding International Development Cooperation*. London: Zed Book Ltd.

Diop, A (1991); *Civilization or Barbarism*; Lawrence Hill Books.

Douglas, K. B (1999); *Sexuality and the Black Church: A Womanist Perspective*; Orbis Books.

Durkheim, E (2014) *The Rules of Sociological Method: And Selected Texts on Sociology and its Method*. New York: Free Press.

Durkheim, E, Mauss, M (2009); *Primitive Classification*; Taylor & Francis.

Ehrman, B. D (2003); *Lost Scriptures: Books that Did Not Make It into the New Testament*; Oxford University Press, Inc.

Elias, N (2014) *The Civilizing Process*. Oxford: Blackwell Publishing.

Engberg-Pedersen, P, Gibbon, P, Raikes, P, Udsholt, L (1996) *Limits of Adjustment in Africa: The Effects of Economic Liberalization, 1986-94*. Suffolk: James Curry Ltd., Heinemann, Reed Publishing.

Engels, F (1947); *Anti-Dühring Herr Eugen Dühring's Revolution in Science*; Progress Publishers.

Foner, P (2002); *The Black Panther Speaks*; Da Capo Press.

Fanon, F (1964); *Toward the African Revolution*; Grove Press.

Fanon, F (1965) *A Dying Colonialism*; Grove Press.

Fanon, F (1969); *The Wretched of the Earth*; Penguin Books.

Fanon, F (2008) *Black Skin, White Masks*; Pluto Press.

Feuerstein, G (1998); *Tantra: The Path of Ecstasy*; Shambhala Publications, Inc.

Foucault, M (1998) *The History of Sexuality Vol. 1: The Will to Knowledge*; Penguin Books.

Foxe, J (2001); *Foxe's Book of Martyrs*; Bridge-Logos Publishing.

Franco, J. L (1996); "Maroons and Slave Rebellions in the Spanish Territories." In R. Price (Ed), *Maroon Societies: Rebel Slave Communities in the Americas*; The John Hopkins University Press.

Freeden, M (2013); "The Morphological Analysis of Ideology." In M. Freeden, L. T. Sargent, and M. Stears (Eds), *The Oxford Handbook of Political Ideologies*; Oxford University Press.

Gahlin, L (2007); *Egypt: Gods, Myths and Religion*; Anness Publishing Ltd.

Gentles-Peart, K (2016); *Romance with Voluptuousness: Caribbean Women and Thick Bodies in the US*; University of Nebraska Press.

Gilroy, P (1999); *The Black Atlantic: Modernity and Double Consciousness*; Verso.

Gladwell, M (2002); *The Tipping Point: How Little Things Can Make a Big Difference New Edition*; Abacus.

Gladwell, M (2009); *Outliers: the Story of Success*; Penguin Books.

Gleick, J (1998); *Chaos: The Amazing Science of the Unpredictable*; Vintage Books.

Goldman, E (1911); *Marriage and Love*; Mother Earth Publishing Association.

Gordon, L (2012); "Requim on a Life Well Lived: In Memory of Fanon." In N. Gibson (Ed), *Living Fanon: Global Perspectives*; Palgrave Macmillan.

Grady-Willis, W. A (2005); "The Black Panther Party: State Repression and Political Prisoners." In C. E. Jones (Ed), *The Black Panther Party [Reconsidered]*; Black Classic Press.

Gramsci, A (1971); *Antonio Gramsci: Selections from the Prison Notebooks*; Lawrence &Wishart Ltd.

Graves-Brown, C (2010); *Dancing for Hathor: Women in Ancient Egypt*; Continuum Books.

Green, E (2020); *Dark Mind Control Techniques in NLP: Powerful Mindset, Language, Hypnosis, and Frame Control*; Modern Mind Media.

Grinker, R, Lubkemann, S, Steiner, C (2010); *Perspectives on Africa: A Reader in Culture, History, and Representation Second Edition*; Blackwell Publishing Ltd.

Hardt, M, Negri, A (2000) *Empire*; Harvard University Press.

Harman, C (1999); *Economics of the Madhouse*; Bookmarks Publications Ltd.

Harrison, L (2002); "On Cultural Nationalism." In P. Foner (Ed), *The Black Panther Speaks*; Da Capo Press.

Harvey, D (2006); *Limits to Capital*; Verso Book.

BIBLIOGRAPHY

Hawass, Z (2006); *The Royal Tombs of Egypt*; Thames & Hudson Ltd.

Hayes, F. W, III, Francis, K. A, III (2005); "'All Power to the People': The Political Thought of Huey P. Newton and The Black Panther Party." In C. E. Jones (Ed), *The Black Panther Party [Reconsidered]*; Black Classic Press.

Herring, G (2006); *Christianity: From the Early Church to the Enlightenment*; Continuum International Publishing Group.

Heywood, A (2017); *Political Ideologies: An Introduction*; Palgrave.

Hill, N (2004); *Think and Grow Rich Revised and Expanded by Dr Arthur R. Pell*; Vermillion London.

Hudson, M (2021) *Super Imperialism: The Economic Strategy of American Empire Third Edition.* Dresden: ISLET-Verlag.

Ibn Katheer Dimashqi, H (2006); *Book of the End: Great Trials and Tribulations*; Maktaba Dar-us-Salam.

Imseis, A (2010); "Speaking Truth to Power: On Edward Said and the Palestinian Freedom Struggle." In A. Iskandar and H. Rustom (Eds), *Edward Said: A Legacy of Emancipation and Representation*; University of California Press.

Intelexual Media (2023); *A Short History of Masturbation*; [ONLINE] Available at: https://www.youtube.com/watch?v=0aoY6Ihjips. [Accessed 29/11/2023].

Islam, S (2024); *Godbodyism: How Adamology Leads to a True Black Thearchy Black Divinity Series Vol 5*; Divinity Black People Ltd

Jackson, S. A (2009); *Islam and the Problem of Black Suffering*; Oxford University Press.

Jacobs, M (1992); *Key Figures in Counselling and Psychotherapy: Sigmund Freud*; Sage Publications Ltd.

Johnson, O. A (2005); "Explaining the Demise of The Black Panther Party: The Role o Internal Factions." In C. E. Jones (Ed), *The Black Panther Party [Reconsidered]*; Black Classic Press.

Jones, W. R (1998); *Is God a White Racist? A Preamble to Black Theology*; Beacon Press.

Josephus, F (2013); *The Works of Josephus: New Updated Edition*; Hendrickson Publishers.

Karenga, M (1989); *Introduction to Black Studies*; University of Sankore Press.

Katz, A (2008); *The Holocaust: Where Was God? An Inquiry into the Biblical Roots of Tragedy*; Burning Bush Press.

Keen, D (2012); *Useful Enemies: When Waging Wars is More Important than Winning Them*; Yale University Press.

Khalfe, A. (2019); *An Outpouring of Subtleties upon the Pearl of Oneness Volume 1: Divinity*; Sunni Publications.

Killah Priest (1996); "B.I.B.L.E." In: *Liquid Swords* [CD]; Geffen/MCA.

King, M. L, Jr (1986); *A Testament of Hope*; HarperCollins Publishers.

King, M. L, Jr (1992); *I Have A Dream; Writings and Speeches That Changed the World*; HarperCollins Publishing.

Koester, C. R (2014); *Revelation: A New Translation with Introduction and Commentary*; Yale University Press.

Koestler, A (1976); *The Thirteenth Tribe*; Random House, Inc.

Kolawole, M. E. M (1997); *Womanism and African Consciousness*; African World Press.

Kropotkin, P (2002); *Anarchism*; Dover Publications Inc.

Kropotkin, P (2006); *Mutual Aid: A Factor of Evolution*; Dover Publications Inc.

Kumar, D (2012); *Islamophobia and the Politics of Empire*; Haymarket Books.

Lady Gaga (2009); *Poker Face (Official Music Video)*. [ONLINE] Available at: https://www.youtube.com/watch?v=bESGLojNYSo. [Accessed 31/12/2023].

Lenin, V (1968); *V. I. Lenin Selected Works*; Lawrence and Wishart Ltd.

Lenin, V (2010); *Imperialism: The Highest Stage of Capitalism*; Penguin Books.

BIBLIOGRAPHY

Lenin, V (2014); *State and Revolution*; Haymarket Books. Square Press, Inc.

Lenin, V (2020); *What Is to Be Done? Burning Questions of Our Movement*; Science Marxiste.

lil' bill (2023); *How Black Elites LIE to Us*; [ONLINE] Available at: https://www.youtube.com/watch?v=Uu-X_E8cwaA. [Accessed 29/11/2023].

Littlewood, R (2006); *Pathology and Identity: The Work of Mother Earth in Trinidad*; Cambridge University Press.

Lizokin-Eyzenberg, E & Shir, P (2021); *Hebrew Insights From Revelation*. Israel: Jewish Studies for Christians.

Luxemburg, R (2004); *The Rosa Luxemburg Reader*; The Monthly Review Press.

Lyotard, J (1986); *The Postmodern Condition: A Report on Knowledge*; Manchester University Press.

MacCulloch, D (2010); *A History of Christianity*; Penguin Random House.

Mackenzie-Grieve, A (1968); *The Last Years of the English Slave Trade Liverpool 1750-1807*; Frank Cass & co. Ltd.

Malatesta, E (1922); *At the Café: Conversations on Anarchism*; KDP Amazon Publishing.

Malcioln, J (1996); *The African Origins of Modern Judaism*; Africa World.

Marx, K (1986); *Capital Volume I*; Lawrence &Wishart Ltd.

Marx, K (1958); *Selected Works vol 3*; Foreign Languages Publishing House.

Maxwell, M (1998); *Revelation: Doubleday Bible Commentary*; Bantam Doubleday Dell Publication Group, Inc.

M'Bantu, A, Muller, G (2013); *The Ancient Black Hebrews and Arabs*; Pomegranate Publishing.

Mbembe, A (2019); Necropolitics; Duke University Press.

McHugo, J (2019); *A Concise History of Sunnis & Shi'is*. London: Saqi Books.

McRobbie, A (2008); *Pornographic Permutations*; Routledge.

Meiu, G. P (2011); "'Mombasa morans': embodiment, sexuality and Samburu men in Kenya." In S. Tamale (Ed), *African Sexualities: A Reader*; Pambazuka Press.
Meyer, M, W (1992); *The Gospel of Thomas: The Hidden Saying of Jesus*; Harper.
Moltmann, J (1993); *Theology of Hope: On the Ground and Implications of a Christian Eschatology*. Minnesota: Fortress Press.
Mellino, M (2011); "Notes from the Underground, Fanon, Africa, and the Poetics of the Real." In *Living Fanon: Global Perspectives* (Ed). Nigel C. Gibson; Palgrave Macmillan.
Muhammad, E (1965); *Message to the Blackman of America*; Muhammad's Temple of Islam No. 2.
Muhammad, E (1973); *The Fall of America*; Muhammad's Temple of Islam No. 2.
Newton, H (2002); *The Huey P. Newton Reader*; Seven Stories Press.
Nkrumah, K (2006); *Class Struggle in Africa*; Panaf Books.
Nkrumah, K (2009); *Consciencism Philosophy and Ideology for De-Colonization*; Monthly Review Press.
Nkrumah, K (2022); *Neo-Colonialism: The Last Stage of Imperialism*; African People's Conference.
Nye, J S, Jr (2004); *Soft Power: The Means to Success in World Politics*; Public Affairs Books.
Nzegwu, N (2011); "'Osunality' (or African eroticism)." In S. Tamale (Ed), *African Sexualities: A Reader*; Pambazuka Press.
Patterson, O (1996); "Slavery and Slave Revolts: A Sociohistorical Analysis of the First Maroon War, 1665-1740." In R. Price (Ed), *Maroon Societies: Rebel Slave Communities in the Americas*; The John Hopkins University Press.
Philo (2016); *The Works of Philo: Complete and Unabridged New Updated Edition*; Hendrickson Publishers Marketing, LLC.
Priestley, D (2013); *Entrepreneur Revolution: How to Develop Your Entrepreneurial Mindset and Start a Business that Works*; Capstone Publishing Ltd.

Raja, M (2020); *Decolonizing Literary Theory: Some Tentative Thoughts | Zahiriyya and Bataniyya Philosophy*; [ONLINE] Available at: https://www.youtube.com/watch?v=Ez7UZUCM8wo. [Accessed 06/12/2023]

Rand, N. T (1994); "New Perspectives in Metapsychology: Cryptic Mourning and Secret Love." In N. T. Rand (Ed), *The Shell and the Kernel*; University of Chicago Press.

Rand, N. T (1994); "Secrets and Posterity: The Theory of the Transgenerational Phantom." In N. T. Rand (Ed), *The Shell and the Kernel*; University of Chicago Press.

Roberts, A (2011); *Evolution The Human Story*; Dorling Kindersley Limited.

Roberts, J. D (2012); "Dignity and destiny: black reflections on eschatology." In *The Cambridge Companion to Black Theology*, eds. Dwight N. Hopkins and Edward P. Antonio. Cambridge: Cambridge University Press.

Rogers, K (1976); *The Gambler*. [ONLINE] Available at: https://www.youtube.com/watch?v=7hx4gdlfamo. [Accessed 31/12/2023].

Rowland, C (1985); *Christian Origins: An Account of the Setting and Character of the most Important Messianic Sect of Judaism*; SPCK.

Said, E (2003) *Orientalism*. London: Penguin Books.

Saraswati, S (2012); *Kundalini Tantra*; Yoga Publications Trust.

Sardar, Z, Abrams, I (2012); *Introducing Chaos: A Graphic Guide*; Icon Book Ltd.

Schimek, J-G (2011); *Memory, Myth, and Seduction: Unconscious Fantasy and the Interpretive Process*; Routledge.

Seale, B (2002); "The Ten-Point Platform and Program of the Black Panther Party." In P. Foner (Ed), *The Black Panther Speaks*; Da Capo Press.

Seleem, R (2004); *The Egyptian Book of Life*; Watkins Publishing London.

Seligman, C. G (1966); *Races of Africa*; Oxford University Press.

Sheller, M (2012); *Citizenship From Below: Erotic Agency and Caribbean Freedom*; Duke University Press.

Singh, N. P (2005); "The Black Panthers and the 'Undeveloped Country' of the Left." In C. E. Jones (Ed), *The Black Panther Party [Reconsidered]*; Black Classic Press.

Skousen, M (2017); *The Big Three in Economics: Adam Smith, Karl Marx, and John Maynard Keynes*; Routledge.

Smif-N-Wessun (1995); "Home Sweet Home." In *Dah Shinin'* [CD]. New York: Wreck Records, Nervous, Inc.

Smif-N-Wessun (1995); "PNC." In *Dah Shinin'* [CD]. New York: Wreck Records, Nervous, Inc.

Snoop Doggy Dogg (1994); *Doggystyle*; Death Row Records.

St. Augustine (1958); *City of God*; Bantam Doubleday Dell Publishing Group, Inc.

Stourton, E (2005); *In the Footsteps of Saint Paul*; Hodder Headlin Ltd.

Strong, J (1990); *The New Strong's Exhaustive Concordance of the Bible*; Thomas Nelson Publishers.

Strachey, J (1936); *The Theory and Practice of Socialism*; Victor Gúllancz Ltd.

The Holy Bible: King James Version (2002); Michigan: Zondervan.

The Holy Qur'an: Maulana Muhammad Ali Translation (2002); Ohio: Ahmadiyya Anjuman Isha'at Islam Lahore Inc.

Torok, M (1994); "The Illness of Mourning and the Fantasy of the Exquisite Corpse." In N. T. Rand (Ed), *The Shell and the Kernel*; University of Chicago Press.

Turman, E. M (2018); "Heaven and Hell in African American Theology." In *The Oxford Handbook of African American Theology*, eds. Katie G. Cannon and Anthony B. Pinn; Oxford University Press.

Turner, L (2011); "Fanon and the Biopolitics of Torture: Contextualizing Psychological Practices as Tools of War." In N. Gibson (Ed), *Living Fanon: Global Perspectives*; Palgrave Macmillan.

Tyldesley, J (2011); *The Penguin Book of Myths & Legends of Ancient Egypt*; Penguin Books.

Umoja, A. O (2005); "Set Our Warriors Free: The Legacy of The Black Panther Party and Political Prisoners." In C. E. Jones (Ed), *The Black Panther Party [Reconsidered]*; Black Classic Press.

Van Loon, H (1960); *The Story of Mankind*; Washington Square Press, Inc.

Vanee, L (2023); *End the Genocide* [ONLINE] Available at: https://www.facebook.com/reel/1584869658715687. [Accessed 17/12/2023].

Wacquant, L (2016) "Bourdieu, Foucault, and the Penal State in the Neoliberal Era." In D. Zamora & M. C. Behrent (Eds), *Foucault and Neoliberalism*. Cambridge: Polity Press.

Watterson, B (2013); *Women in Ancient Egypt*; Amberley Publishing.

Williams, D. S (1993); *Sisters in the Wilderness: The Challenge of Womanist God-Talk*; Orbis Books.

Williams, D. S (2011); "Black Theology and Womanist Theology." In D. N. Hopkins & E. P. Antonio (Eds), *The Cambridge Companion to Black Theology*; Cambridge University Press.

Williams, J (1928); *Hebrewisms of West Africa From the Nile to the Niger with the Jews*; Africa Tree Press.

X, M (1968); *The Autobiography of Malcolm X*; Penguin Books.

X, M (1989); *Malcolm X: The Last Speeches*; Pathfinder.

X, M (2004); *Why I am Not an American*; Citizens International.

www.ingramcontent.com/pod-product-compliance
Lightning Source LLC
Chambersburg PA
CBHW050512170426
43201CB00013B/1931